In the Shadow of the Sultan

EDITORIAL BOARD OF THE CMES MONOGRAPH SERIES

Eva Bellin
Cemal Kafadar
Habib Ladjevardi (Chair)
Roy Mottahedeh
Tom Mullins
Roger Owen

HARVARD MIDDLE EASTERN MONOGRAPHS
XXXI

In the Shadow of the Sultan

Culture, Power, and Politics in Morocco

EDITED BY
Rahma Bourqia and Susan Gilson Miller

WITH CONTRIBUTIONS BY
Rahma Bourqia, M. Elaine Combs-Schilling,
Mohamed El Mansour, Gary S. Gregg,
Abdellah Hammoudi, Mohamed Kably, Abdelfattah Kilito,
Susan Gilson Miller, Henry Munson, Jr.,
Daniel J. Schroeter, and Susan E. Waltz

DISTRIBUTED FOR THE
CENTER FOR MIDDLE EASTERN STUDIES
OF HARVARD UNIVERSITY BY
HARVARD UNIVERSITY PRESS
CAMBRIDGE, MASSACHUSETTS

Cover illustration: "The Emperor Mawlay 'Abd al-Rahman,"
by Eugène Delacroix. From *L'Ilustration: journal universel*,
21 September, 1844.

Copyright 1999 by the President and Fellows of Harvard College
ISBN 0-932885-20-9
Library of Congress Catalog Card Number 98-89330
Printed in the United States of America

04 02 01 00 99   6 5 4 3 2 1

Contents

Preface vii
Acknowledgments ix
Note on Transliteration xiii

1 · An Introduction to the Discussion   1
SUSAN GILSON MILLER AND RAHMA BOURQIA

PART ONE: ANTECEDENTS

2 · Legitimacy of State Power and Socioreligious Variations in Medieval Morocco   17
MOHAMED KABLY

3 · Speaking to Princes: Al-Yusi and Mawlay Isma'il   30
ABDELFATTAH KILITO

PART TWO: PERIPHERIES

4 · The Sanctuary (*Hurm*) in Precolonial Morocco   49
MOHAMED EL MANSOUR

5 · Royal Power and the Economy in Precolonial Morocco: Jews and the Legitimation of Foreign Trade   74
DANIEL J. SCHROETER

6 · *Dhimma* Reconsidered: Jews, Taxes, and Royal Authority in Nineteenth-Century Tangier 103
SUSAN GILSON MILLER

PART THREE: CENTERS

7 · The Reinvention of *Dar al-mulk*: The Moroccan Political System and Its Legitimation 129
ABDELLAH HAMMOUDI

8 · Performing Monarchy, Staging Nation 176
M. ELAINE COMBS-SCHILLING

9 · Themes of Authority in the Life Histories of Young Moroccans 215
GARY S. GREGG

PART FOUR: PROSPECTS

10 · The Cultural Legacy of Power in Morocco 243
RAHMA BOURQIA

11 · The Elections of 1993 and Democratization in Morocco 259
HENRY MUNSON, JR.

12 · Interpreting Political Reform in Morocco 282
SUSAN E. WALTZ

Glossary 307
A Selective Bibliography 311
Contributors 321
Index 325

Preface

Centuries ago, that most famous of Maghribi Muslim thinkers and writers, Ibn Khaldun (1332–1406), pointed out what he saw as the three key factors of political authority: religious allegiance and fervor, group feeling (*'asabiya*), and a strong royal power. Ever aware of the inherent tendency of these elements to wax and wane in any given society, he described how this vacillation also caused legitimacy and power to flourish and then decline. The present volume offers an overview of the various methods by which successive Moroccan dynasties in the premodern and postcolonial eras managed to cultivate and sustain their authority and its perceived legitimacy through one or another combination of Ibn Khaldun's three elements.

More than that, the present studies also probe, in different ways, the social, economic, religious, and political dimensions of the legitimacy claimed by, and accorded to, the *makhzan* (government) in premodern and contemporary Morocco. They demonstrate various approaches to thinking about the means of exercising power, the symbolisms, and the discursive representations of legitimacy used by different rulers of Morocco since medieval times. The range of topics and methods employed by the contributors reflects both the disciplinary diversity of the scholars involved and the breadth of their individual scholarly perspectives.

It is worth noting that a significant aspect of the collection is the transatlantic collaboration that it represents. For over a decade now, the Harvard Center for Middle Eastern Studies has been the fortunate recipient of support from the Ministry of Higher Education of the Kingdom of Morocco for a Moroccan and Maghribi Studies Program. This program has allowed us to offer new courses on the Maghrib to Harvard undergraduate and graduate students, to sponsor a monthly public forum on Morocco, to engage in faculty exchanges with our counterparts at Mohammed V University in Rabat, and to develop lasting contacts with Moroccan scholars at various Moroccan universities. Moroccan scholars have visited Harvard, teaching alongside our faculty and carrying out their own research in the fine North African collection of Widener Library, and Harvard faculty and students have spent time in Morocco, pursuing their scholarship and augmenting their language skills. Genuine collegial work and personal as well as professional friendships have resulted.

These chapters stem from these contacts and exchanges. They are taken from the papers given at a workshop on 7–8 April 1994, at Harvard University entitled "Representations of Power in Morocco and the Maghrib: Historical and Contemporary Perspectives." A reciprocal workshop was held in Rabat in the spring of 1996 on the subject of "Law and Society in the Maghrib." Both meetings have moved us farther down the road of closer intellectual cooperation and exchange. The publication of the present volume is another tangible sign of the growing importance of shared inquiry among researchers from this country and those of North Africa and the Middle East, as we prepare our scholarly agendas for the coming century.

William A. Graham
Professor of the History of Religion and Islamic Studies
Director of the Center for Middle Eastern Studies (1990–96)
Harvard University

Acknowledgments

In the Shadow of the Sultan: Culture, Power, and Politics in Morocco is a project of the Moroccan Studies program at Harvard University. This program is funded by the Moroccan government through a grant administered by the Moroccan Ministry of Higher Education. The purpose of the Moroccan Studies program, founded in 1985, is to promote public awareness and high-level scholarship about Morocco within the American university community and throughout American society more generally. The editors wish to thank the benefactors of the program for their generosity and support, while at the same time acknowledging the spirit of openness and respect for academic freedom they have shown toward all aspects of the program and its activities.

Harvard's Moroccan partner is Mohammed V University in Rabat, where the moving force behind the collaboration was the former Rector (now retired) Professor Abdellatif Benabdeljlil, scholar and diplomat, who lent his support to all aspects of its realization. His counterpart in Cambridge was Professor William A. Graham, former director of the Center for Middle Eastern Studies, the home to the Moroccan Studies program since its creation. Professors Graham and Benabdeljlil personified the cooperative aspect of the Moroccan Studies agenda through their own friendly relations. That ambiance of good feeling has continued under the present leadership of the Rector Abdelouahed Belkeziz and current CMES Director Roger Owen, who together have given renewed strength and dynamism to Moroccan Studies at Harvard.

Our thanks, too, to the scholars who participated in the conference "Representations of Power in Morocco and the Maghrib: Historical and Contemporary Perspectives," which was the starting point for this book. To those names that appear here, we add those of Edward (Terry) Burke, Abdesslam Magraoui, Wilfrid Rollman, and Ahmed Toufiq, each a distinguished scholar of Morocco in his own field. We wish to recognize their contributions to the proceedings and their important presence in the overall endeavor.

At the Center for Middle Eastern Studies, we were fortunate to have a number of colleagues interested in Morocco and the Maghrib who helped with crucial tasks. Nakeema Barbero, Deborah Gilman, Leslie Poe, Eric Evans, and Naghmeh Sohrabi were cheerfully involved and made things go infinitely more smoothly than they might have gone. Professor Abdelhaï Diouri of Rabat, visiting Moroccan scholar at CMES in 1996–97, read parts of the manuscript and gave excellent critical comments. Other useful input on individual chapters came from Terry Burke, Abdellah Hammoudi, David Miller, Henry Munson, Jr., and I. William Zartman. Emily Gottreich copyedited the first draft and did some translating. Seth Graebner, Marie-Dominique Boyce, and Michael Cooperson also did translations, grappling heroically with difficult texts. Margaret Owen took on the task of polishing a manuscript fraught with inconsistencies and raising it to a high professional standard, a task she accomplished with skill, humor, and dispatch. Finally, we would like to mention Rachida Kabbaj of the Secretariat of the University in Rabat and Helen Ives at CMES, who made their own transatlantic connection, arranging travel for the conference and transmitting the final papers.

Other thanks are due to Habib Ladjevardi of CMES, who lent

his managerial ability to seeing the book through to publication, and to Roger Owen, who stepped in at a critical moment, giving the project a much-needed push toward completion. We share with all those mentioned above the satisfaction of seeing this joint venture, so long in the making, finally achieved.

> Susan Gilson Miller and Rahma Bourqia
> Cambridge, Massachusetts and Rabat, Morocco
> 25 July 1998

Note on Transliteration

Transliteration of words from standard Arabic follows a simplified version of the system used in the *International Journal of Middle East Studies*. There are no diacritical marks, *ta marbuta* is "a" in the construct state, the *'ayn* is indicated by ('), and *hamza* is indicated by ('). Spellings common in English have been used, particularly for personal and place names. Likewise, where people have adopted romanized spellings of their family names, it has been retained. In some cases where dialectical Moroccan Arabic appears, the words have been translated phonetically.

In the Shadow of the Sultan

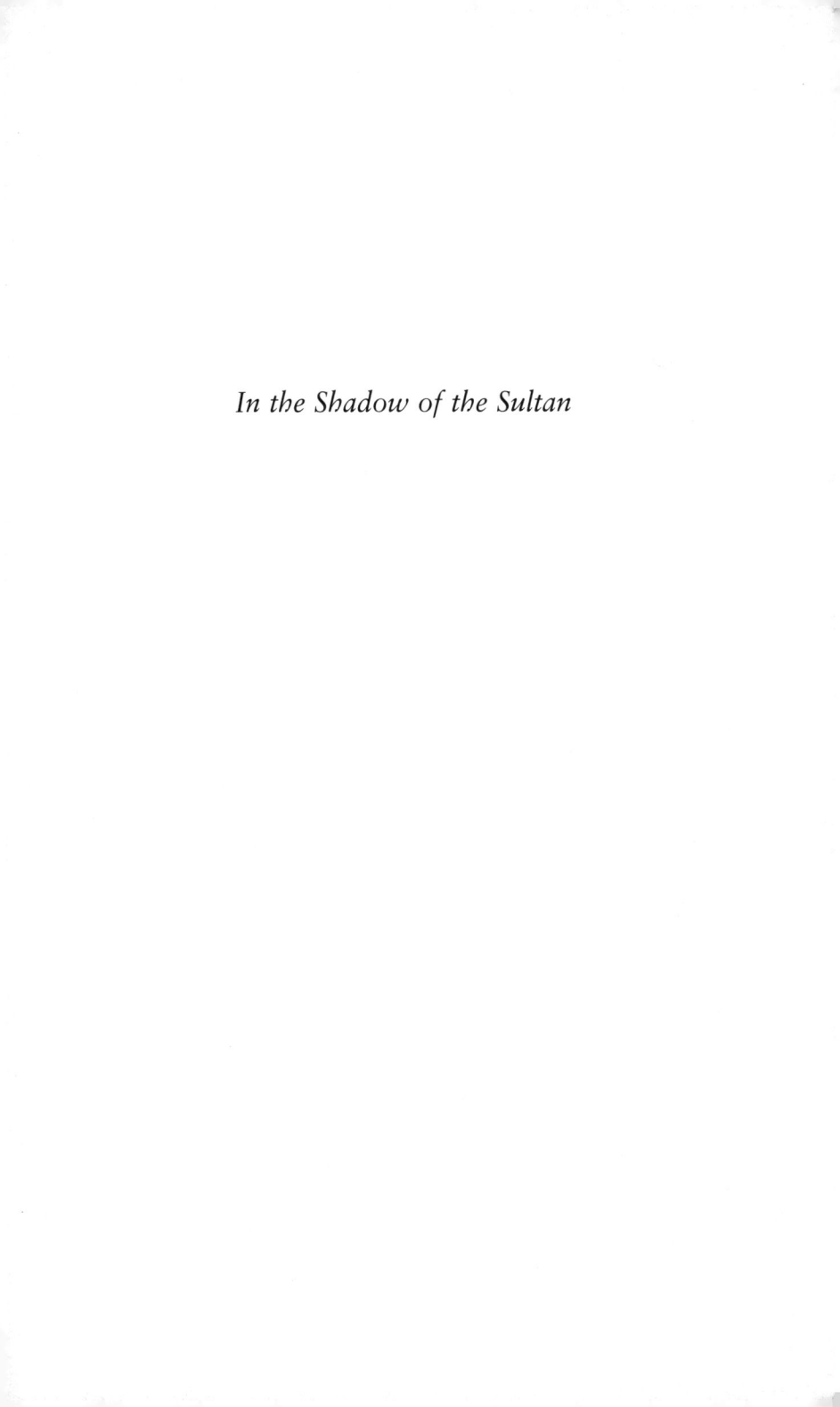

· ONE ·

An Introduction to the Discussion

Susan Gilson Miller and Rahma Bourqia

I

The field of Moroccan studies has exerted an influence on contemporary social thought by introducing into scholarly debate striking examples of the interrelationships between power, culture, and society. The purpose of this book is to contribute to that discussion by reexamining connections between state power and the individual in Morocco, in the light of the new approaches and methodologies being used by a younger generation of postcolonial scholars. The prevailing theme is the question of power and its changing forms and expressions within Moroccan society at various historical moments, from the eleventh century to the present. The contributors include historians, political and social scientists, and a literary critic, each writing from his or her own disciplinary perspective. The book does not pretend to be panoptic; rather, it is a series of snapshots that, when taken together, offer the reader a sense of what recent scholarship has to say about central problems in contemporary Moroccan studies.

In Morocco, power usually means royal authority, and pivotal to our discussion is the topic of the monarchy and the means by which it has established and maintained its legitimacy in the social sphere. Compared to other Maghribi (Muslim North African) and Middle Eastern states, the Moroccan political system has preserved a remarkable constancy over time. Since the early ninth century, Morocco has been more or less continuously ruled by a sultan-king who has monopolized the levers of government. The present dynasty, the 'Alawis, first came to power in the seventeenth century and has governed the country ever since in an extraordinary unbroken chain of rule. This striking longevity invites questions about the institutions and social forms that have given substance to monarchical power and the role they have played in implanting it so deeply in society. The question of culture is critical to this analysis, and a strong emphasis on cultural matters over political or economic ones shapes our point of view. This orientation is reflected not only in the multidisciplinary interests of the contributors but also in the privileging of the discussion of power as an aspect of social experience. When operating successfully, culture is located at the meeting point of politics and society, binding state actions and individual destinies together in an ideological continuum that gives coherence to daily life. Does the richly nuanced popular culture in Morocco constitute an implicit support for the legitimation of monarchical authority? In response to this question, many of the contributors have interrogated social practices to examine the extent to which they reflect processes and attitudes that reinforce the current political system. Mohamed El Mansour's chapter (Chapter 4) on the institution of the *hurm* (sanctuary) and its functioning as a key political and social escape valve vividly demonstrates this point, as does Gary S. Gregg's on socialization and personality formation within the family (Chapter 9).

The emphasis on social experience has its source not only in the magnetic pull of popular culture, so extraordinarily rich in the Moroccan case, but also in a turning away from the top-down methodologies of an earlier generation of researchers who looked for large, explanatory theories of a political, social, economic, and even aesthetic nature that would somehow capture the Moroccan essence. The impact of Edward Said's *Orientalism* had its reverberations in North African scholarship, causing soul-searching among Western specialists on Morocco and stimulating a reexamination of the foundation texts written in the protectorate period (1912–56). Now that the colonial era is past, scholars have become aware of the extent to which the interests of the colonizers scripted our understanding of North African society. While appreciating the ethnographic detail of Robert Montagne's studies of the High Atlas Berbers or Roger Le Tourneau's encyclopedic knowledge of Fez, one must nonetheless remain alert to their underlying political agenda.[1] In terms of recent social science research, this has led to a rereading of the known sources and a search for undiscovered ones that are more expressive of an indigenous point of view. Almost every chapter in this collection illustrates this tendency, which of course is not exclusive to Morocco but generalized throughout the fields where contemporary scholarship has grown out of the soil of colonial inquiry.

A return to the sources has been felt to be especially significant for those topics associated with a specifically Moroccan experience. Western scholarship has been fascinated, for example, by the phenomenon of saints and saint worship. Social scientists have been drawn to this issue, sometimes with too much hubris and too little understanding of its eclectic origins and deep psychic roots; the results were often oversimplified and ahistorical assertions about saintly personalities and their relationship to political authority. Returning to the abundant textual and oral sources concerning saints and using new methods of interpretation, contemporary Moroccan scholars have expanded vastly our understanding of this exemplary type, showing that it encompasses a multiplicity of social, historical, and political roles. As the registers of possibility concerning saint worship and local phenomena such as ceremonies, rites of passage, and other practices multiply, we are rewarded with fresh insights into Moroccan social phenomena over which no single school or ideological point of view prevails. Instead, as the present collection attests, we see the emergence of paradigms that are refreshingly nonconformist.

However, the transition to a more reality-based mode of scholarly inquiry is not without its elements of risk. Recent scholarly studies touch on some of the most sensitive areas of social and political concern, such as slavery, gender relations, ethnic and minority relations, and the nature and operations of state power.[2] Research has begun to expose social and political mechanisms once occluded or simply not discussed, and in so doing, it has provoked a lively public debate. The ferment has been accompanied by the production of high-quality monographs, the appearance of collections from university colloquia and seminars, the editing of major theses, the growth of private publishing houses interested in intellectual topics, and, most important of all, the rise of a small but avid reading public. Flowing outward from its university-based origins, this new thinking confronts the inhibitions of a political and social system whose perennial attitude toward change has been ambivalent at best. Therefore, it is not surprising that considerable heat is being generated along the edges of the encounter.

The present volume brings to English-speaking audiences for the first time a broad sampling of some of the latest scholarship on Morocco emanating from the revisionist point of view. Each chapter in its own way breaks the cake of custom, proposing alternative readings of long-held beliefs about the nature of authority in Morocco. Since much of the really significant research on Morocco today is in Arabic, a language not accessible to most Western readers, the book renders a service by making available to nonspecialists who may have an interest in the topic, the region, or in postcolonial studies in general a taste of what Moroccan scholarship has to offer. It is not intended to be the final word, only a provisional one, and for each author included, there are many others who are not, both within Morocco and outside it, whose work is of equal and enduring value. Such collaborative efforts between scholars from the Maghrib and beyond are destined to increase as transnational research becomes the scholarly norm and joint efforts become more common.

II

What do we mean by power in Morocco? Where is it located, how does it work its way through society, bending people to its will? A conceptualization of power begins with the state. According to Max Weber, the state is "a compulsory political association [that] successfully upholds a claim to a monopoly of legitimate use of force in the enforcement of its order."[3] In the Weberian model, power is the coercive element at the basis of state action, and no state can function without it. Moreover, the manner in which power is exerted becomes the very defining quality of the state. In the rational (Western, modernist, progress-oriented) state, according to Weber, power is used to reinforce societal goals and to mobilize the means to achieve them. In contrast with this paradigm is a traditional system like Morocco's, where power is sustained in order to promote loyalty to a chief and solidify a system of personal authority.[4] According to Weber, traditional rule is legitimized in one of two ways: (1) in terms of the traditions themselves, which set the parameters of power, or (2) by the will of the ruler, backed by an obedience founded on a personal loyalty to him that is "essentially unlimited."

So far so good, for there is much here that fits the Moroccan case. However, Weber goes on to propose a second paradigm of power that also echoes down the long corridors of Moroccan experience. This is power in its symbolic and performative mode, which he calls "charismatic" authority, defined as "a certain quality of an individual personality by virtue of which he is set apart from ordinary men and treated as endowed with . . . exceptional powers."[5] Charismatic authority is characterized by an informal organization with no set discipline, setting it apart from the more stylized traditional authority that operates within a formal system of rules.[6] Recognizing the rich possibilities of this notion when applied to the Moroccan situation, Clifford Geertz embroidered on it, calling charismatic power (or *baraka*) not only "combustible" and "extravagant" but the very leitmotif of political life in Morocco, where the power of God appeared in "the exploits of forceful men, the most considerable of whom were kings."[7] Whether conceived of in its more sober traditional form or in its more wildly charismatic one, both constructions of power left a residue of unanswered questions. For example, we might ask what differentiates the formal from the informal rules under which each kind of authority operates, and is there really a distinction between them? In other words, Weber's conceptual categories do not really fit concrete situations of power, and when put into action, they have to be adjusted to local conditions.

Furthermore, recent historical research informs us that traditional Morocco was more than a cauldron of raging *baraka,* where kings were dispensers of magic and "charismatic adventurers were constantly arising on all sides," as Geertz so boldly puts it.[8] It was also the site for the operation of widely accepted and deeply inculcated ethical norms that could, if wielded properly, elicit unified patterns of coherent and goal-oriented social action (popular protests and jihad, for example). In other words, not only were charismatic and traditional power complementary, they were also superseded by yet another kind of political authority that was also culturally based. A recognized system of norms, laws, and procedures governed public and private life: it may not always have been transparent to the outsider but nonetheless functioned with economy and efficiency. These norms and regulations were not necessarily tied to the person of the monarch, although he struggled to personify them; rather, they stood over and above the office of the sultanate and beyond its reach, finding their home in a societal consensus about the nature of just rule. This consensus would not be captured in typologies of royal power, nor would it necessarily inhere in kingship's idea of itself. More truly, it is embedded in social experience, from where it exerts a decisive authority over political and social affairs. In order to locate it, one has to turn away from formal abstractions of power such as Weber's, useful and enlightening so far as they go, and move to the materiality of history and social life where other levers of action become manifest. Let us now examine some symbolic and expressive aspects of power that are not alluded to in the classical discussion but that nonetheless have contributed significantly to a revisionist reading of Moroccan social experience.

The first point is regarding the concept of legitimacy and how it may be understood in the Moroccan context. The operation of royal power in the social field rests on the idea that a command given will eventually be obeyed. But the probability of that happening depends to a large extent on the popular perception of the legitimacy of the political order. Most observers agree that the concept of legitimacy in Morocco is based on a combination of factors deriving from the Islamic tradition and other sources and that popular adherence to the monarchy is more a deeply felt sentiment, fabricated out of cultural and religious symbols, than an attachment to any Hobbesian social contract or national idea. If we agree that royal authority in Morocco conforms to a traditional charismatic model, then how does power manage to sustain itself over time? Inheriting *baraka* from one's ancestors is no guarantee of regime longevity; rather, it is the popular perception of royal power and the way it is integrated into social life that renders it truly functional as a commanding force. Miracles, wonder-working, and other symbolic artifacts are constructed over an ethical substratum that gives them meaning and efficacy. Symbolic references provide the nexus between the imaginative and the pragmatic by providing orientation in a confusing universe of ideas and by helping to reassemble, out of bits and pieces of experience, the "archaic elements of identity."[9] A legitimacy made up of symbols, as Mohamed Kably points out (in Chapter 2), has greater flexibility, resilience, and longevity than one based on formal structures, utopian ideals, or political platforms that are vulnerable to wars, economic failures, and ecological disasters. After reading Professor Kably's chapter, one may well conclude that the prominent place of symbolic content in the legitimation of the Moroccan monarchy has contributed in no small way to its impressive durability.

A further point about power is the relationship between it and its representations. By this we mean the conscious and unconscious ways in which rulers talk about themselves, display themselves, and, in general, shape the discourse about authority within a given society. Monarchies by their very nature lend themselves to ceremonial display, and the implicit merits of public ceremony have been energetically manipulated in the Moroccan case, as we see in M. Elaine Combs-Schilling's contribution (Chapter 8). Ceremonies that center on the king, his family, and his close associates enhance the prestige of the ruler, lend aura to his designated heir, and reinforce hierarchies of deference and dominance. How this representation is sustained in a world in which external means of representation (satellite television, the international press, the Internet) can circumvent the control of local authorities is an unprecedented situation in Morocco and a characteristically modern dilemma for all forms of political rule. A negative image of the monarchy created by an unfriendly exposé can be a threat, and the need to show a good public face influences the ways in which the political process is managed. Henry Munson, Jr.'s treatment of the Moroccan elections of 1993 (Chapter 11) and Susan E. Waltz's discussion of recent developments in human rights (Chapter 12) are as much concerned with popular perceptions of authority as they are with the nature of the political process per se. More than ever, public discourse about power has become an intrinsic factor in shaping that power.

This leads us directly to the next point, which concerns the language of power as it is spoken by the people and the extent to which it is a sensitive indicator of how authority is perceived. The lexicon of power is vast, and as Rahma Bourqia points out in her chapter (Chapter 10), the discourses about it flowing through society are practically limitless. They range from the metaphorical use in everyday speech of words representing institutions of authority—*makhzan* is a good example—as a surrogate for "awesome power," to the use of other expressions that are deeply embedded in historical experience. Historians have been especially creative in showing how power is reproduced in society through language. By returning to overlooked or underexploited texts and extracting key concepts from them, they underscore the vividness and potency of forgotten speech. A lexicon of key social concepts—terms such as *harka* (royal progress), *ztata* (safe conduct), *azma* (crisis), and *fitna* (rebellion)—has been informally compiled, pinpointing the social phenomena that form the "tissue of relations" connecting diffuse elements in society to the apparatus of the state.[10] By highlighting the language of power, historians have opened up new perspectives on state-societal relations. The criss-crossing of the fields of social action by dynamic concepts representing negotiation and exchange between center and periphery is an important new element in our understanding of how power actually operates at the local level.

The reconceptualization of relations between the state authority and subordinate groups has also radically changed our notions of how so-called marginal elements in society, such as Jews, slaves, and women, were integrated into their social milieu and even exercised some control over it. Revisionist readings offered here by Susan Gilson Miller (Chapter 6) and Daniel J. Schroeter (Chapter 5) stress that economic necessity was not always the leading factor governing majority-minority relations; of equal importance were a sense of geographical place, the role of communal leadership, the work of shared cultural values, and a general desire for peace and intercommunal harmony. Social scientists who enter the archives, and historians who go into the field, find abundant evidence to prove that the neat categories drawn by a previous generation of scholars do not conform to the shifting, porous, and often vague boundaries that actual experience erects between supposedly disparate social groups.

When speaking about power at the local level, it is also critical to recall that not all power was monopolized by the state. A singular aspect of the Moroccan cultural landscape is the presence of charisma outside and beyond the reach of the *makhzan*. Local power was distributed among saints and *shurafa'* who played a critical role as alternative centers of social action. Saintly figures populate the Moroccan *imaginaire*, occupying coveted symbolic space at the core of popular feeling. Efforts to define saintly power precisely are impeded by the difficulty of rendering into Western terms concepts having deep roots in the Moroccan psyche. Endowed with special qualities of ethical strength and social efficacy, saints are agonistic heroes who form a counterweight to sultanic authority. As Abdellah Hammoudi points out in his chapter (Chapter 7), saints and sultans share a similar kind of spiritual ascendance that makes their relationship one of tension, rivalry, and mutual attraction. Both possess *baraka*, which levels the field between them and places them on an equal footing in terms of a spiritual claim to rule. This diffusion of religious authority across social space meant historically that charismatic power was scattered across a broad band of social actors, any one of whom could make a claim of legitimacy and raise the banner of dissent. In the preprotectorate period, dramatic episodes of messianic-style protest led by "false" pretenders nearly succeeded in toppling the monarchy more than once.[11]

However, the real importance of saintly power lies more in the realm of the moral than the political. The potency of a saint resides in his capacity to rouse indignation against injustice through minimalist means. The meeting of the historical figure of al-Yusi with the Sultan Mawlay Isma'il has been frequently invoked as a model for the confrontation between "holy-man" power and "strong-man" rule. But as Abdelfattah Kilito shows us with Barthesian wit (in Chapter 3), this epic encounter was not a battle of swords or even of wills but rather one of words. Al-Yusi's instrument was not magic but moral suasion, and his achievement was not to astonish the sultan with wonder-working but to gently admonish him and reduce him to tears through the careful manipulation of words. Saintly discourse offers an authoritative counterweight to official discourses of power, and the prestige of the saint is based less on his ability to respond aggressively to force than on his quiet reminder to the prince of his ethical and social responsibilities. Through the hagiographical literature as it is reproduced in the oral tradition, high ideals of moral authority have been widely disseminated throughout Moroccan society and have taken root in the popular imagination. Saintly narratives offer paradigms of exemplary behavior that are the raw material out of which a broadly accepted normative sense is fashioned.

A final point about symbolic power is its mobility. The accrual of symbolic capital is a historical process that gains momentum over time, and its transfer from one form of political authority to another is an ever-present possibility. By the end of the nineteenth century, courtly protocol had become so elaborate in Morocco that European travelers would comment on its sophistication and capacity to impress the masses. The customs and ceremonies of self-glorification carefully nurtured by one political authority are often appropriated by another, which turned out to be the case in Morocco with the coming of the French in 1912. By that time, the sultanate was exhausted and close to expiration, torn apart by internecine struggles and successive European incursions. Preserved and resuscitated by the French under the protectorate, the monarchy arose from the ashes, stripped of its political power but with its symbolic richness intact and even raised to new heights. In the 1930s and the 1940s, Sultan Mohammed V was reified as the representative of the nation. The palace, in defiance of the French authorities, formed an alliance with the nationalist groups that waged a successful resistance to a crumbling French authority, regaining national sovereignty in 1956.

III

During the period of French rule, structures of power inherited from the Maghribi past were overlaid with other kinds of authority derived from Western sources. After independence in 1956, French and Spanish rule gradually melted away, but the institutions it had imposed on Moroccan political culture remained behind. Rationalism, accountability, and goal-directedness—the legacy of the Enlightenment historical experience—were grafted onto the Moroccan system in the form of bureaucracies, ministries, and a partially secularized judiciary and legal code. Political factions grew up around the principal actors in the nationalist movement, parties were formed, elections held, and parliaments elected. Yet none of these institutions or activities were central to the running of the country, which continued to function mainly through the long-standing amalgam of coercive, traditional, and charismatic power and its attendant networks and associations. The immense capacities of a late-twentieth-century technological state, combined with the affective authority of an age-old theocratic-based legitimacy, synthesized to give the regime the capacity to govern with few constraints other than those imposed by economic necessity. And so the situation continues today. On the surface, the state appears to be rational and coherent; in actuality, it is made up of layers of authority derived from many sources that coexist and interact but without the benefit of any overriding principle or theme. A dual legal system, one respecting Sharia law and another inspired by Western legal codes—the two often in conflict—is only one example of this disjuncture, but there are others too numerous to recount that permeate public and private life.

Meanwhile, on the street level, unfulfilled aspirations continue to stir the mass consciousness, throwing out sparks of discontent and occasionally bursting into open flame in the form of student rebellions, workers' strikes, and vocal demonstrations. The ideological sources of popular protest in Morocco are complex and not readily disaggregated; to a certain extent, they rest on a deep historical sense of social justice made up of memories of past glories, a collective image of the exemplary leader, and a popular notion of moral purity and material generosity arising from the

Islamic tradition. In the political arena, this historical sensibility arising from below meets the ambiguities of power disseminated from above, creating a polyphonic, frequently discordant setting for political life. In the best of times, the system seems purposefully archaic; in the worst of times, paralysis sets in, producing uncertainty and even social crisis. Between these two poles of possibility lie the hopes and fears of the Moroccan people, many of whom ardently wish for a resolution of the difficulties that vex them daily.

The role of the intellectual in such situations is a limited but important one; it is to separate into readable bits the various phenomena—historical, cultural, and social—that combine to produce the current reality by removing the mask of mystery and replacing it with a knowledge (admittedly contingent) based on research, documentation, and critical evaluation. The ideas offered in this book should be understood within that framework of impartial investigation and discovery. The past may not exactly resemble the future "more than one drop of water resembles another," as Ibn Khaldun believed, but there is enough continuity in human experience to make the effort worthwhile.

NOTES

1. Both works are landmark studies of colonial scholarship: R. Montagne, *Les Berbères et le Makhzan dans le sud du Maroc* (Paris, 1930); R. Le Tourneau, *Fès avant le Protectorat*, 2nd ed. (Rabat, 1987).
2. For example, the highly original work of M. Ennaji, *Soldats, domestiques, et concubines: L'Esclavage au Maroc au XIXe siècle* (Casablanca, 1994).
3. T. Parsons, ed., *Max Weber: The Theory of Social and Economic Organization* (New York, 1964), 154; see also L. Anderson, "The State in the Middle East and North Africa," *Comparative Politics* (October 1987): 1–18.
4. Parsons, ed., *Max Weber*, 341.
5. Ibid., 358.
6. Ibid., 361.

7. C. Geertz, "Centers, Kings, and Charisma: Reflections on the Symbolics of Power," in *Local Knowledge: Further Essays in Interpretive Anthropology* (New York, 1983): 121–3, 135.
8. Ibid., 136.
9. We thank Abdelhaï Diouri for this insight. See his *Les Puissances du symbole* (Casablanca, 1997), 9–11.
10. A. Sebti, "Insécurité et figures de la protection au XIXe siècle: la ztata et son vocabulaire," *La Société civile au Maroc* (Rabat, 1992): 47–69; see also, by the same author, "Présence des crises dans la chronique dynastique marocaine: entre la narration et les signes," *Cahiers d'études africaines* 119 (1990): 237–50.
11. Saintly lineages projected themselves onto the political field and provided an alternative to sultanic rule during the so-called maraboutic crisis of the seventeenth century; in the late nineteenth century, messianic figures called *roguis* (false pretenders) again challenged the monarchy and threatened to overthrow it. See J. Brignon et al., *Histoire du Maroc* (Casablanca, 1967), 222–7, 325.

Part One

ANTECEDENTS

· TWO ·

Legitimacy of State Power and Socioreligious Variations in Medieval Morocco

Mohamed Kably

FRAME AND LIMITS

The question of legitimacy often presents itself as a means for understanding the juridical status or the sociopolitical role of power. In the case of medieval Morocco, the question of legitimacy was a constant concern of successive dynasties. Legitimacy pervades the surrounding historiography, as dynasties sought to translate difficult themes of doctrinal discourse—such as the legality of a political rupture, or the orthodoxy of official behavior, or the association of any new project with the obligation to oppose all deviations and innovations (*(bida')*) both politically and militarily—into the simplest of terms. The goal, of course, was to rid society of these disputes altogether. So it happens that either by dint of suggestion or assertion, the power under discussion usually takes on an image that is so well constructed that it resists both evolution over time and criticism. Yet alongside this image we note the persistence of discordant elements, not officially recognized, that betray the existence of realities arising

---

Translated by Seth Graebner and Susan Gilson Miller.

from socioreligious variations that are more or less tolerated or contained.

To fill in this sketch, we must first explain our approach. We begin by replotting against an Islamic background the trajectory that describes the legitimacy of power in medieval Morocco. After that, we take a reading of this curve, with the aim of sorting out its lines of force, its probable mechanisms, and the elements of its basic structure. In order to avoid misunderstandings, we first take the precaution of defining our terms as carefully as possible with regard to their history and meaning.

In speaking of legitimacy, it is useful to recall that when the term is applied to politics, it evokes an outcome that constitutes the endpoint of a process of normalizing a condition that was brought about (or that seems to have been brought about) outside the Islamic norm by aggression against adversaries who themselves claim to share in the common faith of the Koran. Legitimizing such a condition would necessarily mean legitimizing the act of conquest that gave birth to it. The only way to do this in Islam is to invoke simultaneously reform and jihad, a holy war against nonbelievers. Hence the founding link in medieval Morocco between these two terms and all claims to dynastic legitimacy. Every project of reform, even those not systematically supported by jihad, had a tendency to aggregate around a centralized monopoly of power. Since medieval Islamic Morocco, especially in its beginnings, was a melting pot of autonomies and antagonisms of every sort, it might be worth noting that not every power that appeared in that space was necessarily concerned with legitimacy.[1] Only a reforming power, aggressive and monopolistic, would effectively have recourse to it.

In medieval Morocco, the power corresponding to such a profile has a name that comes down to us from a definite past. It is the term *makhzan*, which we find mentioned for the first time in two Almohad texts that are nearly contemporaneous, the *Memoirs of al-Baydhaq* and *Kitab al-ansab*. Probably written between the midtwelfth and early thirteenth centuries, these two texts appear to describe an official hierarchization that most likely dates back to the period of the organization of the Almohad state—that is, to the first half of the twelfth century.[2]

Does this mean that the centralizing state is a latecomer to Morocco? Insofar as the presence of such a state presupposes the demarcation of a territory both unified and differentiated, we may conclude that this territory, and the state associated with it, date back even further in time. The name al-Maghrib al-Aqsa (Muslim furthest West or Morocco) was liberally employed in the writings of the geographer al-Idrisi, who mentions it first in his *Nuzha*, completed in 548/1154.[3] Within this space he locates the movements of the Sanhaja Almoravids after they came out of present-day Mauritania, leading us to believe that the territory of al-Maghrib al-Aqsa came into being at the same time as the Almoravid state—that is, in the middle of the eleventh century.[4] For this reason, we situate the themes discussed here between that date and the period of the emergence of the Sa'di state in the first half of the sixteenth century.

TRACING THE CURVE

Taking into account this demarcation and the preceding definitions, we ask, What trajectory has the legitimacy of state power taken in Morocco? We know that the Almoravid state situated itself unequivocally within the camp of the local Maliki Sunnism and that under the influence of the Andalusian doctors of that rite it hastened to place itself under the authority of the Sunni Abbasid caliphate of Baghdad. In exchange, the caliphate sanctioned and supported Ibn Tashufin's act of unification through jihad by granting him the title of sovereign at the same time that he received the blessings of the illustrious al-Ghazali in writing.[5]

Toward the middle of the twelfth century, the Masmudian state of the Almohads appeared. Breaking systematically with all former allegiances, this state made up of the disciples of Ibn Tumart set itself up at the outset as a caliphate in its own right, with very clear designs on Egypt and beyond.[6] The eclectic legitimacy claimed by the western caliphate invoked principally a

Mu'tazalite Unitarianism adapted to a doctrine of Shi'i Mahdism of the most radical sort.[7]

As for the Marinid state, it came into being and acquired its political initiation in the service of the Hafsids of Tunis. Not long before, the Hafsids had presented themselves as the legitimate heirs to the Almohad caliphate of Marrakesh, now considered as practically defunct. Once they felt strong enough to break away from the Hafsid tutelage, the Marinid amirs placed themselves under the banner of Maliki Sunnism; toward the end of the thirteenth century, they attached themselves to the promotion of Idrisid sharifism. Meanwhile, the Marinids awaited the opportunity to lay claim to the supreme eminence of the former suzerain caliphate of Tunis, which arose in the fourteenth century, especially under Abu 'Inan.[8]

In the case of the Sa'dis, everything suggests that by the beginning of the sixteenth century state power had begun to identify itself with the tradition of southern Mahdism. However, Sa'di power soon began to orient itself to other points of reference, as the evolution of official titles would suggest.[9] In fact, in the case of the Sa'di dynasty (as with the others) official titles faithfully convey the orientation that each of these dynasties took in the process of seeking legitimacy. The sovereign title of the Almoravids was that of *amir al-muslimin,* conferred by Baghdad; the title *amir al-mu'minin* would become the perquisite of the Almohad sovereign, who presented himself as the caliph of the Mahdi Ibn Tumart, who alone had the right to use that title (as well as that of imam) in the particular Shi'i sense of the word. The subaltern title of *amir al-muslimin* reappeared with the Marinids, with the exception of Abu 'Inan, who gave himself the title of caliph and therefore called himself *amir al-mu'minin.* Finally, we note that Muhammad al-Shaykh, for all intents and purposes the first Sa'di sovereign, did not hesitate to adopt Shi'i terminology by bestowing on himself the two titles of imam and mahdi, while his successors, like Ibn Tumart's successors, declared themselves caliphs, thereby retaining the title of *amir al-mu'minin.*[10]

TRANSFORMATION OF POWER

What exactly do these fluctuations signify? By what logic do they proceed, and how may we understand the processes underlying them? The elements of a response begin to emerge from our initial soundings. The most salient findings, it seems, are the following:

1. If we turn our attention back to the period preceding the arrival of the Almoravids, we discover, in the accounts describing the space later known as al-Maghrib al-Aqsa, the presence of all of the legitimizing elements encountered thus far, used alternatively by one or another dynasty in power. In the absence of a politicoreligious map of Morocco at that time, we only note the simultaneous existence of Maliki and Hanafi Sunnism, of Kharijism, Mu'tazilism, of Imamate Shi'ism, and of Idrisism. The numismatics of the period suggest that Idrisism, catalogued first as moderate Zaydi Shi'ism, later tended toward Imamate Mahdism, if not to hard-line Isma'ilism.[11] The titles of the Idrisid Hammudids of Andalusia seem to confirm this fact, given the frequency of the attribution Fatimi as it was applied to Idris or to his offspring.[12] Even early signs of a charismatic sharifism may be discerned, if we are to believe Ibn Hawqal, in the permanent well-being of the "blessed city of Fez" in the fourth/tenth century, as well as in the respectful attitude of the Cordoba Ummayads and Ifriqiya Fatimids.[13]

2. On examining this form of incipient sharifism, we should note that the celebrated Qadi 'Iyad, a well-known Maliki jurist of the end of the Almoravid period, makes it one of the axial points of his famous *Shifa'*.[14] Meanwhile, his contemporary Ibn Tumart presented himself officially as a direct descendent of Idris, while Ibn Tumart's disciple and first caliph 'Abd al-Mu'min alternated between claiming the same Idrisid ancestry and a more simple, purely Qurayshi genealogy.[15] Furthermore, we know from other sources that the future Sa'dis would situate themselves precisely within a collateral branch of this same Idrisid lineage and that the Marinids, for lack anything better,

would be content with making themselves into the historical progenitors of organized sharifism.¹⁶ It would seem that sharifism presented itself as a veritable catalyst for the legitimacy of all those who aspired to power. This is a constant of the first degree that we should keep in mind.

3. Another constant would be the fundamentally autonomous nature of political legitimacy in medieval Morocco at the level of political reality. From the legal point of view, only the case of Almoravid legitimacy would be an exception. By soliciting the blessings of the Abbasid caliphate of Baghdad, the founders of al-Maghrib al-Aqsa created such an anomaly that over the centuries it seems to have been condemned to oblivion. Apart from that, legitimacy in Morocco was tied to its secular autonomy vis-à-vis the eastern caliphate, an autonomy that had its origins in the irreversible rejection touched off by the Kharijites in the year 122 or 123/740–741 and culminating in the politicoconfessional upheaval that more or less framed the Idrisid emirate.¹⁷

4. Another constant characteristic is the binary nature of the jihad, in the sense that this fundamental principle of Moroccan legitimacy in its beginning phases involves, on the one hand, both a stubborn settled population and a resistant, restless, migratory one and, on the other, an enemy threatening from either overseas or from the coast. Whether we look at the Sa'dis, the Marinid-Wattasids, the Almohads, or the Almoravids, these two aspects of the problem could hardly be more clear. Nevertheless, we find that the local aspect of the jihad was much more pronounced in the Almoravid and Almohad periods, no doubt because the schisms went deeper and because doctrinal unification was less necessary after the coming of the Marinids than before. Moreover, we note that among all the Islamic dynasties of the region and the other Islamic dynasties, only the Almoravids and Almohads did not take their names from eponymous ancestors but rather from points of doctrine—*ribat* in one case and *tawhid* in the other—thereby justifying in the eyes of their followers the insertion of their rule into the global historical design of the Islamic revelation.¹⁸

5. Taking into account this important distinction, we should locate with greater clarity the historic phase these two rival dynasties devoted to their mission of proselytism. This is important for two reasons: first, because of the impact of this phase and, second, because it constitutes a period of sorting out, in contrast to the earlier confessional mosaic. In the Almoravid period, the countrywide legitimacy of their later phase would be marked by a renewed reference to Maliki Sunnism.[19] In the Almohad period, in addition to an almost unanimous dissent of the governed, this phase would carry forward an official rejection of Tumartian Mahdism in 626/1229 by the caliphate of Marrakesh, renounced amid a general indifference but at the risk of provoking a reaction from Ibn Tumart's privileged kin. This indifference, perhaps even more than the rejection of Mahdism, was most likely due to the bloody excesses that punctuated the earlier Almohad conquest, as well as to the policy of official segregation. This policy was not apparent at the outset, but we may assume that it had a close and a priori relationship with the spectacular success of pietistic mysticism that came about shortly after the triumphal rise to power of the new masters.[20]

6. The sum total of these various factors meant that the Marinid legitimacy (and the Marinid-Wattasid that followed it) had to deal not only with the Maliki and Sufi reality already on the scene from the end of the preceding period, but also with the chronic irritation of post-Almohad Mahdism encouraged from afar by the suzerain Hafsid caliphate of Tunis. Because they had no reform project they could truly call their own, and because they began by exploiting the legitimacy of this same Hafsid caliphate, the Marinids, having seized Marrakesh, went on to make sure of their control over Sijilmassa and the north in 674/1276, thus using the jihad to establish their own legitimacy. This pragmatic approach had as its initial platform, in addition to the jihad, popular dissatisfaction with the results of Almohad radicalism. For this reason, the Marinids hastened to implement the second phase of their jihad by inaugurating in Fez in 675/1277 a policy of building Sunni colleges (*madaris*) that

sanctioned the fundamental Maliki aspect of their rule. Furthermore, seeking to counterbalance Sufi influence while holding in check Almohad Mahdism (considered by its adherents as sanctified by the Idrisid ancestry of Ibn Tumart), the new power adopted a sharifian strategy based on the cult of Idris I and Idris II, designed to draw benefits from all the branches recognized as Idrisid.[21]

7. Building on the far-reaching consequences of such a strategy, the Sa'di legitimacy developed under the banner of an excentric sharifism in the Draa Valley at the dawn of the tenth/sixteenth century. It tried to succeed where centrist sharifism, represented by al-Juti, the *naqib* of the Idrisids, had failed miserably a half-century earlier, in 869/1465.[22] These two sharifian legitimacies had as their common trait an alliance with Sufi activists no doubt motivated by moral reform, as well as by a jihad adapted to each of their two different sets of circumstances. The Sufi allies of the Sa'dis, however, were far more numerous and operated at a distance from the capital. They would become the tool not only of sharifism but also of the early phase of a triumphant Sa'di legitimacy.[23] We also notice that in the Sa'di case as well as in the Idrisid, the attitude of the Maliki scholars was marked by an exemplary fidelity to the Marinid-Wattasid power; confronting the victorious Sa'dis, some scholars categorically refused to renounce their allegiance to their former masters and heroically chose martyrdom.[24] However, while neither offending nor unnecessarily indulging their ambitious Sufi allies, Sa'di state power put in the forefront representatives of the deeply rooted Maliki rite once victory was achieved. Meanwhile sharifism, now enshrined at the summit of the state, assumed more than ever its secular function as charismatic mediator and preferred emotional catalyst.

AN EVOLVING LEGITIMACY

What conclusions can we draw from this reading? Keeping in mind the foregoing remarks, can we at the very least speak of a palpable evolution in the phenomenon under study and, if so, in what direction? One thing is quite clear: the legitimacy of state power as it was originally defined, located in the space that became known as al-Maghrib al-Aqsa, had at its disposal an arsenal of legitimizing means that, at least potentially, represented an embarrassment of riches. Toward the close of our period, this arsenal seemed to get smaller. In the end, alongside a strengthened Malikism, there remained only sharifism—a sharifism transferred onto a privileged and diverse body, politically heterogeneous and differentially adapted to the particularities of time and place. On the other hand, Sufi power that did not exist prior to the Almoravid period became increasingly structured and influential as time went on. As an element in this overarching transformation, the legitimacy in question gave proof of its selectivity, its dynamism, and its adaptability, while firmly adhering to options that were tried and tested.

Moreover, to return to our trajectory of legitimacy, we cannot help but notice that on the state level, it was a long way from the legitimacy associated with the Almoravid and Almohad phase to the more durable legitimacy that followed. On the one hand, we are dealing with an approach that is frankly dogmatic and, for all practical purposes, is a legitimacy of doctrine, rigid and essentially closed. On the other, we see an approach that is more flexible, leading to a legitimacy that is responsive, polyvalent, and as pragmatic as one could wish. The evolution from one phase to the other is no doubt explained by the profound effect on the governed society of the crushingly monolithic character of the Almoravid and Almohad systems, which varied in severity from one regime to the other. It might also be explained by an internal refusal of an approach perceived of as Islamically exclusive. Along the way, these underlying reactions became apparent and compounded the difficulties of the governing class.[25] Consequently, in the end it was a legitimacy that was neither capricious nor unremittingly exclusionary but rather malleable and, if need be, quite energetic. Constructed by means of a functional accumulation, early on it chose to abandon exclusivity in favor of flexibility, responsiveness, and an openness to continual change.

NOTES

1. Valid for the Maghrib in general, this situation appears more accentuated in the farthest west, in what was later called al-Maghrib al-Aqsa, where, in addition to sects, subsects, and their roughly corresponding social divisions, we note the persistence of deep-rooted and autonomous entities considered heretical. On these beginnings, see M. Talbi, "La Conversion de Berbères au harigisme ibadito sufrite et la nouvelle carte politique du Maghreb au IIe/VIIe siècle," *Etudes d'histoire ifriqiyenne et de civilisation musulmane médiévale* (Tunis: Université de Tunis, 1982), 13–80, especially, 47–75; M. Kably, *Variations islamistes et identité du Maroc médiéval* (Paris, 1989), 11–45, and particularly 28–33. On the "heretical" groups, see A. Bel, *La Religion musulmane en Berbèrie* (Paris, 1938), 170–82; G. Marçais, *La Berbèrie musulmane et l'Orient au moyen âge* (Paris, 1946), 126–9; M. Talbi, "Hérésie, acculturation et nationalisme des Berbères Berghouata," *Actes du premier congrès d'étude des cultures méditerranéennes d'influence arabo-berbère* (Algiers, 1973), 217–33; T. Lewicki, "Prophètes, devins et magiciens chez les Berbères médiévaux," *Folia Orientalia* 7 (1965): 3–27.
2. The term *makhzan* in these texts is associated with the category called *'abid al-makhzan* (servants of the *makhzan*), which tends to confirm the relative age of the term compared to the period of the document's composition; see E. Lévi-Provençal, *Documents inédits d'histoire almohade* (Paris, 1928), 46, 70, and also vii–viii. On the history of the institution as such, see M. Buret, *Encyclopaedia of Islam*, 2nd ed., s.v. "Makhzan." On the corps of *'abid al-makhzan*, see J. F. Hopkins, *Medieval Muslim Government in Barbary until the Sixth Century of the Hijra* (London, 1958), 92–3.
3. The name *al-Maghrib al-Aqsa* appears seventeen times in the complete text of the *Nuzha*, while the name *al-Gharb al-Aqsa*, practically equivalent, but undoubtedly older, is used only four times; see al-Idrisi, *Nuzha al-mushtaq fi ikhtiraq al-afaq/Opus Geographicum* (Naples, 1975), 1033 and 1056.
4. Al-Idrisi, *Nuzha al-mushtaq,* 221–5.

5. E. Lévi-Provençal, "Le Titre souverain des almoravides et sa légitimation par le califat 'abbaside," *Arabica* 2, no. 3 (1955): 265–80; M. van Berchen, "Titres souverains d'Occident," *Journal Asiatique* 9 (1907): 245–335; H. Munis, "Sept documents inédits de la dynastie almoravide" (in Arabic), *Revista del Instituto de Estudios islamicos en Madrid* 2, no. 1–2 (1954): 55–84. For the text of al-Ghazali's fatwa, see Bibliothèque Générale, Rabat, Abu Bakr Ibn al-'Arabi, MS K1275, ff. 128–30; for that of his letter to Yusuf Ibn Tashufin, see ff. 130–3, or 'Abd Allah 'Inan, *'Asr al-murabitin wa-al-muwahhidin fi al-Maghrib wa-al-Andalus,* 2 vols. (Cairo, 1964), 1:530–3.
6. Ibn Jubayr, *Voyages,* trans. M. Gaudefroy-Demombynes (Paris, 1949–65), 88–91; Van Berchen, "Titres souverains d'occident"; R. Brunschvig, "Un Aspect de la littérature historico-géographique de l'Islam," in *Mélanges Gaudefroy-Demombynes* (Cairo, 1935–45), 147–58; M. Gaudefroy-Demombynes, "Une Lettre de Saladin au calife almohade," in *Mélanges René Basset,* Publications de l'institut des hautes études marocaines, 2 vols. (Paris, 1923), 2:279–304.
7. On Almohad doctrine, see in particular I. Goldziher, "Ibn Tumert et la théologie de l'Islam dans le Maghreb au XIe siècle," in *Le Livre d'Ibn Tumert* (Algiers, 1903), 1–101; R. Brunschvig, "Sur la doctrine du Mahdi Ibn Tumart," *Etudes d'islamologie,* 2 vols. (Paris, 1976), 1:281–93 and 295–302; D. Urvoy, "La Pensée d'Ibn Tumart," *Bulletin d'études orientales* 27 (1974): 19–44.
8. M. Kably, *Société, pouvoir et religion au Maroc à la fin du moyen âge* (Paris, 1986), 271–91.
9. On the relation between the context of the Sa'di emergence and the tradition of southern mahdism, see Kably, *Société, pouvoir et religion,* 250–6, 277–8; M. García-Arenal, "Mahdi, Murabit, Sharif: l'avènement de la dynastie sa'dienne," *Studia Islamica* 71 (1990): 77–114.
10. On the titles of the first three dynasties, see van Berchen, "Titres souverains de l'Occident"; on that of the Sa'dis, see al-Fishtali, *Manahil al-safa fi ma'athir mawalina al-shurafa'* (Rabat, 1972), 25; Ibn al-Qadi, *Al-muntaqa al-maqsur 'ala ma'athir al-khalifa al-Mansur,* 2 vols. (Rabat, 1986), 1:238, 242; G. S. Colin, ed., *Chronique anonyme de la dynastie sa'dienne* (Rabat, 1934), 5.
11. On these elements, see al-Muqaddasi, *Ahsan al-taqasim fi ma'rifat al-aqalim* (Leiden, 1906), 236–8, and especially Ibn Hawqal, *Kitab*

sura al-ard (Leiden, 1938–39), 79–104; trans. J. Kramers and G. Wiet as *Configuration de la terre* (Beirut, 1965), 90–102.
12. H. L. Beck, *L'Image d'Idris II, ses descendants de Fas et la politique sharifienne des sultans Marinides (659–869/1258–1465)* (Leiden, 1989), 38–51.
13. Ibn Hawqal, *Kitab sura al-ard*, 103–104 (Arabic), 101–2 (French); 'Abd al-Hamid, *Kitab al-istibsar fi 'aja'ib al-amsar*, 2nd ed. (Casablanca, 1985), 181.
14. Beck, *L'Image d'Idris*, 49.
15. Lévi-Provençal, *Documents inédits*, 21–23.
16. On the sharifian lineage of the Sa'dis, see R. Le Tourneau, "La Naissance du pouvoir sa'adien vue par l'historien al-Zayyani," in Institut français de Damas, *Mélanges Louis Massignon*, 3 vols. (Damascus, 1956–57), 3:65–80, and especially 65–70 and 73–5; al-Ifrani, *Nozhet-Elhadi*, trans. O. Houdas (Paris, 1888–89), 3–5; Ibn al-Qadi, *Al-muntaqa*, 1:242–3; Abu al-'Abbas Ahmad Ibn Khalid al-Nasiri, *Al-istiqsa' li-akhbar duwal al-Maghrib al-'aqsa*, 9 vols. (Rabat, 1955–59), 5:5. On the Marinid attitude toward sharifism, see Kably, *Société, pouvoir et religion*, 291–302.
17. Kably, *Variations islamistes*, 29–33.
18. This must be qualified as follows. While it never had the same breadth as in the Almoravid and Almohad period, the local jihad could not have been a higher priority at the beginning of the Sa'di movement because it was intimately and strategically linked to the neutralization of the Bedouins living in the Sous from the middle of the fourteenth century who were, almost two centuries later, still dealing with the Portuguese aggressors. On this point, see Kably, *Société, pouvoir et religion*, 246–53, and García-Arenal, "Mahdi, Murabit, Sharif," especially 99–104. In the latter article, the author, while having the merit of giving many corroborative details, takes care to attribute a citation borrowed from our work, apparently not suspecting that the quote is in fact incorporated in an argument in our text, implying the demonstration taken up again in hers and forming, in the end, her point.
19. We cannot help but note that despite the Almohads' declared and quasi-systematic hostility, Malikism surfaced as an acknowledged reality, not coincidentally, just as the nascent authority of the Marinids began to solidify. On the possible reasons for this reappearance, and on the survival and reinvigoration of the Maliki

madhhab in Marinid Morocco, see R. Le Tourneau, "Sur la disparition de la doctrine almohade," *Studia Islamica* 32 (1970): 193–201; M. Shatzmiller, "Les Premiers Mérinides et le milieu religieux de Fès: l'introduction des médersas," *Studia Islamica* 43 (1976): 109–18; Kably, *Société, pouvoir et religion*, 272–85, and, by the same author, "Hawla ba'd mudmarat al-tashawwuf," in *Al-tarikh wa adab al-manaqib* (Rabat, 1988), 67–9.

20. On the rejection of mahdism, see R. Brunschvig, *La Berbèrie orientale sous les Hafsides: des origines à la fin du XVe siècle*, 2 vols. (Paris, 1940–7), 2:20–2; Kably, *Société, pouvoir et religion*, 20–1; on the social policy and military behavior of the Almohad state, see Kably, "Hawla ba'd mudmarat," 72–8.
21. On this subject, see Kably, *Société, pouvoir et religion*, 68–92.
22. On this attempt and its failure, see M. García-Arenal, "The Revolution of Fas in 869/1465 and the Death of Sultan 'Abd al-Haqq al-Marini," *Bulletin of the School of Oriental and African Studies* 41, no. 1 (1978): 43–66; idem, "Sainteté et pouvoir dynastique au Maroc: la résistance de Fès aux Sa'diennes," *Annales; E.S.C.* 4 (1990): 1019–42, and especially 1027–9; Kably, *Société, pouvoir et religion*, 330–7.
23. García-Arenal, "Sainteté et pouvoir," 1021–4; Kably, *Société, pouvoir et religion*, 334–7.
24. García-Arenal, "Sainteté et pouvoir," 1024–6.
25. Al-Murrakushi, *Kitab al-mu'jib* (Cairo, 1994), 171–7. The translation by E. Fagnan, *Histoire des Almohades* (Algiers, 1893), 147–54, gives an overview of these contradictions and of subsequent reactions to the Almoravid system. For reactions to the Almohad system, see Brunschvig, *La Berbérie orientale*, 20–3, 30–42; Kably, *Société, pouvoir et religion*, 20–53.

· THREE ·

Speaking to Princes: Al-Yusi and Mawlay Isma'il

Abdelfattah Kilito

Ibn al-Muqaffa' advises courtiers not to base their relationships with a new prince on their knowledge of his former character because, as he writes, "character alters with the attainment of power (*mulk*), and presumption on old familiarity may have harmful consequences."[1] This is the lesson Falstaff never learned; after consorting in debauchery with the Prince of Wales, he found himself brutally spurned when the Prince was crowned Henry V.

Al-Yusi (d. 1691) devotes a page of his *Muhadarat* to the remarkable Ibn Abi Mahalli, who declared himself the long-awaited Mahdi and, after winning several victories over Zaydan the Sa'di, entered Marrakesh in triumph.[2] Al-Yusi's account is reserved, if not actually critical, regarding Ibn Abi Mahalli, but the concluding section of the account offers something of a surprise:

> It is claimed that after Ibn Abi Mahalli seized Marrakesh, the brothers of his order (*fuqara'*) sought him out to pay him homage and offer their felicitations. But as they stood before him congratulating him on his newly conquered kingdom, one of their

---

Translated by Michael Cooperson.

number remained silent. The prince pressed the man to speak up and explain himself. He replied, "You are Sultan for the time being. I will not speak unless you give me leave to tell the truth without fear of reprisal." "Granted," said Ibn Abi Mahalli. "Speak up, then!"

"In ball games," said the *faqir*, "some two hundred men chase after a ball and struggle to tear it away from each another, risking blows, injuries, and death, all for the sake of the ball. The whole enterprise results in nothing but fear and pain. And if you examine the ball, you find that it's nothing but *shrawit*—that is, a bundle of rags."

When Ibn Abi Mahalli heard this parable, he understood its meaning and burst into tears. "We intended to restore the faith," he said, "but we have gone astray!"[3]

In this scene, Ibn Abi Mahalli is the recipient of two different types of speech: a laudatory discourse uttered by a group and a reproachful one uttered by an individual. In the latter case, the individual in question does not ask to be heard; he may even wish he could avoid speaking altogether. However, his wary silence contrasts sharply with the talkativeness and high spirits of his fellow visitors. As a result, the prince suspects him of being a spoilsport—sport in this case being precisely the issue. But then why did the man come in the first place if he had no intention of paying homage to Ibn Abi Mahalli? His silence is awkward and disturbing, reminiscent of the tales of teachers who glimpse in the audience an unknown young man who refuses to utter a word: faced with obstinate silence, the teacher imagines any number of possible reasons for it. By setting himself apart from the group, the *faqir* attracts attention to himself, particularly the attention of Ibn Abi Mahalli, who "pressed the man to speak." The *faqir* cannot disobey so direct an order; he has no right to remain silent.

But the remarks he has to make may well place him in danger. He knows that "for the moment" he is no longer dealing with a fellow *faqir* but with a sultan and is unsure of how freely he may speak to him. Because he regards Ibn Abi Mahalli as a sultan, he must in turn regard himself as a subject over whom the prince holds the power of life and death. Thus he asks for a promise of immunity (*aman*), which permits him to speak the truth (*haqq*). This necessarily implies that the others have spoken lies (*batil*, closely correlated to *haqq*). It also means that the truth is unpleasant. Finally, it indicates that the truth is also dangerous; telling the truth places the speaker in jeopardy—just like the ball game, one might add.

Even after obtaining protection from the sultan's wrath, the *faqir* does not address the sultan directly but rather in a roundabout way by using a parable or exemplum (*mithal*). He employs neither the first nor second person; in other words, he neither involves himself directly, nor does he implicate Ibn Abi Mahalli. Instead, he confines himself to generalities, referring to the paltry rewards of power, particularly of power attained through violence. This of course supposes that such is the meaning of the parable, a supposition that may well be false. The parable remains in effect allusive, offering no more than the image of several hundred men pursuing a ball, working themselves into a state of excitement, and injuring one another. The game is an act of folly because they are running after a bundle of rags; but the men are too absorbed in the thrill of the chase to think about it. It never occurs to them to examine the ball.

Also demanding examination is the parable itself, which must be viewed in light of not only its literal and superficial meaning but also its deeper significance—that is, its moral. In general, classical authors spell out the meaning of the exempla and parables they employ. This case, however, is different. Here the *faqir* tosses up a riddle and ceases speaking, taking refuge once again in a suspenseful silence. The ball is now, so to speak, in Ibn Abi Mahalli's court, where he is invited to examine it—that is, to meditate on the parable and its meaning for him. He must renounce his attachment to the external form of the ball, to the literal sense of the parable, and to the appearance of power.

Significantly, al-Yusi does not comment on the parable or on the scene itself. He, too, is strangely silent. However, this may be because the *faqir* himself explains the parable, not after delivering it, as is usually the case, but before, when he says, "You are Sultan for the time being." This ambiguous utterance acknowledges Ibn Abi Mahalli's power while suggesting that that power will not last. The very words that affirm the *faqir*'s submission and dependence allude to the transitory nature of that state of affairs. Ibn Abi Mahalli was not a sultan in the past; he is one "for the time being," but his power is evanescent, provisional, and fleeting, for one day he will be sultan no longer.

Ibn Abi Mahalli grasps the moral, bursts into tears, and replies with a single phrase that summarizes his career: "We intended to restore the faith, but we have gone astray!" His intentions were praiseworthy: he wanted to fortify and consolidate religion (*aradna an najbura al-din*), but he has succeeded only in corrupting it (*fa-atlafnah*).

What do his tears signify?[4] They may represent his recognition of the justice of the *faqir*'s words and thus constitute a form of repentance. Or they may be tears of mourning for a lost innocence, shed in recognition of the painful truth (taught by Greek tragedy and Shakespearean drama) that all power is guilty. Without noticing, Ibn Abi Mahalli has lost his way and lost himself and now stands helpless before the *faqir*. This is the way matters stand, he seems to say, and nothing can be done about it.[5]

In any case, although it is nowhere stated outright, Ibn Abi Mahalli's tears are *laudable:* they signify that his heart has yet to harden and that he remains if not capable of being reformed at least capable of acknowledging truth when he hears it. This is a positive thing, a quality the narrator appears to appreciate, even though he refrains from commenting on the scene—a scene that, we must remember, is taking place before a crowd. The tears the sultan sheds are purifying and cathartic. By confessing his transgressions in public, Ibn Abi Mahalli seems to wash himself clean, to find his own lost self again, and to turn "for the time being" back into a *faqir,* a man no different from his humble interlocutor. He is still sultan, and his power, as Ibn al-Muqaffa' writes, cannot but alter his character; but the admonition can still recall his former nature and lead him back to an original innocence.⁶

Let us turn to another account reported by al-Yusi, in this case from the Long Epistle to Mawlay Isma'il. Here the figures in question are Harun al-Rashid and Sufyan al-Thawri:

> When Harun was declared caliph and began to receive visitors, he opened the treasury and began the distribution of prizes in the hope of receiving a visit from Sufyan, his former teacher. Realizing that Sufyan was not going to appear, Harun wrote him a letter and dispatched 'Abbad al-Taliqani to deliver it. 'Abbad found Sufyan sitting with his companions inside the mosque. On seeing him, Sufyan rose to pray. 'Abbad waited until he had finished and then presented him with the letter, but Sufyan refused to touch it, instead asking his companions to read it for him. The letter said: "We await your coming to visit us; we are mindful of the friendship that binds us," etc. Sufyan said to his companion: "Write my answer on the back of the letter." His disciples said, "Master, write to him on a fresh sheet!"
>
> "On the back of the sheet," he said again. "If he has acquired it by proper means, all the better; but if he has acquired it illegally, we'll be rid of it and avoid any contamination of our religion."
>
> He then dictated the following: "To Harun the misguided, deprived of the sweetness of the Koran." On he went in this manner, saying "You have opened the treasury of the believers and distributed its funds to gratify your desires. Have you asked permission of those who fight on behalf of the faith? Have you asked permission of the widows and the orphans?" and so on in this manner, concluding, "As for friendship, we have broken it off; no tie or affection binds us now. Do not write to us again; for if you do, we shall neither read your letter nor reply to it."
>
> After witnessing this, 'Abbad went to the market, removed his clothing, and replaced it with less costly garments; he then dispatched someone to lead his riding animal back to the palace, and repented unto God Almighty. When he returned with the letter to al-Rashid, the caliph understood the meaning of his change in appearance and cried out, "The messenger has succeeded where his master has failed!"

'Abbad handed him the letter. When he read it, he burst into tears and wept in the most piteous fashion. His courtiers (*julasa'*) said, "Sufyan has demonstrated his impertinence; have someone fetch him here!"

"Silence!" he said, "for you are the ones who have misguided me!"[7]

This account has much in common with the first while also possessing distinctive features of its own. The exchange between the prince and the scholar takes place not orally but in writing, which introduces an element of distance, most obviously in space: the caliph is in his palace and the scholar in the mosque. Most surprising, however, is the audaciously outspoken tone of Sufyan's reply. Sufyan uses no parables or formulas of deference and circumspection. So great is his impertinence that he refuses to touch the caliph's letter and has the reply written (by a disciple!) on the back of the same sheet. Moreover, all this happens in the plain sight of numerous onlookers. The account depicts Sufyan as seated among his disciples (who are shocked when he refuses to write his reply on a blank sheet of paper) and Harun as surrounded by his couriers and intimates. The latter are quick to express their outrage, but the caliph silences them, referring to himself using Sufyan's term of reproach: "Silence, for you are the ones who have misguided me!" That the caliph weeps on reading the admonition is a good thing in itself; for him to reprimand his entourage is even more meritorious. He proves that he has understood the lesson and can in turn speak of virtue to those around him.

Al-Yusi concludes the account as follows: "Harun preserved Sufyan's letter and would take it out from time to time and read it." Al-Yusi does not tell us whether Harun wept at every reading.

This account helps clarify the desired result of an admonition and of admonitory speech (*wa'z*) in general—namely, to move the recipient to tears. 'Umar b. 'Abd al-'Aziz, whom al-Yusi admires as much as any of the rightly guided caliphs, on hearing a sermon "began to weep, shriek, and groan to the point he nearly died."[8] Tears result from fear (*khawf*), and classical texts use *waʿz* and *khawf* interchangeably to refer to the same phenomenon. "Admonish me (*ʿizni*)," the Caliph al-Mansur once said to ʿAmr b. ʿUbayd.[9] "Frighten us (*khawwifna*)," said ʿUmar b. al-Khattab to Kaʿb al-Ahbar.[10] In these examples, the prince himself requests a speech that will frighten him and reduce him to tears.

Admonition undertakes to make the prince weep, just as buffoonery has the aim of making him laugh. It sometimes happens that the same person fulfills both functions. Buhlul, for example, would alternately make Harun al-Rashid weep and laugh.[11] Tears, like laughter, defuse tension and leave the prince amenable to granting requests, according favors, and bestowing gifts (which the buffoon generally accepts and the preacher usually declines).[12]

A brief comparison with panegyric and satire will further clarify the significance of admonition. Panegyric encourages, comforts, and stimulates. Satire, on the other hand, discourages, humiliates, and offends. A satire by al-Aʿsha "made the hardhearted and self-possessed ʿAlqama weep like a slave."[13] But unlike admonition, satire also seeks to provoke laughter: it presupposes an audience (of listeners or readers) who will enjoy the victim's humiliation. The author of the satire weaves a fabric of complicity between himself and others—all others, in fact, with the sole and miserable exception of the victim, who is marked forever by the poisoned arrow. When addressed to a prince, an admonition makes him weep, but he is the only one to feel the effect. His entourage, unmoved by the admonition, most often reacts with anger; they resent the author who has so disheartened the prince. But the prince himself asserts his right to be so treated, for in abasing himself before God, he glorifies himself before men. In this way. he turns the sudden despair that afflicts him to his own advantage, for his humility becomes the stuff of stories that will spread and redound to his greater glory.

One model for admonition appears in the Biblical episode

where Nathan rebukes David for sending Uriah the Hittite to his death so that he can marry Uriah's wife Bathsheba. The parable of the poor man's ewe so moved David that he broke down and for seven days fasted and slept only on the ground (II Samuel XII: 1–16). I mention this episode because al-Yusi is fond of citing the following Hadith of the Prophet: "The scholars of my community are like the prophets of the Israelites."[14] Once prophecy ended with Muhammad, the scholars became the guardians of the Revelation, and their relationship to those in power must be analogous to that of the Hebrew prophets and their kings.

Al-Yusi's principal frame of reference is the epoch of the Revelation and the reigns of the rightly guided caliphs, where he searches for a response to the problems that beset the community. Truth is to be found in the past or, more precisely, in one brief historical period that shone with spectacular glory before vanishing forever. One can no longer expect anything from the future. Al-Yusi has no belief whatsoever in progress; rather, history for him consists of decadence and decay. In his works, he returns obsessively to this theme, complaining time and again of living at the end of days (*akhir al-zaman*).[15] Certainly history may hold agreeable surprises, and the ancient verities may on occasion reassert themselves (as during the reign of the Umayyad Caliph 'Umar b. 'Abd al-'Aziz, according to al-Yusi), but only fleetingly, before the long dark night falls once more.[16]

Among the duties of a scholar is the exhortation to good deeds (*al-amr bi-al-ma'ruf*), but he should carry out this duty, according to al-Yusi, only when two conditions are met: assurance that he will have a favorable reception and certainty that the exhortation will not provoke civil unrest (*fitna*). In the *Muhadarat*, al-Yusi harshly criticizes those quixotic Messianists whose good intentions (often indistinguishable, unfortunately, from the promptings of Satan) have brought about anarchy.[17]

Let us take a closer look at the first condition, the assurance of a favorable reception. On what might such an assurance be founded? How can one make a speech of reproach or admonition acceptable to the prince?

Al-Yusi is fully aware that certain utterances may have unpleasant consequences. This is a perennial theme of *adab*-works: speech is dangerous, particularly when addressed to princes. It is better to remain silent. Paradoxically, however, in order to counsel silence, one must have recourse to speech. Among Ibn al-Muqaffa''s variations on this theme is his double recommendation (which, as it happens, he failed to follow for himself) that one should, first of all, hold one's tongue and, second, avoid the company of princes as much as possible.[18] Although Al-Yusi makes no reference to Ibn al-Muqaffa', citing other sources instead, he follows the second recommendation to the letter. However, his position on the first is more complex. He is aware of the virtue of silence and self-restraint: one who keeps silent, he writes, "enjoys security but is useless; he may even cause harm, should the sultan, or anyone else, mistake his silence for consent."[19] Understood as a sign of approval, silence becomes another form of flattery.

In the Long Epistle, al-Yusi criticizes scholars who flatter and dissemble in their dealings with princes. In the *Muhadarat,* he nevertheless praises kindness (*mudarat*), citing numerous examples of scholars who treated heretics and Christians with consideration in order to serve a greater good.[20] He declares that he himself is temperamentally disposed to mildness and disavows *mulahat*—that is, the practice of berating and rebuking others.[21] It is not always useful or opportune to reveal one's thoughts, and tact is especially called for when addressing the prince. In his own relations with Mawlay Isma'il, al-Yusi demonstrates the rules to be followed in such a case.

Al-Yusi's relation to Mawlay Isma'il is essentially epistolary. As noted above, writing establishes a distance, the sender and the receiver being in two different places. Corresponding to this distancing in space is an interval in time—namely, the interval between the dispatching of the message and its reception.

Among the domains where this relationship at a distance appears is that of the fatwa, or consultation on a point of law. Four of al-Yusi's epistles consist of replies to questions posed by

Mawlay Isma'il—one on the subject of the captives of Larash, a second on the sect of the 'Akakiza, and the remaining two on the status of slave women. One of the scholar's functions is thus to state the law and guide the prince's actions. With regard to the fatwa, the initiative appears to come from the prince, who elicits pronouncements from the scholar.

In other cases, the prince is still the initiator of the interchange. Al-Yusi's Long Epistle is a reply to an epistle sent him by Mawlay Isma'il in which the prince reproaches him for, among other things, avoiding his company. Taken as a whole, al-Yusi's epistle serves as a treatise on the relationship between princes and scholars or, more broadly, between political power and what may be called discursive power. Up to a certain point, these two powers remain separate and usually occupy two different spaces; but they are frequently called on to approach one another more closely. Such is the case with Mawlay Isma'il and al-Yusi. As tense and conflicted as their relationship is, the simple act of writing reveals a wish to find some common ground.

The sultan's letter moreover revolves around the question of utterance. It contains a formal demand that al-Yusi speak: "If you have something to say, say it; reply to our queries point by point."[22] Just as Ibn Abi Mahalli exhorted the *faqir* to speak, so too does Mawlay Isma'il demand speech from al-Yusi. The sultan appears nevertheless to doubt that his interlocutor has "something to say" and seems to think al-Yusi incapable of holding up his end of the conversation—that is, of giving a proper accounting of himself. Unless he responds to the sultan "point by point," al-Yusi will be in the wrong. Should he leave even one point unexplained, he will have lost his credibility. Any failure to explain himself completely will make him culpable.

But al-Yusi does the sultan one better: he comments slyly on his correspondent's doubts about his ability to speak. "What could possibly prevent me from speaking, should I so desire? The language is Arabic, and I have the support of both reason (*ma'qul*) and tradition (*manqul*)."[23] A Berber accused of having nothing to say, he invokes his knowledge of Arabic and evokes the connotations of the verb *a'raba:* "to speak clearly, to employ clear and positive arguments." In citing the *ma'qul* and the *manqul,* he designates the two foundations indispensable to any exchange of opinion.

Yet he still writes under constraint. Various reasons, he says, led him to postpone his reply, the first being *hayba*—that is, the veneration mixed with fear he feels toward the sultan, reminiscent of what the *faqir* must have felt when speaking to Ibn Abi Mahalli. For this reason al-Yusi is tempted at first to be silent but, like the *faqir,* is eventually persuaded by the sultan to speak. He makes no explicit request for *aman,* the promise of safety from the sultan's wrath, but he implies that one is indeed necessary. He reminds the sultan of the unpleasant consequences of speaking out, emphasizing that his hesitation is motivated by fear that the sultan will think him bent on criticism (*muraja'a*), contradiction (*muhajja*), or contentiousness (*munaza'a*). He is equally careful to point out that he is writing only in self-defense—that is, in obedience to the sultan's command (*amr*).[24]

What status is al-Yusi's discourse to occupy? He presents it as analogous to the discourse of scholars when they comment on and discuss the words of older authorities without in any way disparaging their predecessors. It is in this spirit that he will comment on the epistle sent him by the sultan. He will debate the sultan's words but not the sultan himself; as he says, "discourse addresses itself to discourse, not to the author of a discourse."[25] To clarify this disengagement between author and discourse, he asserts that he will actually be debating against the secretaries who drafted the sultan's epistle. This reference to the secretaries implies not only that he is not challenging the sultan but that he is not even challenging his discourse, as if Mawlay Isma'il had no part in the debate at all. The sultan's role thus becomes that of a spectator or referee who will weigh the secretaries' arguments as well as al-Yusi's.[26]

Nor is this all. Just as he places the sultan behind the secretaries, al-Yusi places himself behind the ancients—that is, the great authorities of the past. Certainly it is he who speaks, but he has arranged matters so that his discourse will do no more than echo what his illustrious predecessors have already said. Citation, accordingly, plays an important role in his epistle. Al-Yusi cites Hadith, sayings of the Prophet's companions, edifying tales, proverbs, poems, and fables, including the account of Harun al-Rashid and Sufyan al-Thawri. Taken to its extreme, this technique means that it is not al-Yusi who is speaking at all; or, if he does speak, it is only by hiding behind the names of universally recognized figures, legitimizing himself using their example and their prestige. He is not pleading his own case but rather that of the ancients themselves.

So far, we have seen the scholar under an obligation to write, whether to pronounce a fatwa demanded of him by the prince or to defend himself against accusations leveled at him. In the one case as in the other, the scholar replies to the prince. Having missed the chance to initiate the interchange, he assumes a secondary role. This role is convenient inasmuch as the scholar need offer no justification of his own for taking up his pen.

The situation is different when the scholar decides to write to the prince without being asked, particularly when he allows himself to compose a letter in which he reproaches the prince and reminds him of the principles of justice. Twice al-Yusi found himself in this situation. In the first case, he addressed Mawlay Isma'il in a letter known as the Short Epistle (to distinguish it from the Long Epistle mentioned above); in the second, he wrote a letter entitled "Exhortation of Kings to Do Justice." Unfortunately, neither document is dated, making it impossible either to situate one with respect to the other or to situate both with respect to the Great Epistle, composed in 1096/1685.

In "Exhortation of Kings to Do Justice," al-Yusi describes the transition from caliphal to autocratic government. Only in the very last lines does he mention the sultan, whom he describes as "loving truth, and never swerving from the search for it."[27] The style, measured and circumspect, is that of *mudarat* or affability.

In the Short Epistle, on the other hand, al-Yusi addresses Mawlay Isma'il directly from beginning to end. This oft-cited document is shockingly audacious, adopting the tone of *mulahat* or reprimand. It consists of an admonition in the style of Ibn 'Abbad's address to the Marinid Abu Faris. As we have seen, the admonition of princes is a genre with a long pedigree in Arabic culture; for one reason or another, however, this epistle of al-Yusi made a particularly strong impression on his contemporaries.[28] The reader who examines it today still does so in stunned admiration.

Al-Yusi was well aware of his own temerity. The letter contains evidence that he sought to soften the impact of his criticism using various oratorical precautions. It contains examples of the traditional means of persuasion, including propitiatory formulas, praise of the addressee, prayers on his behalf, protestations of submission and fidelity, sermonizing passages, and the like. But its most arresting feature is that al-Yusi presents it as if the sultan had actually requested it: "For some time I have noted that our sovereign seeks out exhortations (*mawa'iz*) and advice (*nush*) and desires to see the portals of prosperity and success open before him. I thus resolved to address to our sovereign a letter that, should he take notice of it, shall permit me to hope that he attain the bounties of this world and the next and ascend to the highest of honors; and albeit I am unworthy to pronounce exhortations, I hope that our sovereign be worthy to receive them and to abstain from reproaches."[29] Al-Yusi insidiously suggests that he composed his admonition in response to an eager wish on the part of the addressee. In other words, the initiative once again falls to the sultan.

In response to the question of whether a prince should prefer to be loved or to be feared, Machiavelli states that "he should be both; but in view of the difficulty of combining the two, it is safer to make oneself feared than to make oneself loved, if one must choose one or the other."[30] For his part, al-Yusi argues that a wise prince does not base his policies on a desire to be loved, since "men serve kings out of fear or greed, and fear makes love superfluous."[31] Citing this old saying in support of his position, he affirms—in terms similar to Machiavelli's—that "for the sultan . . . it is better to be feared than loved (*al-faraqu minhu khayrun min hubbuhi*)."

In actuality, however, the prince behaves as if he will not be satisfied with the fear he inspires in his subjects; he seeks to win their hearts as well. Al-Yusi knows this better than anyone else: in his letters, he describes not only the veneration and fear (*hayba*) he feels before the sultan but also the affection (*muhabba*) he bears for him. One must conclude that power cannot be absolute unless based on a union of love and fear.

NOTES

1. Ibn al-Muqaffaʻ, *Al-adab al-kabir*, ed. Y. Abu Halqa, 3rd ed. (Beirut, 1964), 20.
2. On Ibn Abi Mahalli (d. 1613), see J. Berque, "L'Homme qui voulet être roi," in *Ulémas, fondateurs et insurgés du Maghreb* (Paris, 1982), 45–80, and ʻAbd al-Majid al-Qadduri, *Ibn Abi Mahalli al-faqih al-thaʼir* (Rabat, 1991).
3. *Al-muhadarat*, ed. M. Hajji and A. S. Iqbal, 2 vols. (Beirut, 1982), 1:262–3. I cite this passage from the translation by J. Berque, *Al-Yousi: problèmes de la culture marocaine au XVIIe siècle* (The Hague, 1958), 87.
4. Tears, according to al-Jahiz, "are a sign of delicacy and sensibility. . . . The pious use weeping to better approach God and beg his mercy. . . . Sufyan b. Muhriz wept so many tears he lost his eyesight. Many are those praised for [the readiness with which] they wept, including Yahya and Haytham, both nicknamed 'The Weeper'." *Le Livre des avares*, trans. C. Pellat (Paris, 1951), 8. Recent research has come to address the history of tears. For France in the eighteenth and nineteenth centuries, see A. Buffault, *Historie des larmes* (Paris, 1986).
5. Al-Ifrani reproduces the scene reported by al-Yusi, placing before it a passage describing the transformation Ibn Abi Mahalli underwent after his victory: "When Abu Mahalli made his entry into the caliphal palace at Marrakesh, he did as he pleased there. . . . The intoxication of power (*nashwat al-mulk*) turned his head, causing him to forget the fear of God and the asceticism on which he had based his conduct." Al-Ifrani, *Nuzha al-hadi*, 2nd ed. (Rabat,

n.d.), 207. "He did as he pleased": this evocation of arbitrariness, intemperance, and abuse of power alludes to a well-known Hadith: "If you have no shame, you can do as you please." In giving in to his passions and neglecting the precepts of moderation, Ibn Abi Mahalli is no longer subject to reason, *'aql*, a term whose etymological meaning is "cord" or "leash" and, by extension, restraint and wisdom.

6. Or perhaps not. In his work *Islit al-khirrit*, Ibn Abi Mahalli evokes his childhood and the figure of his father: "He came to beat me after first tying me up with a cord, having taken notice of my escapades and my enthusiasm for chasing sparrows, playing ball, and attending weddings" (cited by 'Abd al-Majid al-Qadduri, *Ibn Abi Mahalli*, 39). This narrative shares several features with the account given by al-Yusi:

- *The ball* The adult Ibn Abi Mahalli has changed little since his childhood. He still plays ball! His childhood escapades never end but rather continue into his erratic and unsettled adulthood.
- *The weddings* The marriage ceremony affirms the power of the male, who, by virtue of his nightly exploit, becomes the focus of attention and admiration. See M. E. Combs-Schilling, *Sacred Performances: Islam, Sexuality, and Sacrifice* (New York: Columbia University Press, 1989), 192–4. An analogous ceremony can be said to take place when Ibn Abi Mahalli becomes sultan and the crowd throngs to the palace to congratulate him.
- *The sparrows ('asafir)* These transitory winged creatures prefigure the people of the lower orders (*'awamm*) who were to follow him (*Muhadarat*, 1:262). The classical authors spared little rancor in choosing terms for the common people, and comparisons to fowl were common. Al-Yusi (*Muhadarat*, 1: 108) notes that commoners scamper after every raven that croaks (*na'iq*). Inconstancy, instability, and frivolity were presumed common to both the common people and the sparrow. The expression *hilm al-'asafir* (literally, "the forbearance of a sparrow") refers to stupidity, mindlessness, and dullness. Most remarkable is the analogy between the father and the *faqir*, the latter appearing as a substitute for the former. Both chastise Ibn Abi Mahalli, one

by beating him after tying him with a cord and the other by reproaching him and making him see reason (*'aql*), which here again signifies a bridle, cord, or hobble. Ibn Abi Mahalli's tears are the same he shed when his father punished him.

7. Al-Yusi, *Rasa'il,* ed. F. al-Qabli, 2 vols. (Casablanca, 1981), 1:192–3.
8. Ibid., 253.
9. Al-Sharishi, *Sharh maqamat al-Hariri,* 4 vols. (Cairo, 1952–3), 2:182.
10. Al-Ibshili, *Al-mustaraf,* ed. A. al-Tabba' (Beirut, 1981), 105.
11. Al-Naysaburi, *'Uqala' al-majanin,* ed. al-As'ad (Beirut, 1987), 140–2.
12. One notes in passing that Louis XIV wept after hearing a sermon by the Père de la Rue. See E. Lavisse, *Louis XIV,* 2 vols. (Paris, 1978), 2:709.
13. Al-Qayrawani, *Questions de critique littéraire,* tran. C. Pellat (Algiers, 1955), 19.
14. Al-Yusi, *Rasa'il,* 1:243.
15. On the topos of the "convicium saeculi," see Berque, *Al-Yousi,* 83–4.
16. This nostalgia for origins is nothing new. What scholar has not seen history as an exile? See A. Laroui, "Islam et état," in *Islam et modernité* (Paris, 1986), 34–6. In al-Yusi's case, however, nostalgia takes on a particular emphasis, combining nostalgia for the past with longing for his birthplace. Al-Yusi is a nomad and a man of the desert ("ana rajulun badawi," he proclaims in the Long Epistle, *Rasa'il,* 1:170). As such, he deplores the city, which represents constriction, crowding, sedition, greed, and hypocrisy. City life corrupts social mores, including diet (excessive consumption of meat), conjugal relations (male loss of power over ever more demanding wives), and parental authority (children corrupted by the loose morals of the town) (166–7). By way of contrast, al-Yusi paints an idyllic picture of his stay in the country, where he finds peace, innocence, generosity, and transparent simplicity. He notes that the term *badiya* (country, wilderness) originally signified the visible, the clear, and the externally apparent (182). Renewing one's ties to rural places is to go back in time and renew the link to one's origins.
17. *Muhadarat,* 1:257–60.

18. Compare the ambiguous relationship between the sage Bidpai and the King of India in *Kalila wa-Dimna;* see also the *Hiero* of Xenophon and the excellent study by L. Strauss, *De la tyrannie,* trans. H. Kern (Paris, 1954) [in English: *On Tyranny: An interpretation of Xenophon's Hiero* (New York, 1948); revised and expanded, ed. V. Gourevitch and M. Roth (New York, 1991)].
19. *Rasa'il,* 1:154.
20. *Muhadarat,* 2:398–401.
21. Ibid., 1:375.
22. *Rasa'il,* 1:232.
23. Ibid.
24. Ibid., 1:132.
25. Ibid., 1:133.
26. Ibid.
27. Ibid., 1:255.
28. Al-Qadiri, *Nashr al-Mathani li-ahl al-qarn al-hadi 'ashr wal-thani,* ed. M. Hajji and A. Tawfiq, 4 vols. (Rabat, 1977–86), 3:25–6.
29. *Rasa'il,* 1:237. I cite this passage as it is translated by E. Fumey, *Archives marocaines* 9 (1906): 111.
30. Machiavelli, *The Prince,* in *Oeuvres complètes* (Paris, 1952), 339.
31. *Rasa'il,* 1:218.

Part Two

PERIPHERIES

· FOUR ·

The Sanctuary (Hurm) in Precolonial Morocco

Mohamed El Mansour

The *hurm* as a concept and an institution appears often in ethnographic and anthropological literature dealing with North African societies but has never been singled out as an independent subject of investigation. When tackling this issue, other related concepts necessarily emerge, such as *zwag*, *'ar*, and *shafa'a*, all of which involve some form of sacred protection. In fact, the semantic fields of these concepts tend to overlap for the simple reason that all of them convey in one way or another the idea of holy protection. As will be seen here, even the concept of *hurm* bears more than a single meaning.

SACRED TERRITORY

The most common meaning of *hurm* (*haram* in standard Arabic) is that of a "sacred place, a place set apart from the space of ordinary existence."[1] Obviously, this definition is incomplete, since the idea of *hurm* encompasses not only space but also a number of domains that are both material and immaterial. Thus saints and shurafa' speak about it, in the plural form, under which we find not only the sacred territory but all kinds of moral and social privileges. These *hurumat* belong in principle to God, but who is better qualified than God's friends and the people of the Prophet's household (*ahl al-bayt*) to claim them? A *hurm* or a sanctuary is seen as the extension of the divine realm that is worthy of respect and veneration, a place where people are compelled to refrain from all forms of violence. Because a sanctuary is the locus of the divine presence, it is often a place of worship, but its religious role tends to be overshadowed by the social function of serving as an asylum or place of refuge.

The idea of sanctuary is as old as religious belief itself. As W. Robertson Smith has shown, the institution of the sanctuary was an integral feature of Semitic religious belief. The Hebrews had a number of cities of refuge, and in pre-Islamic Arabia there were also sacred places called the *haram* or *hima,* the most important of them being the sanctuary of Mecca.[2] North Africans also seem to have been familiar with the idea of holy protection, and the custom of *zwag* (seeking protection) was most probably present among the Berbers long before the Arab conquest in the seventh century. In other parts of the world, traditional and tribal societies in particular needed some form of holy protection that served as a guarantee against tyranny and power abuse. Even in Islam, which aimed at establishing a righteous world order and providing guarantees against "the strong hand," the right of sanctuary was not abolished; on the contrary, it was confirmed. In addition to establishing the *haram* of Mecca, the new religion added a warning that all transgressors would be threatened with "the curse of God, his angels and all men."[3]

In the Maghrib the *hurm* is usually identified with the shrine of a saint and its immediate surroundings. E. Westermarck collected abundant data on sacred places in Morocco at the beginning of this century and defined the *hurm* as "the sacred domain of a saint."[4] The concept of the *hurm* in Morocco was directly inspired by that of the holy sanctuary of Mecca. In fact, the Moroccan royal decree (*zahir*), which established or recognized existing *hurumat,* referred to the Meccan sanctuary, granting local sites the same attributions, such as the prohibition of the shedding of blood, hunting, or even the cutting of trees. Every living thing within the sanctuary was considered to be holy, or at least to be enjoying the holiness of the place, and therefore was worthy of protection. The limits set around the *hurm* and the ritualization of visitation to the shrine of the *hurm* master were also structured in a way that clearly invoked pilgrimage to Mecca.[5]

Each *hurm* had well-defined limits, sometimes specified in the written documents. The *hurm* of Mawlay 'Abd al-Salam Ibn Mashish in northern Morocco, for instance, extended over a large area that included the whole or parts of several tribal territories. Although this area did not enjoy the same degree of holiness as the saint's shrine itself, it did, nevertheless, offer asylum to anyone who placed himself within its limits. In Fez, the sanctuary of Mawlay Idris included a number of streets and blocks of houses surrounding the holy shrine. In principle, any person fearing reprisals from an enemy or a government agent could feel secure within the *hurm* limits, which were clearly indicated.[6]

In Morocco, not all sanctuaries were of equal sanctity. A person looking for a safe refuge had to study very carefully the map of sacred ground available to him. Usually saints' shrines came first on the list of sanctuaries. Westermarck observed that mosques, for instance, were rarely used as asylums despite their sacred character. Popular piety tended to accord a much greater value to a saint's shrine at the expense of "God's abode" (*bayt Allah*).[7] Moreover, saintly shrines themselves were not treated equally. If we were to draw a map of the sacred, we would end up with a multitude of spots of different shades of color depending on the intensity of holiness attributed to each sanctuary.

The degree of respect and veneration enjoyed by the sanctuary depended on many variables, the most important of which was popular recognition and the association of the *hurm* with a prestigious saintly lineage or a celebrated Sufi order. With the rise of sharifism during the last five centuries, the sharifian *hurumat* tended to become holier and, in people's eyes, to enjoy more *baraka*. However, *baraka* alone was never enough to command authority, and a sanctuary with a strong group cohesion behind it was more likely to draw respect. Thus *hurumat* such as those of Mawlay 'Abd al-Salam Ibn Mashish or Mawlay Idris acquired more importance, not only because of their greater sanctity, derived from a prestigious sharifian descent, but also because of the solidarity shown by their *shurafa'* in face of transgression. The history of Morocco abounds with examples. While a sultan such as the 'Alawi Sidi Muhammad Ibn 'Abd Allah (ruled 1757–90) could easily attack the *hurm* of the Sharqawi *zawiya* in 1785 and restore it to *makhzan* authority, he never attempted to dislodge his rebellious son, Mawlay al-Yazid, from the Mashishi sanctuary. Had he done so, he would have certainly aroused against him the feelings of both the powerful Idrisi *shurafa'* and a much larger public opinion than in the case of the Sharqawis.

AN EXAMPLE OF A *HURM*: THE SANCTUARY OF MAWLAY 'ABD AL-SALAM IBN MASHISH

The 'Alami *shurufa'* of northern Morocco, like other Idrisi *shurufa'*, saw their religious prestige greatly enhanced as a result of the rehabilitation of sharifdom during the Marinid period (thirteenth to fifteenth centuries). They also benefited from the rise of Shadhili Sufism, since Mawlay 'Abd al-Salam Ibn Mashish (d. 1228) was also the Sufi shaykh of Abu al-Hasan al-Shadhili. The veneration of Ibn Mashish grew with time, and his shrine became the object of an annual pilgrimage, considered in the popular tradition as "the pilgrimage of the poor," a substitute for those who could not afford the journey to Mecca.[8]

However, it was only in the sixteenth century that the Mashishi *hurm* came under the official aegis of the Sa'di sultan, Ahmad al-Mansur (d. 1603). Following the battle of Wad al-Makhazin against the Portuguese (4 August 1578) in which the 'Alami *sharif* Sidi Ibn Raysun played a prominent role, Ahmad al-Mansur issued a royal decree that formally established the Mashishi sanctuary. Al-Mansur, who was proclaimed sultan on the battlefield, had won a decisive victory by defeating not only the Iberian challenge from the north but also the Ottoman ambitions from the east. The Sa'dis reaped enormous prestige from their success, but they were in no position to take all the credit for themselves. These *shurafa'* who came from the southern fringes had legitimized their rule with a victory won far from their own political base, in a territory traditionally known to be the stronghold of the Idrisi *shurafa'*. The religious prestige of their Idrisi cousins was such that the Sa'dis could hardly remain insensitive to them. The least they could do to reward them for the role they had played in repulsing the Christian threat was to grant them a number of privileges. In fact, the Sa'dis were eager to show their willingness to share power with the northern *shurafa'*, although in a limited and symbolic way.

The privileges granted to the 'Alami *shurafa'* included tax exemption, the right to share in the income of the shrine of Mawlay Idris in Fez, and above all, the making of a vast territory around the shrine of Mawlay 'Abd al-Salam into a sanctuary. The *hurm* was established in the name of Mawlay 'Abd al-Salam and his ancestor Sidi Mizwar and extended over the lands of several tribes of the Jbala.[9] It was declared inviolable, which meant that it lay outside *makhzan* jurisdiction, and any fugitive who took refuge in it was immune from pursuit. The decree issued by al-Mansur, and renewed regularly by sultans thereafter, emphasized the immunity of the *hurm,* stating that the "*makhzan* could in no way come near the *hurm* or circumambulate it" (*la yaqrabuhu wa-la yatufu bih*) and that its status was identical to that of the *haram* of Mecca, meaning that no one would be allowed to shed blood or cut trees on it. The last sultan to have renewed the Sa'di *zahir* was Mawlay al-Hasan at the end of the nineteenth century. "We have taken on ourselves," says the decree, "to respect [the sanctuary] within its limits as an inviolable *hurm* for whoever takes refuge in it."[10]

OTHER MANIFESTATIONS OF SACRED PROTECTION

The *hurm* as a place of asylum was one form of sacred protection among several that assumed different forms. In addition to sacred space, there was sacred time, during which violence was prohibited. The phenomenon is pre-Islamic and was certainly found in many tribal societies where the diffusion of power necessitated some accommodation among the various groups to ensure the continuity of the social and economic order. It is well known, for instance, that the nomadic tribes of the Middle Atlas used to refrain from violent behavior at certain times of the year to allow basic economic activities such as plowing or harvesting to take place.[11]

In southern Morocco, saints intervened to regulate the use of violence by appointing a particular time during which hostilities were temporarily halted. Thus during the power vacuum preceding the rise of the Sa'di dynasty in the sixteenth century, a saint in the Sous named Muhammad Ibn Mubarak succeeded in imposing peace on the tribes of the region for three days a week, which became known as "Ibn Mubarak's days."[12] Prohibitions in effect at the holy *haram* of Mecca were respected during these days of peace, including the ban on the shedding of blood and the killing of animals or even insects. Ibn Mubarak's days became so respected, we are told, that a murderer could meet the son of his victim without fear of revenge. According to a local author, the tribes of the Sous, both Arab and Berber, adhered to the system devised by Ibn Mubarak and respected it.[13] In this particular case, a saint, although he did not have a material sanctuary of his own, was nevertheless able to create a symbolic *hurm* that, during three days a week, extended over a large area.

In fact, living saints extended their holy protection to places far from their own *zawiya,* or retreat. In principle, there was no spatial limit for a "friend of God" who shared in the divine power, since his kingdom was that of God himself. Hagiographic writings are full of instances in which saints provided protection to persons who were then able to travel long distances without being molested. Thus 'Abd al-Salam al-Qadiri (d. 1698) reports the case of a runaway slave who, in the time of Mawlay Isma'il (1672–1727), took refuge in the *zawiya* of Ahmad Ibn 'Abd Allah Ma'n in Fez and, after having received the saint's protection, was able to travel to very distant places without being captured by government agents.[14] The slave belonged to a dignitary, and the sultan wanted to take him away from him to be enlisted in the famous *'abid* black army. But the slave was so attached to his master that he decided to take refuge in the *zawiya*. The sultan became furious and ordered the slave to be killed. When the saint noticed the slave's anxiety, he went to him and gave him a stick, saying to him: "Just leave this place, and do your prayers regularly. No harm will reach you." On hearing this, we are told by al-Qadiri, "the slave traveled to the Mashriq, where he carried out the pilgrimage several times, and then returned to the Maghrib and roved as he pleased without suffering the least injury during his voyage, thanks to the *baraka* of our Lord Ahmad, may God be pleased with him."[15]

'Abd al-Salam al-Qadiri mentions another miracle of Ahmad Ibn 'Abd Allah in which the saint extended his protection to a deserter from the city militia (*rumat*) of Fez. After he had spent some time in the sanctuary, Sidi Ahmad looked at him one day and said: "Just go. You have nothing to fear!" The deserter left the *zawiya* and found work transporting sand and limestone from one part of the city to another. When people met him in the streets, they could not believe their eyes because they knew that *makhzan* officials were pursuing him, but he just smiled and went on his way without the least bit of trouble. Finally he was dropped from the *rumat* roster and was never bothered again, according to al-Qadiri.[16]

Many miracles are attributed to this saint, who lived in the city of Fez at the time of the powerful sultan Mawlay Isma'il (d. 1727), who used every means to curtail the traditional liberties of the people of Fez. In the face of an authoritarian ruler, the saint stepped in to defend the city and provide protection to the helpless. Thus while Ibn Mubarak intervened to compensate for the absence of political authority, Ahmad Ibn 'Abd Allah in

Fez intervened at a time when people were suffering from too much of it. The two cases clearly show the role of saints and the *hurm* institution in preserving equilibrium between two extremes—that of lawlessness on one hand and of despotism on the other.

The realization of such an equilibrium in society was the task not only of saints but also of all others who shared in sanctity—namely, the *shurafa'*. With the consolidation of sharifian ideology in Morocco from 1500 on, the idea developed about the essential role of the Prophet's lineage in protecting not only the *umma* but the whole of creation. By virtue of their special relationship to God, the *shurafa'* enjoyed his special protection, which they passed on to the rest of humankind. "The people of my House," said the Prophet, "are like those on Noah's Ark; whoever gets on is safe, and whoever is left behind is lost."[17] According to the prophetic tradition, they are the guarantors of peace and harmony on earth. Some sharifian groups such as the Wazzanis claim that they can even guarantee salvation in the world to come.[18]

As a group enjoying a special relationship with God, the *shurafa'* are entitled to a number of privileges that take the form of *hurumat*. In the Moroccan context, they are known as the people of *al-taqwir wa-al-ihtiram* (consideration and respect) and therefore worthy of reverence.[19] The maltreatment of members of the holy lineage is seen as "a violation of God's domain" (*qasr hurumat Allah*), which never passes without a divine punishment.[20] According to Muhammad Ibn al-Tayyib al-Qadiri (d. 1773), the political turmoil and the natural calamities that affected the country following the death of Mawlay Isma'il were the result of the many abuses to which the *shurafa'* were exposed.[21] In Fez the presence of Mawlay Idris and his descendants was always considered to be an essential factor in the well-being and prosperity enjoyed by the city. If the people of Fez were able to endure the many hardships that befell them, it was thanks to the patron saint, Mawlay Idris, and the heavy concentration of the *shurafa'* within the city walls.[22]

THE SOCIAL SIGNIFICANCE OF THE *HURM*

As we have seen in the case of the Mashishi *hurm*, the sanctuary is the property of the group and is counted among the privileges enjoyed by that group. But it is more than just a privilege or a source of benefit, whether material or moral. As Jacques Berque observed for the Seksawa, sacred places symbolize the group's identity and continuity.[23] They also stand for the unity of the group and its cohesion within the rest of society. The historical role of the Idrisi *hurm* in Fez as a pole of attraction for the various sharifian families is significant in this respect.

The sanctuary also answered a social need. It provided a shelter against injustice and allowed the community to solve its problems by means other than those of violence. When *makhzan* authority weakened, *hurumat* represented a substitute for the central power. In this sense they constituted an answer to the crisis of the state. To take the example of Fez, it is quite clear from the local histories that in the seventeenth and eighteenth centuries, in periods of a power vacuum, the *hurumat* became more numerous and were more frequently solicited.[24] In a milieu characterized by instability and violence, sanctuaries provided islands of peace. They allowed tribes and other social groups to work out nonviolent solutions, thus serving as violence regulators.

But even during periods of strong authority, sanctuaries did not remain inactive. They provided shelter against abuses of power and especially against the arbitrary rule of local despots. When the demands of the *makhzan* or the local potentate became unbearable, the common person found relief in the *hurm*, where the sultan's kingdom did not reach.

Finally, the presence of sanctuaries symbolized a certain delimitation between different sources of power in society. The acceptance of the *hurm* institution by sultans and the granting of considerable privileges to the groups associated with them reflected a power distribution between the temporal authorities and the religious groups. This problem of the distribution of power had its origins with the sharifian families in the first place. In fact, from the sixteenth century, the sharifian dynasties that ruled Morocco found themselves in an ambiguous and embarrassing situation. First, the Sa'di and the 'Alawi *shurafa'* who founded these new dynasties were geographically marginal since they came from the southern fringes, far from the traditional concentrations of sharifdom in Fez and northwestern Morocco. Second, they were in a sense second-class *shurafa'* insofar as they lacked the preeminence (*zuhur*) and the prestige (*jah*) enjoyed by the Idrisis.[25]

The rehabilitation of sharifdom was a historical process that took shape around the Idrisi *shurafa'* under the Banu Marin in the fourteenth and fifteenth centuries.[26] Therefore, the coming to power of the southern *shurafa'* must have been a disappointment to the Idrisis. Both the Sa'dis and the 'Alawis were aware of this and tried persistently to provide the Idrisis with compensation by redistributing power among the various sharifian lineages. The aim of the ruling dynasty was to confine the other *shurafa'* to the religious field by granting them a wide range of privileges in the form of donations, tax exemptions, decrees of distinction (*al-taqwir wa-al-ihtiram*), land grants, and the right of sanctuary. Idrisi *shurafa'* such as the Wazzanis found compensation by establishing a Sufi *tariqa* and by taking comfort in the fact that spiritual leadership of the universe was more important than worldly dynastic rule. In fact, the Wazzanis and the other Idrisi *shurafa'* did not always content themselves with the spiritual realm, but a form of personal insurance, a guarantee of access, a kind of civic responsibility sometimes developed into strong regional powers through the *hurm* institution and the exercise of other privileges.[27]

THE TEMPORAL POWERS AND THE *HURM* INSTITUTION

The Islamic conception of power does not make a distinction between temporal and spiritual power since the caliph usually holds both. Moroccan sultans, like other Islamic rulers, were as much political figures as they were religious leaders. Moreover, the sultan as *shurafa'* holds as much *baraka* as any other descendent of the Prophet, if not more. Yet in everyday life it is the temporal aspect of a sultan's rule that is most manifest. In the exercise of their daily functions, sultans appealed constantly to the *shurafa'* and the *murabitun* (saints). These religious figures were in effect part of the royal ceremonial whether the sultan was in his capital or on the move throughout the countryside. Their presence was essential not only in conferring legitimacy on the sultan's actions but also in helping him carry out the daily tasks of government, particularly through the process of mediation.

In the same way, the *hurm* as a religious institution played an essential part in the overall politicoreligious order. Far from being an institution totally directed against the sultan and his *makhzan*, the sanctuary could at times be of great help to the central government itself. By providing refuge to a rebellious prince, for instance, the *hurm* usually presented the sultan with a peaceful alternative for resolving a political crisis that, if allowed to end in violence, could be both costly and risky. The *hurm* as the symbol of nonviolence offered a necessary mechanism for arranging a negotiation between the contending parties. For the loser in the political game it offered a face-saving device and a way out of a deadlock. The sanctuary also served as a safety valve for the *makhzan* by providing an outlet for suppressed frustrations and feelings of despair. When a tribal group resorted to the *hurm* to protest the abuses of a governor, it was a signal to the sultan that something had to be done to redress an unjust situation. In such cases the sultan would either dismiss the governor or arrange for a reconciliation between the two parties.

Under a strong centralizing sultan there was usually a tendency to curtail the powers of the religious groups by limiting their sanctuary privileges.[28] However, efforts in this regard never went so far as to threaten the existence of the institution itself.

Actually, sultans sought to control and regulate the *hurm* privileges, particularly through the promulgation of the special decree (*zahir al-taqwir wa-al-ihtiram*). Many of these documents are nothing more than routine texts granting the beneficiaries "consideration and respect," which in practical terms meant preferential treatment by local *makhzan* officials and exemption from arbitrary taxes. But some decrees of this type were more elaborate when they were delivered to *hurm* holders. Thus a *zahir* by Sidi Muhammad Ibn 'Abd Allah to the Raysuni *shurafa'* reiterated the old Sa'di privileges—namely, the concession made to the Raysunis of lands in the region of the battle of Wad al-Makhazin.[29] The same document also granted these *shurafa'* the right to control a weekly market held within the limits of their traditional sanctuary at Tazrut.

As a *sharif*, the sultan was perhaps nothing more than an equal to the rest of the *shurafa'* but as head of the Islamic community, his means of intervention in the affairs of the various religious groups were considerable. Just as he could intervene in the internal affairs of a *zawiya* to support one candidate to the shaykhdom against another, he could also easily decide to appoint a particular person or a particular group to run the sanctuary at the expense of others. In such a way he could increase considerably his leverage among the religious groups. One way to control sanctuaries was to appoint from among the elite of the sharifian groups a *naqib* (manager of sharifian affairs) who was well disposed to the *makhzan*. The sultan's manipulative power was even greater when dissension appeared within a particular group. Thus taking advantage of the divisions that undermined the sharifian groups in Fez, Mawlay 'Abd Allah (ruled 1728–57) conceded the *hurm* of Mawlay Idris to the 'Imrani *shurafa'* at the expense of other branches of the Idrisis.[30]

THE SULTAN AS *HURM* MAKER

Sanctity alone is not enough to make a *hurm* respected. A sanctuary that has behind it a strong religious group or that enjoys the favors of the *makhzan* is more likely to gain respect and popularity. Holiness and might seem to have gone hand in hand. After all, isn't the fear of mighty forces at the origin of religious belief in the first place? Two historical examples illustrate this fact.

The first relates to the elevation in Fez of the *zawiya* of 'Abd al-Rahman al-Fasi to the rank of sanctuary by the 'Alawi sultans. The second deals with the emergence during the last three centuries of a purely *makhzan* sanctuary—the *zwag al-madfa'*, the sanctuary of the cannon.

The Fasi Zawiya

Between the mighty sultan Mawlay Isma'il (d. 1727) and the city of Fez, relations were always rather tense. The authoritarian and centralizing policies of this sultan necessarily clashed with the *esprit frondeur* of an urban community that was very jealous of its traditional liberties. In fact, to subdue and rule a city like Fez proved to be a much harder task than anything else Mawlay Isma'il had to face during his long reign. Sheer force was used extensively to curb the rebellious spirit of the city, but it was of limited efficacy. The people of Fez resented above all the *makhzan*'s heavy taxation and the sultan's grandiose scheme of building a black army by recruiting former slaves (*haratin*). Mawlay Isma'il realized that his heavy-handed policy needed to be softened with what the French were to call later *la politique des égards*. In other words, the sultan tried to gain support inside the city by granting privileges and by coopting the religious elite of the city itself.

One of the pillars of Mawlay Isma'il's policy in Fez was the special relationship he forged with some of the most eminent of the ulama of the time, 'Abd al-Qadir al-Fasi and his son Muhammad Ibn 'Abd al-Qadir al-Fasi. The grandfather of 'Abd al-Qadir, 'Abd al-Rahman al-Fasi (d. 1526), was a great mystic who founded a *zawiya* in the Qarawiyin sector of Fez. As a gesture of good will toward the al-Fasi family, Sultan Mawlay

Isma'il decided to aggrandize the *zawiya* of 'Abd al-Rahman al-Fasi and endow it with a much greater importance as a religious institution within Fez society. The city historian, Muhammad Ibn al-Tayyib al-Qadiri (d. 1773), mentions that in the year 1680 Mawlay Isma'il ordered his governor in Fez to enlarge the *zawiya* after he bought a number of adjacent houses.[31] When the construction was completed, the *zawiya* was four times its original size.[32] Moreover, the sultan endowed this religious lodge with a number of *ahbas*, or endowments, making it an important place of worship and learning in the city. At some time it even began to play a role similar to that of the Qarawiyin mosque, a kind of city hall where the sultan's messages to the city were read and crucial issues debated.[33] Gradually it acquired the status of a *hurm* where those seeking asylum were safe from prosecution. According to al-Qadiri, the *zawiya* became a refuge for offenders and those who failed to pay *makhzan* taxes. Mawlay Isma'il did not harm those who took refuge in it, and none of his governors dared to touch them, whatever were their crimes.[34]

Al-Qadiri mentions at least two instances in which political runaways preferred the al-Fasi *zawiya* to other traditional asylums in the city. In both cases the rebels felt that the *zawiya* would be a safer place than even the prestigious shrine of Mawlay Idris because the sultan held it in such high respect. One of these rebels, we are told, left the *hurm* of Sidi Ahmad al-Shawi, one of the main sanctuaries in the city, to settle in the *zawiya* of 'Abd al-Rahman al-Fasi. From there he was able to travel to the capital of Meknes and ask for the sultan's forgiveness. "On this event," wrote al-Qadiri, "its *hurm* became even more reputable and respected as a result of our Lord's consideration for it."[35]

The Canonization of Cannons

There is probably nothing that better illustrates the relation between might and sanctuary than the so-called *zwag al-madfa'*, or the cannon sanctuary. This institution is a relatively recent one and does not seem to be more than two or three centuries old. In 1765, a French naval attack on the port of Larache ended in a military disaster for the enemy and a great victory for the Moroccan *mujahids*. However, in the popular tradition, credit for the victory did not go to the *makhzan* or even to the *mujahids*, but to a cannon, which, because of its effectiveness in battle, ended up in sainthood. The famous cannon of Larache became known as Sidi Mimun, or the lucky saint. Just as any human saint, Sidi Mimun acquired a *baraka* of its own, becoming an object of popular veneration. It also developed the reputation of ensuring the protection of those seeking asylum. How do we explain this sanctification of a cannon? Did it reflect popular religiosity and the sense of gratitude for its role in the jihad? Or was it simply a fascination with the fire power of this dreadful engine?

During the nineteenth century the cannon sanctuary became a well-established institution. Al-Nasiri mentions that during the expedition of Mawlay al-Hasan to the Middle Atlas in 1888, tribesmen from the Ichqiren tribe sought refuge in a cannon sanctuary as a means of regaining the sultan's favor. The next morning, he wrote, their women and children arrived, placed themselves under the protection of the cannon (*istajaru bi-al-madfa'*) and begged the sultan for forgiveness.[36] At the beginning of the twentieth century, when the French established the Mission Scientifique in Tangier, the custom was still in use, and Georges Salmon was able to provide details about its ritual.[37]

The *zwag al-madfa'* practiced on the eve of the French protectorate appeared to be devoid of religious content. The *hurm* seeker had only to reach a piece of artillery that belonged to the *makhzan* and then ask for the sultan's intervention. This non-holy sanctuary was accessible to non-Muslims and was used by Jews too. But the significance for the *makhzan* was far greater than is normally assumed. By creating a sanctuary of its own, the *makhzan* not only contributed to the secularization of this holy institution but seemed to infringe on a territory that the religious groups considered to be theirs.

SHARIA, *HURM*, AND *'AR*

In Moroccan popular practice, the *hurm* institution was associated with other customs known as *'ar* or *zwag*. To cast *'ar* on someone was a means of asking the protection of a person of influence. The custom received a great deal of attention from European ethnologists, such as Westermarck, who saw it as one of the most sacred customs in the country.[38] The definition he gave to *'ar* was that of a conditional curse, meaning that if the solicited person refused to comply with the demands of the petitioner, he would come under the threat of a curse or some supernatural malediction. Therefore, resorting to the *'ar* custom was a sure way of acquiring the protection of someone who in principle had the power and the means to satisfy the petitioner's request.[39]

However, by the standards of the Sharia, the *'ar* practice carried the earmarks of paganism. First, the sacrifice, the basis of the *"ar"* ritual, was made without pronouncing the name of God *(basmala)*, as is the rule in Islamic law.[40] To be acceptable, a sacrifice has to be dedicated to God and given as alms to the needy. But when the *basmala* is not pronounced, the consumption of meat becomes illegal (*haram*). Some *'ar* rituals also involved what is called *t'arguiba* (the crippling of a bull by cutting its tendons), an extremely questionable practice in terms of the Sharia. The ulama were also hostile to a sacrifice intended to serve as compensation for a service either rendered by the saint or simply expected from him (*nadhr*). However, the most objectionable aspect of the *'ar* custom was the compulsion that the petitioner intended to exert over the solicited saint. Casting *'ar* on saints is a great sin according to the ulama. Veneration due to God's friends does not allow any form of compulsion or threat to be addressed to them. According to al-Kittani, "It is not permitted to make a sacrifice with the intention of casting *'ar* on [the saint], as it is done by many ignorant and weak-minded people. Such behavior is clearly improper because the meaning of *'ar* in both language and custom is to commit a misdeed involving insult and prejudice. Thus when one says, 'May the *'ar* be on you, So-and-So, if you do not fulfill my request,' he is committing a great discourtesy toward God's friends."[41]

The ulama had further reason to be hostile to the *'ar* custom. For them, it was part of tribal customary law, a survival from pre-Islamic times. Tribesmen preferred to settle their affairs in accordance with custom, at the expense of God's law. In many cases the *'ar* practice was even used as a means to transgress the Sharia by forcing people to act against the precepts of the divine law. So strong was suspicion of the *'ar* custom that some *zawaya* rejected it as a means of requesting holy protection. For instance, there is an established tradition among the *shurafa'* of Wazzan whereby all forms of *'ar* supplication were turned down. Instead of adopting a custom involving compulsion and possible embarrassment, the Wazzanis offered a highly respectable *hurm* and a *baraka*-based intercession.

Nevertheless, in terms of the Sharia, the *hurm* itself was a matter of debate. While the *shurafa'* and the *zawaya* defended the institution as a privilege to which they were strongly attached, the ulama and the *makhzan* had a different view. In principle, any religious sanctuary, even that of Mecca, cannot be above the law of God. The *haram* of Mecca itself cannot shelter an offender whose guilt is beyond doubt. In fact, what sanctuaries provided was a temporary protection and the opportunity for the fugitive to reach a negotiated arrangement with his pursuer. Sultans were aware of the Sharia rulings in this respect. If they generally refrained from attacking the grounds of the *zawiya*, it was mainly out of consideration for the *hurm* masters and out of respect for a tradition to which the people were strongly attached. However, when they felt powerful enough to impose their will on refractory religious groups, they never lacked the juridical argument to justify their action. In his contest with the *zawiya* of Wazzan, for instance, Mawlay Sulayman rejected the *hurm* privileges of the *zawiya* and, basing himself on Sharia prescriptions, went ahead with the enforcement of *makhzan* authority in the town of Wazzan. To the recalcitrant shaykh of the *zawiya*, the sultan wrote:

> You certainly are not one of those ignorant people who by their attachment to worldly prestige tend to make of their abode a better place than Mecca or Medina, since these two places are not allowed to shelter a law-breaker. . . . The role of a *zawiya* is to serve as a refuge for the oppressed who seeks God's protection; it cannot serve as a shelter for the offender.[42]

But how does one distinguish between what the *makhzan* considers an offender and the genuinely oppressed who is entitled to God's protection? The same Sultan succeeded in obtaining a fatwa from the ulama authorizing him to invade *zawiya* grounds if they were used as a means to transgress the divine law.[43] Later in the nineteenth century, Mawlay 'Abd al-'Aziz also obtained a fatwa allowing him to invest the *hurm* of Sidi Rahhal near Marrakesh and arrest a mutinous governor.[44]

The gradual erosion of *hurm* privileges cannot be explained only in terms of the *makhzan*'s centralizing policy. The ulama had also their share in this process. Under the influence of Middle Eastern reformist ideas many religious scholars became increasingly hostile to the Sufi brotherhoods and the privileges they enjoyed. This tendency became particularly obvious during the latter part of the nineteenth century and acquired a more radical tone under colonial rule. As a result, the rift grew wider between the religious scholars and the upholders of Sufi ideology. Reformist ulama attacked popular religion as practiced by the *zawaya* and the religious brotherhoods. In their discourse, the *hurm* institution figured as a *bid'a* (innovation), to which they became increasingly hostile. "Among their [the *zawaya*] most reprehensible practices," wrote a twentieth-century *'alim*, "is the one of making the shrines of their shaykhs equal in sanctity to the Holy Ka'ba, providing them with a *kiswa* (the cloth covering the saint's tomb), and fixing territorial limits within which criminals are considered immune."[45] The point here is that the ulama played a significant role in delegitimizing the *hurm* institution and that the *makhzan* was able to rely on their support to undermine the privileges of many influential religious groups.

THE *HURM* CHALLENGED: "CHRISTIAN PROTECTION RATHER THAN THE TYRANNY OF A MUSLIM RULER"

The importance of religious institutions and religious figures in *makhzan* politics has been often underlined by historical and anthropological studies. The sultan, despite the fact that he was a *baraka* holder himself, could not dispense with the *baraka* of others. While on the move throughout the countryside, he was always accompanied by a saintly figure who served as mediator between him and the various social groups. However, during the latter part of the nineteenth century, the sultan's relation with the religious groups deteriorated steadily, partly because of the *makhzan*'s failure to put off European imperialist designs. The centralizing tendencies of the *makhzan,* together with increasing European pressures for the abolition of privileges traditionally enjoyed by religious groups, also contributed to this deterioration. The *hurm* was among the traditional privileges that were affected. State centralization went hand in hand with the belief that in order to overcome the crisis, the *makhzan* had to curtail these privileges. As a result the *makhzan*'s respect for the *hurm* institution suffered, and the religious groups connected with it were affected.

Between Mawlay al-Hasan's accession to the throne in 1873 and the coming of the protectorate in 1912 there were many instances of *hurm* violation. Some of these violations turned into major political crises. Thus in 1896 Mawlay 'Abd al-'Aziz forced the rebellious *qa'id* of the Rahamna, Tahar Bensliman, out of the *hurm* of Sidi Rahhal, obtaining a fatwa from the ulama to justify his action.[46] The right to religious asylum, the ulama argued, cannot be valid unless the person in question meets the basic requirements of religion—namely, submission to the head of the Islamic community.

In 1902, a more serious *hurm* violation occurred in relation to the killing of a British missionary, David Cooper, who had ventured into the sanctuary of Mawlay Idris in Fez in breach of an established custom prohibiting non-Muslims from having access to sacred places. The assassin took refuge in the shrine of Mawlay Idris and refused to be handed over to *makhzan* authorities. Finally, he was induced by the sultan to leave the shrine after he received all the customary assurances by the Idrisi *shurufa'*. However, Mawlay 'Abd al-'Aziz, who was under heavy European pressure, chose to disregard the *hurm*-related customs and ordered the execution of the killer. According to rumors that rapidly spread throughout the country, blood trickled out of the saint's tomb in Fez when the sentence was carried out. The handling of the Cooper affair was perceived of as a direct challenge to the Idrisi *shurufa'* and a dangerous violation of one of the holiest places of the Maghrib. The psychological shock left by this incident prepared the way for a series of political upheavals that led to the installation of the French protectorate in 1912.[47]

These two examples of *hurm* violation were not the first of their kind. By 1875, the *sharif* of Wazzan, whose prestige at the time was unparalleled, already deeply resented the sultan's transgression of the *zawiya*'s traditional rights in matters of protection. In that year he offered his good offices to bring about the submission of Abu 'Azza al-Habri, a rebel in eastern Morocco, and provided him with the necessary guarantees (*aman*) that allowed him to leave the sanctuary. However, Mawlay al-Hasan disregarded the *sharif*'s moral commitment and imprisoned the rebel. Sidi 'Abd al-Salam al-Wazzani was deeply offended and saw in the sultan's behavior a severe blow to his prestige.[48] In fact, at stake was the whole system of religious privileges and the traditional mechanism on which it rested. Furious at what he considered to be an insult to his religious credit, al-Wazzani openly defied the head of the Islamic community by placing himself under the protection of France shortly after the al-Habri incident. "Christian protection rather than tyranny," he declared (*al-nsara wa-la al-dsara*).

Thus the traditional holy protectors became the protected people of the Christians! Under such conditions the saintly figures who used to provide asylum for the oppressed were no longer able to play that role. After the *sharif* of Wazzan placed himself under the protection of the French, *hurm* seekers still came to him and requested his protection, but the protection they were looking for now was that of a strong Christian nation. On its side, the *makhzan* suffered too from the rupture with the religious groups. The sanctified image it drew from its connection with the *baraka* holders was irremediably shattered. In the people's eyes, the sultan was able to remain in power only as long as he had the support and the protection of the saints.[49] Once this protection was withdrawn, he and the country were exposed to great danger. The popular image acquired by Mawlay 'Abd al-'Aziz as "the sultan of the Christians" was to a large extent the result of his repeated transgressions of the sanctified norms that regulated the social and moral order. Under similar circumstances one can understand how a *makhzan* whose legitimacy was seriously compromised attempted to replace the traditional *hurm* institution with that of *zwag al-madfa'*, which symbolized the violent aspect of a discredited state backed by firepower rather than sanctity.

CONCLUSION

The *hurm* institution played a crucial role in the equilibrium of traditional society in Morocco. Sacred protection, whether it took the form of a particular place of asylum or a moral protective authority, served as an important device in the regulation of power and the curbing of "the strong hand," particularly in a society in which central authority oscillated between despotism and political impotence. In a situation in which the state was either too oppressive or too weak to ensure social peace, individuals and groups found in the *hurm* institution a most effective shield against the vicissitudes of power.

Seen from another angle, the *hurm* served as a buffer institution between the central government and the various loci of religious power. In a society characterized by the strong presence of religious groups, the Islamic state was in no position to monopolize religious legitimacy. Sufi orders, local *zawaya,* and sharifian families all shared in that legitimacy and claimed a number of consequent privileges. The ability to mediate conflicts and provide protection for those in need of it figured among the basic attributes of saints and *shurafa'*; moreover, their social credibility depended on their ability to provide such services. The state itself recognized the *hurm* institution and respected it as a basic element in the overall social equilibrium. However, as the Moroccan state entered the era of modernization and centralization during the nineteenth century, traditional privileges enjoyed until then by religious groups became exposed to a gradual process of erosion. The main results of this development were the breakup of those traditional institutions that served as intermediate bodies between the state and society, the exacerbation of tensions between the *makhzan* and the religious groups, and ultimately, the discrediting of the ruling elite.

NOTES

1. *The Encyclopedia of Religion,* ed. Mircea Eliade, s.v. "Sanctuary" (New York, 1987), 12, 59.
2. W. Robertson Smith, *Lectures on the Religion of the Semites* (London, 1901), 142–6.
3. A Hadith of the Prophet reported by al-Bukhari in his *Sahih,* chap. 1. See A. J. Wensinck, *Concordance et indices de la tradition musulmane* (Leiden, 1967), 6, 128.
4. E. Westermarck, *Ritual and Belief in Morocco,* 2 vols. (New York, 1968), 1:64.
5. This is the case, for instance, of Mawlay 'Abd al-Salam Ibn Mashish in northern Morocco. See al-'Ayyashi al-Marini, *Al-fihris fi nasab al-shurafa' al-Adarisa* (Tangier, 1986), 52. On the status

of the holy places in Mecca, see J. Chelhod, *Les Structures du sacré chez les arabes* (Paris, 1964), 230–2.
6. The *hurm* of Mawlay Idris in Fez included the shrine and the surrounding blocks of houses. Its limits were indicated by wooden bars that cut across the neighboring streets and that can still be seen today.
7. Westermarck, *Ritual and Belief,* 1:561.
8. On Mawlay 'Abd al-Salam Ibn Mashish and the 'Alami *shurafa'* of northern Morocco, see al-Tahar al-Lihiwi, *Hisn al-Salam bayna yaday awlad Mawlay 'Abd al-Salam* (Casablanca, 1978).
9. The *hurm* of Mawlay 'Abd al-Salam Ibn Mashish extended over a large area that included all or parts of the following tribal territories: Bani 'Arus, Sumata, Bani Layt, Bani Yider, Bani Yissef, and Ahl Srif. See al-Marini, *Al-Fihris,* 34, and the text of the royal decree by Mawlay al-Hasan (d. 1894) in al-Lihiwi, *Hisn,* 389.
10. al-Lihiwi, *Hisn,* 389.
11. See W. B. Harris, "The Nomadic Berbers of Central Morocco," *The Geographic Journal* 6 (June 1897): 638–45.
12. Al-Mukhtar al-Susi, *al-Ma'sul,* 20 vols. (Casablanca, 1960–2) 18:167.
13. Ibid., 168.
14. 'Abd al-Salam Ibn al-Tayyib al-Qadiri, *Al-maqsad al-Ahmad fi al-ta'rif bi sayyidina Ibn 'Abd Allah Ahmad,* 2 vols. (Fez, 1932–3) 2:217.
15. Ibid.
16. Ibid.
17. Hadith quoted by Muhammad Ibn al-Tayyib al-Qadiri (d. 1773), *Nashr al-mathani,* 4 vols. (Rabat, 1977–86), 4:225.
18. See Mohamed El Mansour, "Sharifian Sufism: The Religious and Social Practice of the Wazzani Zawiya," in *Tribe and State: Essays in Honour of David Montgomery Hart,* ed. E. G. Joffe and R. Pennell (Wisbech, Cambridgeshire, 1991), 69–83.
19. Muhammad Ibn al-Tayyib al-Qadiri, *Muhammad al-Qadiri's 'Nashr al-mathani': The Chronicles,* ed. and trans. N. L. Cigar (Rabat, 1978), 57.
20. al-Qadiri, *Nashr al-mathani,* 3:243
21. Ibid., 4:225.
22. al-Qadiri, *Muhammad al-Qadiri's 'Nashr al-mathani',* 34
23. J. Berque, *Structures sociales du Haut-Atlas* (Paris, 1955).

24. This is particularly clear in al-Qadiri's *Nashr* and also in hagiographic works such as *Al-maqsad al-Ahmad* by 'Abd al-Salam Ibn al-Tayyib al-Qadiri.
25. The Sa'dis' sharifdom was even contested by some sharifian families such as the 'Alawis of Tafilelt. See A. al-Zayani, *Al-bustan al-dharif*, ed. Rashid al-Zawiya, 2 vols. (Rabat, 1992), 1:31.
26. On the rehabilitation of sharifdom in Morocco during the Marinid period see M. García Arenal, "The Revolution of Fas in 869/1465 and the Death of Sultan 'Abd al-Haqq al-Marini," *Bulletin of the School of Oriental and African Studies* 41, no. 1 (1978): 43–66, and Muhammad al-Qabli, "Musahama fi tarikh al-tamhid li dawlat al-Sa'diyyin," *Majallat Kulliyat al-adab* (Rabat) 3–4 (1978): 7–59.
27. This was the case of the Sharqawi and Wazzani *zawiya*s. See, for instance, the decree issued by Sidi Muhammad Ibn 'Abd Allah (ruled 1757–90) in favor of the Wazzani *shurafa'*, who were granted considerable concessions, particularly in the form of administrative autonomy, in M. al-Du'ayyif, *Tarikh al-Du'ayyif*, ed. A. al-'Amrani (Rabat, 1986), 189–90.
28. Among the centralizing sultans who sought to limit the *hurm* privileges was Mawlay Sulayman (ruled 1792–1822). When he was proclaimed sultan, he abolished his father's concessions to the Wazzani *zawiya* and succeeded in obtaining fatwas that allowed him to invest sanctuaries when *makhzan* interests were at stake. See Mohamed El Mansour, *Morocco in the Reign of Mawlay Sulayman* (Wisbech, Cambridgeshire, 1990), 159, 166.
29. See Sidi Humammad Ibn 'Abd Allah's decree in 'Ali al-Raysuni, *Rijal wa mawaqif* (Tetuan, 1982), 19.
30. al-Du'ayyif, *Tarikh*, 158.
31. al-Qadiri, *Nashr al-mathani*, 2:294.
32. Ibid., 3:153.
33. Ibid., 3:117.
34. Ibid., 3:153.
35. Ibid., 2:204.
36. Ahmad Ibn Khalid al-Nasiri, *Kitab al-istiqsa' li-akhbar duwal al-Maghrib al-'aqsa*, 9 vols. (Casablanca, 1954–6), 9:200.
37. G. Salmon, "Le Droit d'asile des canons," *Archives Marocaines* 3 (1905): 144–53. [The Mission Scientifique was a French research

institute established in Tangier in 1903–1904 that published the revue *Archives Marocaines*.—Eds.]
38. Quoted in K. Brown, "The Curse of Westermarck," *Ethnos* 47 (1982): 202.
39. The definition of "conditional curse" given to '*ar* by Westermarck has been challenged by Kenneth Brown, who believes that '*ar* "concerns *honouring and shame* rather than *cursing and sin*" (Brown's italics); ibid., 204.
40. Charles Pellat, s.v. "'*Ar*" in *Encyclopédie de l'Islam,* supplement, pt. 1–2, 204.
41. Muhammad Ibn Ja'far al-Kittani, *Salwat al-anfas,* 3 vols. (Fez, 1899), 1:54–5.
42. al-Du'ayyif, *Tarikh,* 269.
43. See text of the fatwa in al-Mahdi al-Wazzani, *Al-nawazil al-sughra,* 4 vols. (Rabat, 1993), 3:106.
44. Salmon, "Le Droit d'asile," 140.
45. 'Abd al-Salam al-Sarghini, *Musamara fi al-sunna wa-al-bid'a* (Fez, n.d.), 35.
46. Salmon, "Le Droit d'asile," 140.
47. On the Cooper affair and the political upheaval that followed it, see E. Burke III, *Prelude to Protectorate in Morocco, 1860–1912* (Chicago: University of Chicago Press, 1970), 61–7.
48. E. Michaux-Bellaire, "La Maison d'Ouezzane," *Revue du Monde Musulman* 5 (1908): 50–1.
49. E. Westermarck, *The Moorish Conception of Holiness (Baraka)* (Helsinki, 1916), 9.

· FIVE ·

Royal Power and the Economy in Precolonial Morocco: Jews and the Legitimation of Foreign Trade

Daniel J. Schroeter

The prosperity of Morocco's capital cities and the strength of the monarchy ruling from them has always been linked to long-distance commerce. When this commerce involved trade with the "land of the infidels" (the term often used to refer to Christian Europe), the state needed to justify it on ideological grounds. From the sixteenth century, the consolidation of royal power by both the Sa'di and 'Alawi dynasties was based on long-distance commerce linked to trade with Europe, because of both the revenue that such trade could generate and the commodities it brought, especially gunpowder and arms. In earlier periods when Morocco was a competing Mediterranean power, exchange with the Christian world may have posed less of an ideological problem. But the sharifian period coincided with the growing disparity in power between Morocco and Europe. The political independence of Morocco was threatened by Iberian expansion from enclaves on the Atlantic and Mediterranean coast. Thus, while peaceful trade was a necessary precondition for the consolidation of royal power by the 'Alawi state, the very legitimacy of the dynasty was connected to its ability to defend Muslim territory from foreign powers by jihad, the duty of the Muslim ruler.[1]

Trade as the economic foundation of royal power and jihad as the basis to the legitimacy of 'Alawi claims to sovereignty were two somewhat incompatible needs that constantly had to be reconciled. The question of foreign trade became particularly acute in the nineteenth century when the coercive imposition of unfavorable commercial treaties by the Christian powers seriously impaired the ability of the sultan to rule. Among some of the ulama, foreign trade was seen as one of the major causes of the weakness of Islam. Underlining this weakness was the belief that many of the merchants involved with foreign exchange were Jews. But as foreign interference in Moroccan affairs grew, the costs of running the state and strengthening the military also increased to meet the challenge of external intervention. Foreign trade consequently became more important for consolidating the position of the *makhzan* at a time when European intervention was simultaneously undermining its sovereignty.

In this chapter, I focus on this particular conjuncture in history, examining the means by which the state derived revenue from foreign trade and the ways in which these methods were legitimized during the age when the sovereignty of the sultan was facing the challenge of European imperialism.

Even in periods when the Islamic state was strong in relation to Europe, trade with the non-Islamic world was often seen by the Moroccan ulama as problematic for two essential reasons. First, the sale of certain items might strengthen the position of the enemies of Islam and, in turn, weaken Muslim society. In particular, the sale of articles seen as potentially strengthening the enemy's military force was discouraged by the Maliki *madhhab*, the dominant school of jurisprudence in the Maghrib.[2] Also, the export of grains and other foodstuffs, which might in times of shortage cause discontent, was discouraged. Second, traveling outside of the Islamic world and contact with foreigners was shunned. Maliki jurisconsults looked unfavorably on Muslim travel to or residence outside the lands of Islam, where it was believed that a Muslim could be corrupted and exposed to forbidden practices or his faith undermined.[3] Some jurists argued the necessity for Muslims to migrate (*hijra*) from the realm of unbelief (*dar al-kufr*), while others felt that residence outside of Islamic sovereignty could be justified if it were for a legitimate purpose, such as propagating Islam.[4] Such doctrinal issues had been particularly important in previous centuries in Spain, as Muslims in increasing numbers were coming under Christian rule.

By the sixteenth century, the practice of Islam had been proscribed in Spain, and for Morocco, the object of a new Iberian expansion, the question of the obligation of *hijra* would no longer have any practical applications. Few Moroccan Muslims would venture to Europe, with the exception of a handful primarily from Fez. The ulama of Fez were generally opposed to contact with foreigners, and as commerce with Europe increased in the nineteenth century, they voiced their opposition to the relations of Muslim merchants with Christians.[5] In the late nineteenth century, one scholar, Muhammad Ibn al-Madani Gannun, saw the travel of Fasi merchants to Europe as a kind of treason.[6] The sultan himself sought to strictly control his subjects' travel to Europe.[7] Muslim travel to Europe had to be legitimized as necessary for the benefit of the community and the defense of Muslim lands from foreign incursions.[8] For instance, one Fasi merchant who traveled to Marseilles for commerce confided in the French consular agent in Essaouira that he had a special commission from the sultan to find out all he could about French aims in Algeria.[9]

Those merchants who did travel to conduct trade in foreign countries, unlike their Christian counterparts who came to Morocco, did not have the protection or assistance of a permanent diplomatic representative abroad. Morocco's diplomats resident in foreign countries were limited to ports along the pilgrimage route to Mecca: Tunis, Malta, Alexandria, and Cairo.[10] Moroccans had no permanent embassies in those European countries with which Morocco had significant commercial relations.[11] An attempt at establishing a consulate in Marseilles in the early nineteenth century, with Jewish representatives, was short-lived.[12] There was a more permanent diplomatic establishment in Gibraltar in the nineteenth century. However, the main duty of these agents was not to represent the interests of Moroccan merchants but rather to deal with the exchange of foreign currencies.[13] On the rare occasions that Morocco appointed a resident representative in Christian countries, a Jew generally fulfilled this post (often because the individual Jew already had members of his family living in the country of destination), but the nature of his duties, the duration of his position, and his precise relationship with the *makhzan* was left nebulous and open to negotiation.[14]

While the various treaties between Morocco and the European states stipulated the extraterritorial rights that foreign nationals would enjoy on Moroccan soil, no such provisions were specified for Moroccans abroad. Within the Muslim world, Islamic law was not considered territorial—that is, confined to the political boundaries of specific states.[15] Instead, it was personal, transcending political boundaries, and consequently, a Moroccan traveling in the Muslim world would not have had the need for extraterritorial rights. The notion of extraterritoriality was therefore alien to the Islamic concept of the law. For this reason, a permanent Moroccan embassy abroad, run by Muslims, was conceptually problematic. Consequently, the state relied on diplomatic embassies dispatched for a limited period of time.[16]

Given these obstacles to foreign trade, how then could the ruler possibly legitimize the profit derived from commerce with the unbeliever? Paradoxically, it was the concept of jihad that gave the legal basis for the involvement of the state in commerce with the Christian enemy. Foreign trade was permissible to the extent that the revenue from trade would consolidate the power of the ruler whose duty it was to conduct jihad. Profits could be gained by the state through the activities of officially sponsored corsairs and through trade conducted by commercial treaty. Even grain exports to the infidels could be allowed for the purpose of jihad.

Until the demise of Moroccan corsair ships in the eighteenth century, the state was able to derive significant revenue through piracy, or jihad at sea, as it was known and sanctioned by the 'Alawi state. The sultan would receive one-fifth of the booty according to the Sharia.[17] While jihad always remained a requirement, this did not mean that the state had to engage constantly in warfare. The sultan could also conclude a temporary peace with a Christian power if the purpose was to restore the strength of the state in the interest of Islam, so that jihad could be waged at some future time.[18] Maliki jurisconsults stress the point that if peace is concluded with the infidels, it should preferably be of short duration.[19]

The promotion by the state of jihad at sea also did not preclude trade with those countries with which it had commercial treaties. But the fact that Morocco had no merchant marine of its own made it dependent on foreign ships and merchants coming to its soil. Piracy was the leverage that Morocco employed to compel Christian countries to trade on its own terms. Foreign states were required to pay an annual tribute for the privilege of conducting trade without their ships being attacked. Thus, a commercial treaty could be concluded with one power, and the revenues derived from trade with it could then be used for engaging in jihad against another power. In the 1670s, for example, there were officials at several Moroccan seaports who used the revenue generated from port taxes on trade with Christians for outfitting corsairs.[20]

As long as jihad at sea was conducted simultaneously with commerce by treaty and tribute, foreign trade presented few ideological problems for the sultan. Sidi Muhammad Ibn 'Abdallah (1757–90), who concluded numerous commercial treaties with the European countries in the latter half of the eighteenth century, is also praised for successfully waging jihad.[21] Thus, foreign relations with the Christian powers were seen as being conducted from a superior position. The purpose of diplomacy and trade with Europeans was to promote jihad, while truces could be justified for the purpose of liberating Muslim captives. In fact, Sidi Muhammad differentiated between jihad by land (for example, his capture of Mazagan, henceforth called al-Jadida, and attempts to capture Melilla and Ceuta) and peaceful maritime relations and treaties with the Christian powers. Trade with Europe became increasingly important for the sultan, despite the objections of the ulama. The jurisconsults objected to the export of grain, which the sultan traded in exchange for guns, ammunition, and the return of Muslim captives. The sultan forced a reluctant ulama that was hostile to dealings with the European states to issue fatwas favorable to foreign trade.[22] Once the ability to conduct jihad at sea was undermined, however, the legitimacy of foreign trade became much more problematic.

Sidi Muhammad Ibn 'Abdallah, even prior to his reign, saw the advantages of foreign trade as a means of securing revenue. He established relations with Christian and Jewish merchants in Safi in 1747, and through the extension of foreign trade he was able to secure control of the Hawz, the Shiadhma and the Haha, regions along Morocco's Atlantic flank, building his military power as a result, and enabling him to become the effective ruler from Marrakesh (which was reconstructed and strengthened) with the support of the major tribes.[23] From Marrakesh he established his authority in southern Morocco. Foreign trade thus helped Muhammad's succession to the throne after the death of Mawlay 'Abdallah. Through the foreign merchants of Safi, he traded for materials to outfit his corsair ships, and he also ordered the building of fortifications in Rabat, Sale, and Tangier for his *mujahids*.[24]

The creation of the royal port of Essaouira in 1764 was justified, according to Sultan Muhammad's contemporaries, by the need to build an excellent harbor to conduct jihad at sea (the other reason mentioned was that dissidents were profiting from an active contraband export trade from Agadir, and the new port would undercut this clandestine trade).[25] This never happened (though the sultan conducted jihad from elsewhere and especially met with success in the capture of Mazagan from the Portuguese), and Essaouira was never anything but a town of trade, mainly performed by Jews and foreign merchants who were settled in the town by the sultan. Despite this fact, in the royal discourse Essaouira's character was to be Muslim, and the ulama were to establish the Islamic institutions of urban civilization there.[26] Even twentieth-century narratives of Essaouira's history emphasize the Muslim character of the town: the achievements of the noted ulama are described in detail,[27] while the Jews, who constituted between 30 and 40 percent of the town, are hardly mentioned at all. Jews were everywhere and invisible at the same time. But the assertion of the Muslim character of the town could not disguise the fact that jihad at sea was becoming a thing of the past and that peaceful foreign trade, conducted mostly by Jews and foreigners, was the principal activity of the port of Essaouira.

One of the important means by which the *makhzan* derived revenue from foreign and domestic trade was through the levying of non-Koranic taxes (*maks,* plural *mukus*). Customs duties (if paid by Muslims), various tolls, and market and excise taxes would fall under this category. As a matter of principal, the *mukus* were considered by the ulama to be problematic. The only justification for raising non-Islamic taxes was for the purpose of jihad. Throughout the history of the 'Alawi dynasty, such taxes were imposed and abolished on numerous occasions and were often the cause of confrontations between the ulama and the sultan. The burden of the *maks* fell most heavily on the town dwellers, and its abolition was seen as a measure that would increase production of crafts and reduce impediments on trade. On the other hand, it would also weaken the revenue of the state.

In 1695, Mawlay Isma'il initiated the *mukus* in all Moroccan cities,[28] and Jewish tax-farmers were the major instruments of this policy.[29] The taxes levied by Mawlay Isma'il weighed heavily on the population and invoked the criticism of the noted *'alim* al-Yusi.[30] During the years following the reign of Mawlay Isma'il, when the government was contested by numerous members of the 'Alawi dynasty, the *mukus* were abolished by one of the contenders for the throne, Sidi Muhammad Ibn Ariba.[31] Sidi

Muhammad Ibn 'Abdallah reinstated the *mukus* at the beginning of his reign, clearly hoping to gain more revenues from his expansion of foreign trade. The ulama did not give their unqualified approval but issued a fatwa that simply reiterated the position of the Sharia regarding *mukus*—that *maks* was permissible only during such a time that funds were not available in the treasury to pay the soldiers.[32] The governor of Fez, the Hajj Muhammad al-Saffar, reportedly purchased the *mukus* of the city for 23,000 mithqals.[33]

Sidi Muhammad Ibn 'Abdallah was not the first Moroccan sultan to attempt to consolidate the economic base of the state through foreign trade and the imposition of *mukus*. The difference, however, was the degree to which Morocco's foreign trade was monopolized by the state and the extent of this trade.[34] Numerous commercial treaties were concluded, and many of Morocco's trading partners had to purchase their right to trade by paying an annual tribute.[35] The sultan gave incentives to foreign merchants to settle in Essaouira by lowering duties and made large loans to Moroccan merchants (*tujjar al-sultan*), mostly Jews, to conduct trade from the new town. These Jewish merchants also initially received reductions or exemptions in customs duties. The Jews, in turn, would pay back the sultan in monthly installments through the port authorities. Sometimes financial arrangements would be made through the agents of the Jewish merchants living in Marrakesh, who repaid their debts directly to the ruler. Since loans in accordance with the Sharia had to be interest-free, the sultan would, in effect, receive interest indirectly, through repayment of loans at varying exchange rates via Jewish agents in the court, through the collection of duties generated by the commerce of his royal merchants, and through market taxes that the import and export trade produced. In order to redress the disequilibrium between foreign and indigenous traders, the government also often gave credit on duties to the Moroccan merchants or exemption from duties for a period of time, about which the European merchants constantly complained. Such a system of trade could well be defined as royal banking, with the royal bank (*bayt al-mal*) contracting loans and extending credit of all sorts to merchants.[36]

The important position of Jews in the sultan's system of royal trade, the general growth in foreign commerce, especially when it involved the exportation of grains, and the increasing numbers and influence of Christian merchants in the country met with the disapproval of some sectors of the population. Sidi Muhammad also founded the port of Fadala (Mohammedia today) in 1772–73, explicitly to export the grain of the adjoining regions to Europe.[37] Christians were ordered to build houses there, and customs officials from Rabat and Salé, as well as Jewish officials, arrived there. The new port was soon bustling with the grain trade: "Camels were arriving like clouds day and night," wrote al-Du'ayyif in his chronicle of the period. Al-Du'ayyif disapproved of the fact that the town was "filled with Jews, Christians, and Muslims striving to sell grain . . . and anyone who would see this would have been alarmed."[38]

The increase in foreign trade with Europeans, and the growing prominence of Jews in this trade, was clearly disturbing to al-Du'ayyif. Toward the end of the reign of Sultan Muhammad, the grain trade with the Iberian Peninsula increased considerably, especially from the port of al-Dar al-Bayda (Casablanca).[39] Following the death of the sultan, al-Dar al-Bayda was besieged by the Madyuna tribe, with the intention of plundering the town and the Christian merchants, but they were repelled by Christian ships.[40] Al-Du'ayyif may well have reflected a popular sentiment of growing hostility toward foreign and Jewish merchants, both of whom seemed to be receiving preferential treatment. This hostility was exploited by Mawlay al-Yazid during his short but violent reign (1790–92). A number of prominent Jewish courtiers who had served the previous sultan were executed,[41] and general pillaging of the Jewish quarters (*mallah*) was encouraged by this sultan. Al-Du'ayyif wrote: "And he [the sultan] ordered that the Jews be plundered wherever they be found and in every *mallah* in every town of Morocco because he [the sultan]—may God save him—hated Jews and Christians."[42] Despite Mawlay al-Yazid's aversion to Christians and Jews—a popular reaction against the policies of his predecessor, Sidi Muhammad[43]—the sultan continued to employ Jews and conduct commercial relations with Europe.[44] The Genoese merchant Francesco Chiappe, who had been appointed by Sidi Muhammad Ibn 'Abdallah in 1784 as secretary for foreign relations, also continued to serve the sultan.[45] The port of Agadir, which had been closed to commerce with the development of Essaouira, was reopened for commerce, and the merchants of Essaouira who had formerly resided in Agadir were ordered to return.[46]

After the death of Mawlay al-Yazid, the throne was contested by a number of 'Alawi pretenders before the authority of Mawlay Sulayman (who reigned from 1792 to 1822) was widely accepted. During this period of dynastic struggle, al-Du'ayyif complains of the growing numbers of Christians in the cities actively engaged in the grain trade, not only corrupting the morality of the population but also causing prices to rise and the poor to get poorer. An illicit trade in grains with Europeans continued on both the Atlantic and Mediterranean coasts, which Mawlay Sulayman sought to suppress.[47]

Foreign observers often remarked that Mawlay Sulayman was averse to commerce, and clearly, foreign trade was drastically reduced during his reign. Moreover, the sultan relied strictly on Koranic taxes, and reportedly the abolition of *maks* was a precondition the Fasi ulama made before giving their support to the new sultan, during the period when his reign was contested by other 'Alawi pretenders.[48] The Islamic reformist tendency has been pointed out as the reason for Mawlay Sulayman's rejection of non-Koranic taxes, but it might also be attributed to the fact that since the sultan's level of trade with the Christian powers was reduced to a minimum in the age of the Napoleonic wars,[49] the amount that he would have derived from *mukus* would have been reduced.

Mawlay Sulayman, though wishing to distance himself from his father's reliance on foreign trade and decrying the negative impact that Christians were having on the Muslim population, still depended on trade with the European powers in Essaouira and Rabat in order to raise revenue to purchase weapons. In exchange for arms and frigates, grain and livestock were traded abroad.[50] Almost all of Morocco's foreign trade was concentrated in the hands of a few Jewish merchants in an effort to strictly control it. It seems that the privileges extended to a few Jews, mainly in Essaouira, were also aimed at curtailing some of the commercial activities of Muslims who, it was believed, were being corrupted by their contact with Christians.[51] When this policy was protested against by the Muslim merchants, the sultan defended his policy of employing Jews by citing the *Muwatta'*, the principal work of Malik Ibn Anas, the founder of the Maliki school of jurisprudence, which allows the government to employ Jews if they have paid *kharaj* and *'ushr*.[52]

As trade with Europe accelerated in the nineteenth century, more and more of this commerce was concentrated in Jewish hands.[53] For centuries, Moroccan Jews had a trading diaspora in most of the principal seaports of Europe. The elite Jewish merchants of the sultan often had family members permanently residing in European commercial centers. To be sure, there were also Muslim merchants, especially from Fez and Tetuan, involved in foreign trade with Europe, but they were preeminent in the domestic and trans-Saharan trade. There were numerous Muslim traders who had close economic ties with the Jewish *tujjar*, and the Jews relied on the extensive network of Muslim traders and intermediaries in the interior. Often the Jews were creditors for the Muslim traders in the port towns and along the interior trade routes.[54] But Jewish merchants engaged in the European trade were disproportionately more numerous. In Essaouira, the principal port trading with Europe for most of the nineteenth century, there were never more than four or five Muslims who figured among the top twenty shippers in the nineteenth century, and usually they numbered one or two.[55]

The concentration of trade with the "lands of the infidels" in the hands of Jewish merchants served the needs of the state. Although there may have been some qualms about leaving such an important sector of the economy in the hands of Jews, it was in many respects ideologically preferable than having Muslims in direct contact with the Christians. The royal merchants were closely tied to the *makhzan* in a relationship of credit and debt, which kept them dependent on the sultan. This relationship was the same for Muslims as it was for Jews. But for the Jews, there was the additional relationship of dependency because of their status as *ahl al-dhimma* (people of the covenant), defined by law as protégés of the Islamic state. Considering them inferior to Muslims, the state was obligated to protect them provided that they accepted their subordinate status and paid their annual capitation tax (*jizya*). The notion of protection was also related to the *dhimmi*s' profitability. Although the ulama sometimes disputed the extent to which the intermingling of Jews and Muslims was to be allowed, it was recognized that the sultan could collect funds necessary for conducting jihad against the infidels from the Jews residing in his territory.[56]

The idea and practice of protection also implied a sense of possession, comparable in some ways to the theory prevalent in Europe that regarded Jews as "serfs of the chamber"—that is, property of the ruler (or of the church) who received special protection and whose property, goods, and money belonged to the ruler.[57] The *tujjar al-sultan*, and especially the Jewish *tujjar*, were in many respects regarded as the property of the ruler in Morocco. No matter how much profit they were able to make for themselves, the Jewish merchants were always in debt to the sultan. In Essaouira, the principal houses of the major Jewish merchants were leased as *makhzan* property in the casbah, the residential quarter of the ruling elite. As property of the sultan, the Jews could be moved by him to a new location (again, as in the case of Essaouira). They were not allowed to travel abroad without authorization, which was accorded only after they had pledged their property and goods as pawns, and often they were required to leave their wives behind.[58] Requests for travel outside *dar al-islam* had to be made to the sultan himself. For example, the governor of Essaouira transmitted to the sultan the request of the merchant Judah of Essaouira to travel to London, where his brother, who was his business partner, had died. He asked permission to travel to collect his money and the money belonging to the sultan, from an outstanding debt totaling 788,816 mithqals. He claimed that all his money was in London, and he would go bankrupt if not allowed to travel. He declared that he had merchandise in his property in the *mallah* and would delegate the *dhimmi* Ben Mashsas to pay his monthly installment until he returned.[59]

The status of royal merchant was passed down within the family of merchants and renewed by each successor to the throne by an official letter. The sultan would offer protection to the merchant and, in the language of these documents, referred to them as "our Jews," emphasizing the profit that these special Jews would gain for the treasury. For example, an edict of Sultan 'Abd al-Rahman in 1857 proclaimed the importance of Jacob and Abraham Corcos, underlining how much the treasury had profited from them.[60] To the new governor of Essaouira, the *khalifa* Muhammad demanded in 1857 that his protection be granted to Jacob and Abraham Corcos, who were among the most profitable of the sultan's Jews.[61] While the letters from the palace to individual Jewish *tujjar* would stress the friendship between the merchant and the sultan, the relationship was legitimized in terms of their profitability for the treasury.

While individual Jews might be praised, the sultan would maintain, in the official discourse, disdain for them as a collectivity: the major function of *ahl al-dhimma* was as a tax-paying body. This reflected the essential ambivalence that the state had toward the Jews. On the one hand, out of necessity it allowed the Jews to develop a quasi-monopoly of the European trade and consequently became dependent on Jewish merchants. On the other hand, the desire not to be dependent on the Jews created contempt. This disdain for the Jews as a collectivity worsened as the Muslim world was threatened by imperialism; for it was the subservient position of the *dhimmi* that gave prominence to the superiority of Islam. As the sharifian dynasty was threatened by external, Christian forces, and as increasing numbers of Jews were seen as evading their *dhimmi* status as protégés of foreign powers, both clerical and royal discourse sharpened its tone regarding the *dhimmi*.[62] This, however, did not necessarily alter the individual patron-client relations between the sultan and the Jewish *tujjar*, and the personal ties between individual Muslims and Jews that transcended the formally defined boundaries between them as collectivities.

The 1844 attack against the Moroccan ports by the French exacerbated feelings against the Jews. Mawlay 'Abd al-Rahman wrote Bu Silham Ibn 'Ali, the governor of Tangier in 1846:

> The news has reached us that wealthy Jews, may God curse them, have been increasing the trips [abroad] of their children claiming that they are going [on pilgrimage] to Jerusalem. But they are not returning. Consequently, Islam is harmed in two ways: first, in the diminishing [revenue from] *jizya*, and second, they are becoming reconnoiterers, directing the enemy to the weak spots of the Muslims. On receiving this letter, prevent all of them from traveling from the ports of Larache and Tangier. Be indefatigable in your efforts with them. May God destroy them.[63]

It could be suggested that the sultan had cause for concern, since many Jews, after the conquest of Algiers by the French in 1830, migrated to Algeria to profit from new possibilities for trade. The collection of *jizya* continued to be a major concern for the sultan, and the phrase "May God curse them," an epithet commonly used toward Jews and Christians in Muslim writings, is repeated in the official discourse.[64]

These tensions did not undermine the fundamental interdependence between the state and Jewish merchants. The sultans always had their favorite Jewish merchants whom they protected scrupulously from the officials in their bureaucracy. The patrimonial relationship between ruler and Jewish merchant was extended to other members of the family. For example, after the death of 'Abd al-Rahman's principal Jewish merchant and emissary, Meir Macnin, the palace protected the rights of his daughter Blida to enjoy usufruct from the properties formerly held by her father, despite the considerable debts he owed the *makhzan* at the time of his death.[65] These rights were also protected by Mawlay 'Abd al-Rahman's successor, Sidi Muhammad.[66]

The concentration of the European trade in the hands of Jewish *tujjar* was part of the effort to control and limit contact with Europe while simultaneously profiting from the possibilities of European trade. In the age of aggressive European expansion, the contradiction of this policy became increasingly apparent. By the end of Sulayman's reign and during the reign of 'Abd al-Rahman (1822–59), foreign trade again began to accelerate, but the *makhzan* had few means to profit from this trade. After the 1844 French attack, the tributes still paid by a few countries were annulled, and trade with Europe was increasingly seen as harmful. The nineteenth-century historian al-Nasiri despairs of the growing number of foreign merchants and travelers in the Moroccan ports "mixing and intermingling with the population." He continues to explain how trade in merchandise formerly prohibited was now allowed and how foreign coins became more prevalent than the Moroccan currency. These changes were causing higher prices and monetary inflation.[67]

An important method used by the *makhzan* to maintain control of the European trade and to gain revenues for the state was through monopolies (*kuntradat*). Commercial monopolies were farmed out to merchants, and again, there were disproportionately more Jewish than Muslim merchants who received government contracts. The granting of monopolies to Jews connected to the European trade also served the state well ideologically. For the Jewish tax-farmer, there was the possibility of profit; but being engaged in an activity of questionable legality that could undercut the efforts of producers and traders made him vulnerable and dependent on the sultan for protection. The dissatisfaction caused by the monopoly system could thus be expressed against the Jews and deflected from the state. Sometimes the rights to trade for a whole seaport could be farmed out. At the beginning of the reign of 'Abd al-Rahman, one merchant, Meir

Macnin, and members of his family were given control of the trade in a number of Morocco's seaports: Larache, al-Jadida, Casablanca, and Safi.[68]

More often, however, monopolies on specific commodities were farmed out, quite frequently to Jewish businessmen. Monopolies on specific commodities did not begin with Mawlay 'Abd al-Rahman but had been employed by all the sultans as a strategy for gaining revenue. Even Sultan Mawlay al-Yazid, despite the upheaval during his reign and his purges against Jews, did not abandon trade with Europe and continued to grant privileges to certain Jewish merchants, such as Mordechai Delamar, who received the exclusive privilege to export wax from all the ports.[69]

The number of monopolies diminished significantly in the first decades of the nineteenth century. In 1844, there is evidence only of a monopoly of leeches sold to a Jewish merchant, Yamim Acoca.[70] But a growing sense that it was losing control of foreign commerce after 1844 led the *makhzan* to increase its monopolies. Among the major products sold as monopolies were iron, cochineal, sulfur, tobacco, and skins.[71] A Jewish merchant in Tetuan, Yehuda Ibn Shlomo Halevi, who had been authorized to export wool and skins (*makhzan* monopolies) from Tetuan, Rabat, and Casablanca, proposed in 1850 that he be given a monopoly over the export of henna from the port of Tetuan and that its export from the other ports should be disallowed for a period of five years. For this monopoly, the *makhzan* was to receive an annual payment of 1,000 mithqals.[72]

While Jewish merchants had a preponderant role in the system of monopolies, there were also a number of Muslim merchants who served as royal merchants and tax-farmers, often from the elite of Tetuan or Fez. Following the 1844 war, the *makhzan* may have wanted in part to give preference to Muslim merchants over Jewish, since the latter had close ties with foreigners. Four Tetuani merchants linked to the ruling elite were sent to Essaouira with a large amount of credit and with the exclusive privilege of making delayed payment on export duties. Despite these advantages, they were unable to supplant the Jewish merchants already established in the port.[73] After the 1844 war, the *makhzan* also accorded monopolies to Muslim traders. In 1845, it was reported that iron could be imported only by the Moroccan consul at Gibraltar, Sidi Muhammad al-Razini or his agents; iron was to be seized from the houses of other merchants by the government.[74] Before the administration of the ports became more systematized in the 1860s, often customs duties on specific commodities were auctioned. Among the principal purchasers of these rights were Mustafa al-Dukkali and al-Makki al-Qabbaj.[75] In 1850 *mukus* taxes were imposed by Mawlay 'Abd al-Rahman on the sale of skins and cattle. Traders had to sell the products to the government agents to whom the monopoly had been farmed out. Al-Dukkali and al-Qabbaj were granted this monopoly.[76]

This system of *kuntradat* proved to be untenable because of the harm done to merchants, which probably diminished the revenue generated from foreign trade. Many of the monopolies were disregarded by other traders. Foreign influence also forced the sultan to gradually relinquish most of the monopolies, though there were always a number of items maintained as government monopolies. For example, the tax-farmer Yamim Acoca seems to have held the monopoly for gunpowder for a number of years, evidenced by a report on a lively contraband trade in 1870.[77] In addition to gunpowder, tobacco and hashish (*tarqa*) were maintained as government monopolies. But by 1854, the import and the export of the major products in Morocco's trade were no longer farmed out by the monopoly system. The commercial treaty with Great Britain in 1856 that imposed a standard 10 percent ad valorem duty on imports and a fixed tariff for exports signaled a major change in the royal system of trade. The Anglo-Moroccan treaty became the standard for commercial relations with all nations engaged in trade with Morocco. The *makhzan* sought to preserve its revenues by fixing a separate exchange rate for customs so that the duties would not be adversely affected by monetary inflation.[78]

The commercial treaty with Britain made it effectively impossible to maintain a monopoly system on the principal articles of export in the Moroccan trade since it established a fixed tariff. But the tax taken by government officials from the sale of skins in the markets lasted for much longer. What this meant, in effect, is that the *makhzan*, no longer able to benefit from the sale of monopolies to the elite royal merchants, further exploited the masses of urban dwellers who produced and sold skins in the markets and who had to pay market taxes. This met with considerable opposition from the ulama and resistance by the population, such as when the tanners of Fez rioted in 1873.[79]

After the war with Spain in 1860, Morocco was forced to pay a huge indemnity, which bankrupted the royal treasury. Payments on the debt to Spain for the war indemnities and to the British, who loaned the Moroccan government money to pay the Spanish, continued for years. This led Sultan Muhammad IV to impose an octroi on the city gates, also classified as *mukus*, justified by the sultan as being for the good of the community and for the strengthening of Islam.[80] The cost of running the state with its expanding bureaucracy was another reason for the search for new revenues. The taxes were collected, depending on local circumstances and calculations on what would be most profitable, either through tax-farming (also referred to as *kuntradat*), which would go to the highest bidder (or company of bidders), or through excise tax officials (*umana'*).[81] The growing reliance on a professional state bureaucracy for the collection of taxes (*umana' al-mustafadat*) led to the development of a kind of quasi-municipality in the latter half of the nineteenth century that utilized a portion of the revenue generated from the *mukus* to pay for urban expenses.[82]

The *mukus* were finally abolished in 1885 by Sultan Mawlay al-Hasan, with much rejoicing since it was a tremendous burden both to urban merchants and rural traders bringing their goods to the urban markets.[83] This seems to have been a temporary measure to placate growing discontent, for the *makhzan* records demonstrate that in Essaouira and Marrakesh gate and market taxes continued to be paid until the end of the nineteenth century.[84] Gate taxes were formally reintroduced in 1896, with the agreement of representatives of the foreign powers that foreigners and protégés should also pay the tax.[85] The taxes were either auctioned to tax-farmers or collected directly by the *amin al-mustafad*. In Tangier during the preprotectorate period, not only were gate taxes auctioned to tax-farmers under the supervision of the *amin al-mustafad,* but a tax was also levied on the sale of cattle at the cattle market.[86] Monopolies on hashish and tobacco still existed in the preprotectorate period, and these monopolies could be conceded even to foreign tax-farmers.[87]

One of the major reasons for the discontent over the *mukus* was the fact that the masses were saddled with a much heavier burden, while the elite merchants who were protégés of foreign powers and thus beneficiaries of extraterritorial rights were exempt from payment. The abusive expansion of consular protection, especially protection of Jewish merchants, was perhaps the most important cause in undermining the commercial system.[88] Some protégés, it seems, even tried to evade payment of duties. In 1854, Mawlay 'Abd al-Rahman was informed that "the majority of *dhimmi* merchants in our royal ports have declared themselves protégés of the Christians and have taken the protection of the nations and have acquired passports from the consuls of Tangier, and this is one of the stratagems." The merchants are condemned for "evading their humble status," for "showing insolence to Muslims," and finally, the wrath of God is invoked with the cliché: "May God destroy them."[89] One effect of the growth in the number of Jewish protégés was that many were not paying duties owed in the ports, especially in Tangier. Of symbolic importance was the evasion of payment of the *jizya* in some communities by protégés, which meant that unprotected Jews had to assume a greater tax burden than before.[90] The French consular agent in Essaouira, Auguste Beaumier, reported that "today this tax is reduced practically to nothing, as a consequence of the consular protection that the principal Jews have been able to obtain, to the extreme misery of the others."[91] The

Jewish protégés of the *mallah* of Marrakesh began refusing to pay their *jizya,* and the Sultan Sidi Muhammad ordered that those Jews who refused to pay should be expelled from the country and that a *talib* should be appointed to help carry this out.[92]

The evasion of taxes by protégés and foreigners was in theory modified by agreement between Morocco and the foreign powers at the Conference of Madrid in 1880. The Madrid conference determined that all residents in Morocco, protégés and foreigners included, were to pay the *mukus*. But the protests of the foreign merchants and their protégés obstructed the efforts of the *makhzan* to collect these taxes, and in 1885, as we have seen, they were officially lifted.[93]

Al-Nasiri writes how Mawlay al-Hasan solicited the opinion of his subjects and consulted with the ulama regarding the growing pressures of the foreign powers on Morocco for more liberal foreign trade. Should the export of grains, cattle, and other animals, as demanded by the foreign powers, be allowed when this could cause high prices for the poor? Would not reduced tariffs and customs duties cause a diminution of revenue for the *makhzan* needed to pay the military, forcing it to raise taxes and causing greater hardship for the population? The people, according to al-Nasiri, agreed to the suggestion of the sultan to allow the export of these items for a trial period. The export of certain items to the Christians was justified by the profit that the people would gain from selling the merchandise and the revenues that would be derived from tariffs on the exports. The ulama, however, recommended that the exportation demanded by the foreign powers be rejected, outlining the dangerous influence of foreigners and the requirement of jihad, and that any truce with the enemy should only be temporary. Al-Nasiri himself offered a long justification for the sultan's action based on both legal and political implications. While stating the argument based on jurisprudence and the Sharia that prohibits the export of those goods that might strengthen the position of the infidels against the Muslims, al-Nasiri also recognized a certain realpolitik—that the Muslims were ill-prepared to confront the Christian powers and that jihad not only was no longer feasible but would wreak havoc for Islam.[94]

In the late nineteenth and early twentieth centuries, the ulama became increasingly preoccupied with the corrupting influence of foreign trade, seen as the root of vice and immorality. Even the growth in tea consumption was seen as a threat to Moroccan sovereignty. The increasingly frequent intermingling of Muslims with foreigners and Jews was attributed to the weakening of Islam.[95] What had become increasingly apparent was that a growing number of Muslim merchants recognized that considerable profit could be made from commerce with Europe and were becoming more and more linked to Jews and foreigners in the coastal cities engaged in trade.[96] The continued opposition of the ulama to foreign trade in the decades preceding the establishment of the French and Spanish protectorates paradoxically strengthened the power of the sultan to appropriate the profits of commerce for the *makhzan*. Foreign commerce was considered a marginal activity because it was associated with *ahl al-dhimma*, whose activities were entirely outside the jurisdiction or moral authority of the ulama. The ulama could only warn Muslims of the dangers of too much interaction with the Jewish population. It was the state that was responsible for maintaining the protection of the Jews, and this relationship with non-Muslims was legitimized by Islam. The rhetoric of jihad espoused by some of the ulama, such as Muhammad Ibn Ja'far al-Kattani, and its increasingly Salafi reformist agenda were rarely translated into political action challenging the power of the *makhzan*. The deference of the ulama to the sultan's divine authority, together with their religious disapproval of foreign trade, helped to consolidate the sultan's special relationship to his merchants.[97]

The ambivalence of Morocco's rulers toward trade with Christian Europe was shared with other Muslim states. In an age when *dar al-islam* was expanding and could withstand foreign encroachments, trade with Christian powers was justified as a legitimate exercise of the royal prerogative, sanctioned by law for the purpose of jihad. Non-Muslim minorities were prominent in foreign trade both because of their ability to travel abroad and their lack of ideological opposition to dealing with Christians. Rulers encouraged non-Muslims to trade with Europe because the profits derived from customs duties, taxes, and monopolies increased the sultan's power. By investing in *ahl al-dhimma* instead of Muslim merchants, they could deflect the criticism of the ulama, who, as upholders of Islamic morality, cautioned against excessive intermingling between Muslims and Christians. When Jews traded with Christian countries, the profits that came to the state could be justified for the purposes of jihad.

In the age of European imperialism, this system of royal trade became increasingly untenable. The inability of the Moroccan sultans to maintain control over it was due to the unequal relationship of power between Europe and Morocco that led, in the years following the death of Mawlay al-Hasan I, to the imposition of colonial rule. The patrimonial system of royal trade ceased to be viable in an age when relations with Europe were determined by free trade and imperialism. The most entrepreneurial Moroccan merchants were sometimes able to profit from the new relationship, but they often became agents of European economic expansion. The indigenous system of royal trade, based on an ideology that separated the practical goal of gaining revenues for the *makhzan*'s coffers from the moral disapproval of commerce with Europe, could not prevent the development of a class of Moroccan merchants whose economic interests were tied to foreign domination and, eventually, colonial rule.

NOTES

1. See J. de Bakker, "Slaves, Arms, and the Holy War: Moroccan Policy vis-à-vis the Dutch Republic during the Establishment of the 'Alawi Dynasty (1660–1727)" (Ph.D. diss., University of Amsterdam, 1991), 4–9.

2. Ahmad Ibn Yayha al-Wansharisi, *Al-mi'yar al-mu'rib wa-al-jami' al-mughrib 'an fatawa ahl ifriqiya wa al-andalus wa al-maghrib;* Translation by E. Amar in *Archives Marocaines* 11 (1908): 453–6.
3. M. El Mansour, *Morocco in the Reign of Mawlay Sulayman* (Wisbech, Cambridgeshire, 1990), 54–5.
4. M. K. Masud, "The Obligation to Migrate: The Doctrine of Hijra in Islamic Law," in D. Eickelman and J. Piscatori, eds., *Muslim Travellers: Pilgrimage, Migration, and the Religious Imagination* (Berkeley: University of California Press, 1990), 37.
5. M. Kenbib, *Juifs et musulmans au Maroc, 1859–1948* (Rabat: Mohammed V University, 1994), 116.
6. N. Cigar, "Socio-Economic Structures and the Development of an Urban Bourgeoisie in Pre-Colonial Morocco," *The Maghreb Review* 6, no. 3–4 (1981): 67.
7. J.-L. Miège, *Le Maroc et l'Europe, 1830–1894,* 4 vols. (Paris: Presses Universitaires de France, 1961–2), 2:28
8. For example, on the mission to free Muslim prisoners in Spain in 1776–7. Ahmad Ibn al-Mahdi al-Ghazzal, *Natijat al-ijtihad fi al-muhadana wa-al-jihad,* ed. Isma'il al-'Arabi (Algiers, 1984), 33ff.
9. Archives du Ministère des Affaires Etrangères (MAE), Paris, Correspondance Politique, Maroc 5, 16 August 1837, Delaporte.
10. M. Busha'ra', *Al-istitan wa al-himaya bi al-Maghrib, 1280–1311/1865–1894,* 4 vols. (Rabat, 1984–9), 1:58.
11. A point recognized by al-Nasiri in reference to a commercial treaty of 1180/1766–7 between Morocco and France. Ahmad Ibn Khalid al-Nasiri, *Al-istiqsa' li-akhbar duwal al-Maghrib al-'aqsa,* 9 vols. (Casablanca, 1954–6), 8:31.
12. In 1828, Harun Ibn Ishak Isra'il (Aharon ben Yitzhak Yisrael) and, in 1835, Nessim Cohen Solal were appointed, but objections were raised since Muslims would be under the jurisdiction of a Jew. MAE, Nantes, Tanger 82, correspondances et notes relatives aux projects conçus par le sultan de créer un consulat marocain à Marseille, 1827–35, *zahirs* of 23 Dhu al-Qa'da 1243 (6 June 1828) and 27 Safar 12512 (4 June 1835). See Miège, *Le Maroc,* 2:89. Miège also refers to a chargé d'affaires at the royal court of Turin resident in Genoa but is unclear on his source and does not give the period or duration of the appointment. He writes that it was "si discret qu'il disparut sans que personne s'en inquiétât," 2:29.
13. On this role of Gibraltar, see ibid., 2:98–103.

14. The controversial case of the mission of Meir Macnin to London in 1828 is a good example of the deliberate obscurity of the position of Moroccan Jews in diplomacy. This is discussed in my article "Morocco, England and the End of the Sephardic World Order," in N. A. Stillman and Y. K. Stillman, eds., *From Iberia to Diaspora and Beyond* (Leiden, 1998).
15. S. D. Goitein, *A Mediterranean Society*, vol. 1, *Economic Foundations* (Berkeley: University of California Press, 1967), 66.
16. See *Disorienting Encounters: Travels of a Moroccan Scholar in France in 1845–1846: The Voyage of Muhammad as-Saffar,* trans. and ed. S. G. Miller (Berkeley: University of California Press, 1992).
17. de Bakker, "Slaves," 14–15.
18. See Miller's comments, *Disorienting Encounters*, 76.
19. al-Wansharisi, *Al-mi'yar al-mu'rib*, 220–1; E. Michaux-Bellaire, "Un Fetoua de cheikh Sidia," *Archives Marocaines* 11 (1907): 133, 140–5.
20. de Bakker, "Slaves," 52–3.
21. For example, al-Ghazzal, *Natijat al-ijtihad.*
22. See R. A. El-Nasser, "Morocco from Kharajism to Wahhabism: The Quest for Religious Purism" (ph.D. diss., University of Michigan, 1983), 275, 354–5, 373–4; R. Lourido-Díaz, *Marruecos y el mundo exterior en la segunda mitad del siglo xviii* (Madrid, 1989), 414; idem, "El comercio del trigo entre Marruecos y la Peninsula Iberica en el siglo xviii," *Almenara* 9 (1976): 31–3.
23. al-Nasiri, *Al-istiqsa'*, 7:194–5.
24. Ibid., 8:21.
25. Ibid., 8:20. See also al-Ghazzal, *Natijat al-ijtihad*, 38.
26. See D. Schroeter, *Merchants of Essaouira: Urban Society and Imperialism in Southwestern Morocco, 1844–1886* (Cambridge: Cambridge University Press, 1988), 12–18.
27. M. Ibn Sa'id al-Siddiqi, *Iqza al-sarira li-tarikh al-Sawira* (Casablanca, 196-); Ahmad Ibn al-Hajj al-Rajraji, *Al-shamus al-munira fi akhbar madinat al-Sawira* (Rabat, 1935).
28. M. Ibn al-Tayyib al-Qadiri, *Muhammad al-Qadiri's 'Nashr al-mathani': The Chronicles,* ed. and trans. N. L. Cigar (London: Oxford University Press, 1981), 152.
29. P. Mercer, "Palace and Jihad in the Early 'Alawi State in Morocco," *Journal of African History* 18 (1977): 535–8.

30. al-Nasiri, *Al-istiqsa'*, 7:81–6.
31. In 1734, Mawlay Abu al-Hasan 'Ali Ibn Isma'il recommended that Islamic taxes be collected only in Fez, according to al-Nasiri, *Al-istiqsa'*, 7:137. Sidi Muhammad Ibn 'Ariba allegedly abolished the *mukus;* al-Qadiri, *Nashr al-mathani*, 201.
32. al-Nasiri, *Al-istiqsa'*, 8:7–9; R. Lourido-Díaz, *Marruecos en la segunda mitad del siglo xviii. Vida interna: politica, social y religiosa durante el Sultanato de Sidi Muhammad b. 'Abd Allah, 1757–1790* (Madrid, 1978), 132–3.
33. al-Nasiri, *Al-istiqsa'*, 8:17.
34. Morocco's relations with Europe have been studied in detail by Lourido-Díaz, *Marruecos y el mundo exterior.*
35. J. Caillé, *Les accords internationaux du Sultan Sidi Mohammed b. Abdallah (1757–1790)* (Tangier, 1960); idem, "L'Abolition des tributs versés au Maroc par la Suède et le Danemark," *Hespéris* 45 (1958).
36. Schroeter, *Merchants*, 18ff.
37. Lourido-Díaz, *Marruecos y el mundo exterior,* 370–1, 387, 417–8.
38. M. al-Du'ayyif, *Tarikh al-Du'ayyif,* ed. A. al-'Amrani (Rabat, 1986), 76.
39. Lourido-Díaz, *Marruecos y el mundo exterior,* 621–33.
40. al-Du'ayyif, *Tarikh,* 198, 201.
41. See H. Z. Hirschberg, *A History of the Jews in North Africa,* vol. 2, *From the Ottoman Conquests to the Present Time* (Leiden, 1981), 291; S. A. Romanelli, *Travail in an Arab Land,* trans. Y. K. Stillman and N. A. Stillman (Tuscaloosa: University of Alabama Press, 1989), 143; O. Agrel, *Neue Reise nach Marokko* (Nuremberg, 1798), 123–4, 133–8.
42. al-Du'ayyif, *Tarikh,* 202.
43. See El Mansour, *Morocco,* 15, 88.
44. For example, Meir Macnin continued to serve the governor of Essaouira, and Mordechai Delamar received the exclusive privilege to export wax from all the ports. Algemeen Rijksarchief, The Hague (ARH), Consulaat Tanger 1, 15 March 1791, 31 July 1791, Subremont to Blount; Great Britain, Public Record Office, FO 52/10, 27 April 1799, Matra.
45. M. Arribas Palau, "Los hermanos Chiappe en Marruecos," in *La Conoscenza dell'Asia e dell'Africa in Italia nei secoli XVIII e XIX* (Naples, 1984), 1, pt. 2: 825; FO 52/10, 19 October 1791, Matra.

46. FO 52/10, 30 October 1790, Matra; ARH, Consulaat Tanger 1, 20 November 1790, Subremont to Blount.
47. al-Du'ayyif, *Tarikh*, 274–9 passim, 321, 332, 385; Abu al-Qasim Ahmad al-Zayani, *Al-turjuman al-mu'rib 'an duwal al-Mashriq wa-al-Maghrib*, ed. and trans. O. Houdas, *Le Maroc de 1631 à 1812* (Paris, 1886), 104–5 (Arabic) and 194–5 (French).
48. El Mansour, *Morocco*, 45–9; El-Nasser, "Morocco," 397.
49. El Mansour, *Morocco*, 55ff.
50. El Nasser, "Morocco," 439–40.
51. Kenbib, *Juifs et musulmans*, 55.
52. Abu al-Qasim Ahmad al-Zayyani, *Jamharat al-tijan wa-fahrisat al-yaqut wa-al-lu'lu' wa-al-murjan fi dhikr al-muluk al-'Alawiyin wa-ashyakh Mawlana Sulayman*, cited in El-Nasser, "Morocco," 446.
53. See Kenbib, *Juifs et musulmans*, 57ff.
54. See D. Schroeter, "Trade as a Mediator in Muslim-Jewish Relations: Southwestern Morocco in the Nineteenth Century," in M. R. Cohen and A. L. Udovitch, eds., *Jews among Arabs: Contacts and Boundaries* (Princeton, 1989), 122–7; K. L. Brown, *People of Salé: Tradition and Change in a Moroccan City, 1830–1930* (Manchester: Manchester University Press, 1976), 159.
55. Schroeter, *Merchants*, 24–9.
56. From a fatwa concerning a request by the Jews to build a *hammam* in the *mallah* of Fez in 1252/1836–7. P. Paquignon, "Quelques documents sur la condition des juifs au Maroc," *Revue du Monde Musulman*, 9 (1909): 117.
57. S. W. Baron, *A Social and Religious History of the Jews*, 18 vols. (New York: Columbia University Press, 1957), 4:41, 70ff; L. Poliakov, *Les Banchieri juifs et le saint-siège du XIIIe au XVIIe siècle* (Paris, 1965).
58. Miège, *Le Maroc*, 2:28–9.
59. Royal Palace Library, Rabat, Al-Khizana al-Hasaniyya (KH), 24 Ramadan 1270 (20 June 1854), Muhammad Barisha to Mawlay 'Abd al-Rahman.
60. Corcos Papers (CP), private collection, Jerusalem, 7 Ramadan 1273 (1 May 1857); see Schroeter, *Merchants*, 34; this document is reproduced and translated into Hebrew in Michel Abitbol, *Tujjar al-sultan: une élite économique judéo-marocaine au XIXe siècle* (Jerusalem, 1994), 10–11.

61. CP, 11 Rabi' II 1274 (29 November 1857), Khalifa Muhammad to Muhammad Ibn 'Abd al-Salam Ibn Zakur. For a detailed discussion of the Corcos documents and the *tujjar*, see Abitbol, *Tujjar*.
62. See A. Laroui, *Les Origines sociales et culturelles du nationalisme marocain (1830–1912)* (Paris, 1977), 310–19.
63. KH, 23 Jumadi I 1262 (19 May 1846). See Kenbib, *Juifs et musulmans*, 64–5. Numerous Moroccan Jewish pilgrims were arriving in Jerusalem during this period, often via Marseille. See Miège, *Le Maroc*, 2:94.
64. KH, 9 Safar 1266 (25 December 1849), Mawlay 'Abd al-Rahman to 'Abd al-Qadir 'Ash'ash.
65. Levi-Corcos Papers (LC), 19 Rajab 1263 (3 July 1847).
66. LC 8 Rabi' I 1280 (3 August 1863), sultan to qa'id Mahdi Ibn al-Mashawri.
67. Al-Nasiri, *Al-istiqsa'*, 9:54.
68. FO 52/24, translation of the *zahir* of 22 Safar 1239 (19 November 1823). A translation is also found in MAE, Paris, CCC Maroc 28.
69. ARH, Consulaat Tanger 1, al-Jadida, 15 March 1791, Subremont to Blount; FO 52/10, 27 April 1799, Matra.
70. A complaint was lodged that a master of a British vessel was trying to make a purchase of leeches at Agadir. FO 635/5, 19 November 1844.
71. See Miège, *Le Maroc*, 2:234–41.
72. KH, 9 Jumadi I 1266 (3 March 1850); 26 Ramadan 1266 (5 August 1850), 'Abd al-Rahman to 'Abd al-Qadir 'Ash'ash. His request for a reduction in payment of export duties was denied. Several years later it was reported that he still owed a considerable sum of money on export duties and the monopoly of henna. KH, 5 Jumadi II 1270 (5 March 1854), Muhammad Ibn Zakur to sultan.
73. Schroeter, *Merchants*, 123.
74. FO 830/1, 2 June 1845, 18 June 1845, Grace.
75. KH, Mid-Safar 1264 (January 1848), sultan to Busilham Ibn 'Ali. For a number of years al-Dukkali purchased the monopoly on leeches. FO 830/1, 27 October 1853, Grace.
76. Schroeter, *Merchants*, 124–5; Laroui, *Les origines*, 292–3; E. Michaux-Bellaire, "L'Organisation des finances au Maroc," *Archives Marocaines* 11 (1907): 214; KH, 25 Rabi' II 1270 (25 January 1854), Muhammad al-Khattib to Muhammad Barisha; 23

Rajab 1270 (21 April 1854), declaration of taxes of skins in Marrakesh.
77. Mudiriya al-Watha'iq al-Malikiya (DAR), 1 Sha'ban 1287 (27 October 1870), Khalifa al-Hasan to al-Hajj 'Amara Ibn 'Abd al-Sadiq.
78. T. K. Park, "Inflation and Economic Policy in Nineteenth-Century Morocco: The Compromise Solution," *The Maghrib Review* 10, no. 2–3 (1985): 51–6.
79. J. Berque, *L'Intérieur du Maghreb: XVe–XIXe siècle* (Paris, 1978), 489–92.
80. Schroeter, *Merchants*, 152; al-Nasiri, *Al-istiqsa'*, 9:101–2.
81. Sometimes the *makhzan* encountered difficulties collecting its due from the tax-farmers—for example, in Essaouira, Demnat, and Tafilalt in 1867. KH, 12 Shawal 1283 (17 February 1867), Musa Ibn Ahmad to al-Khalifa al-Hasan. On this system of alternating between tax-farming and direct taxes by government officials, see T. K. Park, "Administration and the Economy: Morocco 1880 to 1980. The Case of Essaouira" (Ph.D. diss., Wisconsin, 1983), 307ff; Na'ima Harraj al-Tuzani, *Al-umana' bi-al-Maghrib fi 'ahd al-sultan Mawlay al-Hasan* (Rabat: Kulliyat al-Adab wa-al-'Ulum al-Insaniya, 1979), 121–6.
82. Park, "Administration and the Economy," 293ff.
83. Schroeter, *Merchants*, 160; al-Tuzani, *Al-umana'*, 128–9.
84. Park, "Administration and the Economy," 340–1.
85. E. Michaux-Bellaire, "Les Impôts marocains," *Archives Marocaines* 1 (1904): 65.
86. G. Salmon, "L'Administration marocain à Tanger," *Archives Marocaines* 1 (1904): 20, 53; E. Michaux-Bellaire, "Al Qçar El-Kebir: une ville de province au Maroc septentrional," *Archives Marocaines* 2 (1904–5): 42.
87. Michaux-Bellaire, "Les impôts," 66.
88. The impact of the protection system, the subject of a number of studies, has been most thoroughly investigated by M. Kenbib, *Les protégés: Contribution à l'histoire contemporaine du Maroc* (Rabat, 1996).
89. KH, 5 Jumadi II 1270 (5 March 1854), Muhammad Ibn Zakur to sultan.
90. On the question of the *jizya*, see Susan Gilson Miller's paper in this volume (Chapter 6). In Tangier, protégés who could have

escaped payment paid the *jizya* since it "was a form of personal insurance, a guarantee of access to power, a kind of civic responsibility" (118).
91. MAE, Memoires et Documents, March 1867.
92. KH, 13 Ramadan 1283 (19 January 1867), Sidi Muhammad to Khalifa al-Hasan.
93. DAR, 12 Sha'ban 1298 (10 July 1881), Muhammad Bargash to al-Hajj 'Amara; 16 Sha'ban 1298, al-Jilani Ibn Ya'qub to 'Amara, reports on resistance of foreigners to paying the gate taxes in Essaouira.
94. Al-Nasiri, *Al-istiqsa'*, 9:182–92; Laroui, *Les Origines*, 322–7.
95. E. Burke III, "The Moroccan Ulama, 1860–1912: An Introduction," in N. R. Keddie, ed., *Scholars, Saints, and Sufis: Muslim Religious Institutions since 1500* (Berkeley: University of California Press, 1972), 116; Laroui, *Les Origines*, 327–33.
96. Miège, *Le Maroc*, 3:32–35, 4:404–7; Brown, *People of Salé*, 158–60.
97. It has recently been argued convincingly that the ulama were almost always compliant in face of the power of the sultan. See H. Munson, Jr., *Religion and Power in Morocco* (New Haven: Yale University Press, 1993), 50–5; on Muhammad Ibn Ja'far al-Kattani and his treatise, *Nasihat ahl al-Islam*, see ibid., 87–96.

· SIX ·

Dhimma *Reconsidered:* Jews, Taxes, and Royal Authority in Nineteenth-Century Tangier

Susan Gilson Miller

Among the various forms in which state power is expressed in Morocco, the royal spectacle stands out as an especially rich subject for semiotic interpretation. In the nineteenth century, Europeans who attended the court were dazzled by the elaborate protocol and the veneration in which the sultan was held. The French traveler Eugène Aubin, who visited Fez in 1902, remarked that court ceremonial concentrated attention on the person of the sultan and was "cleverly devised to impress the masses." His account of the ceremony of Feast of the Sacrifice (*'id al-kabir*) carefully noted where each dignitary stood, how the colorful delegations of tribesmen and diplomats approached the monarch, and how the waiting crowd reacted. The whole ritual was organized around the "silent and motionless" figure of the sultan, blinding in its whiteness, shaded by a cherry-red parasol surmounted by a golden bull—a figure that communicated by its mere presence "the virtues of the Shereefian benediction."[1] Multiple layers of meaning seemed to undergird the display, arresting the observer's eye and stirring his imagination.

Ceremonies in general evoke a "complex field of references," making explicit relations of authority and subordination, reflecting realignments in the social order, and elaborating systems of symbolic control that extend beyond the ceremony itself.[2] Yet they do not have to be confined to the highest level of the state in order to be culturally significant. Even those held at the local level can expose relationships of power, especially if they reproduce values that permeate the body politic. Here we examine the ceremonies and social processes associated with the payment by Jews of the poll tax, or *jizya*, an annual ritual that took place in major towns and cities of precolonial Morocco. The setting of our story is Tangier, where tensions implicit in Muslim-Jewish relations were aggravated in the latter half of the nineteenth century by a rising tide of European influence that upset traditional patterns of behavior. In times of rapid change, ceremonies take on heightened importance as avatars of a mythical past, reinforcing in the popular mind a sense of continuity calculated to lessen the pain of transition.[3] Our inquiry shows how the tax-paying ceremony in Tangier helped to reaffirm long-standing relations between Jews and the *makhzan*, at the same time as it revealed currents of change taking place within the Jewish community and between Jews and Muslims.

THE *JIZYA* IN ISLAM AND IN MOROCCO

The *jizya*, the personal tax levied on Christians and Jews (*ahl al-dhimma*, people of the covenant) was a permanent feature of Muslim relations with non-Muslims throughout the lands of Islam. A variety of taxes were imposed on urban and rural populations, but the *jizya* was the only tax reserved especially for non-Muslims. In premodern Morocco there was no Christian minority, so that payments of the *jizya* concerned Jews alone. Our argument is that the ritual of the *jizya* was not simply a mark of subordination; more than that, it was a public display evoking various registers of feeling that specified the relationship between Muslims and Jews. The handing over of the tax was an occasion to act out the particulars of the contract that bound them together—for Muslims to assert their political and religious preeminence and for Jews to demonstrate their loyalty to the ruling authority and their desire for membership in the wider Moroccan community. This understanding of the *jizya* as a multivalent cultural event having subtle social ramifications departs significantly from past readings in which the tax collection was viewed simply in a negative sense, as evidence of the "highly ritualized degradation" that Jews were said to have suffered in Moroccan society.[4]

Another aspect of the *jizya* discussed here, which may have gone unnoticed by the majority but was critical for the minority, was the process of allocating the obligation it imposed. Collecting the tax called for negotiation within the Jewish community that exposed inner fault lines and also produced new solidarities. The following aspects of *jizya* are examined here: first of all, how the payment of the *jizya* functioned as a meeting ground for the conduct of intercommunal relations, and, second, how the Jewish community organized for its payment. Who paid the *jizya* and for what reasons? How did the tax reinforce the social contract between Muslim and Jew? Within the minority group, how did it enhance the power of some over others? Finally, and most important, was the *jizya* a force for cohesion or disintegration in society as a whole?

First, some general comments about the *jizya* as it is specified in Islamic law and carried on in Moroccan practice. According to E. W. Lane's *Arabic-English Lexicon,* the word *jizya* is derived from the Arabic root *jaza'a,* meaning "to compensate" or "to repay." In this sense, it means the tax paid to Muslim authorities by Jews in return for the right to remain within the lands of Islam in a protected status.[5] According to Islamic jurists, the purposes of the tax were several: it was an instrument by which the lower monotheisms of Judaism and Christianity covered their deficiencies and recognized the superiority of Islam; it served as compensation for the *dhimmi*'s refusal to convert; and finally, it was a form of ransom, repaying the state for the nonbeliever's exemption from military service. As J. R. Willis points out, non-Muslims within Islam existed in a weakened state "open to censure, dispraise and rebuke"; nonetheless, they were endowed with a legal personality and had rights and obligations under the law. To enter into *dhimmi* status was to engage in a contract, and like most contracts, this one had an element of reciprocity. Once the *jizya* was paid, certain jurists asserted, the *dhimmi* was free with regard to his person and his wealth, thus introducing "condescendences of respect" into a relationship that otherwise could be characterized by tension and even animosity.[6]

Legal opinion differed regarding the process of paying the *jizya*, giving rise to divergent practices in various parts of the Muslim world. In medieval Egypt, according to S. D. Goitein, the tax (called the *jaliya*) was imposed on males starting from the age of puberty, often calculated from nine years of age. It was paid directly to agents of the state, and the role of the Jewish community as intermediary was minimal. Goitein cites a few instances in which wealthy members of the community covered the tax for poor coreligionists, noting that this was unusual. Generally speaking, the tax was universally applied, and the tax collectors were relentless, turning "the season of the tax" into a time of "horror, dread, and misery."[7]

In Morocco, paying the *jizya* was more often a communal responsibility rather than an individual one, and local Muslim officials rarely interfered in its collection. In Tangier, Jewish community leaders would assign a specific amount to individuals according to their wealth, supervise the collection, and then deliver the total to a representative of the *makhzan*, usually the local governor, or *basha*. This method exempted the poorest and made sure that those most able to pay shouldered the greatest burden. Within the Jewish community, paying the *jizya* became a special category of charity, alongside other charities (*tsedakot*) meant to protect the weak and preserve communal bonds.

Muslim jurists also disagreed regarding the extent to which coercion could be used in collecting the tax, offering variant interpretations of the Koranic text most often cited as the source for establishing the *jizya* in the first place.⁸ If a man could not pay the *jizya*, some argued, corporal punishment should not be used. It was humiliating enough, they claimed, to be singled out for a tax not levied on believers, and there was no need for additional penalties. Other authorities, however, condoned the use of force, and spoke of striking the payee with blows to the head as he handed over the tax or coercing him to wear the receipt for payment around his neck as a mark of subordination. Foreign travelers to Morocco remarked on this aspect of ritualized coercion, among them a shipwrecked American, James Riley, who witnessed the collection of the *jizya* in Mogador (Essaouira) in 1816:

> The Jews soon appeared by classes; as they approached, they put off their slippers, took their money in both their hands, and holding them alongside each other, as high as the breast, came slowly forward to the *talb,* or Mohammedan scrivener, appointed to receive it. He took it from them, hitting each one a smart blow with his fist on his bare forehead, by way of receipt for his money, at which the Jew said, *Nahma Sidi* [*na'am ya sidi,* yes, sir] and retired to give place to his companion. Thus they proceeded through three first classes without much difficulty, when the fourth class was forced up with big sticks. This class was very numerous, as well as miserable. They approached very unwilling. . . . [Some paid the tax, but others did not, in which case the individual] was seized instantly by the Moors, who throwing him flat on his face on the ground, gave him about fifty blows with a thick stick upon his back and posteriors, and conducted him away, I was told to a dungeon, under a bomb proof battery, next to the western city wall, facing the ocean. There were many served in this way.⁹

If this account is accurate (we have no reason to believe it is not), then why the barbarous cruelty? Even if we allow for the effects of a prolonged captivity on the mariner's imagination, the gruesome details cannot be ignored. How widespread this kind of treatment was we cannot know for sure. Collection of tribute, whether from Jews or Muslims, could be the occasion for displays of brute power. Local governors were often free to oppress their subjects with impunity, especially if they ruled in towns like Essaouira that were distant from centers of *makhzan* control. The ceremony of the *jizya* afforded these petty despots the opportunity to flaunt their authority. There is little doubt that the collection of the tax was sometimes carried out in a cruel manner, but whether this was the rule or the exception is less than clear.

Islamic legal opinion was generally unanimous on one point, however, which was the necessity for the *dhimmi* to present himself in person to pay the tax. The taxpayer could not delegate the task to a surrogate, which wealthy *dhimmis* would have no doubt preferred. Some legists went so far as to insist that the taxpayer remain standing while the tax collector sat; others prescribed that the hand of the collector had to be above that of the *dhimmi*, who should offer the tax with outstretched palm.[10] Moreover, the handing over of the tax was to be performed in a public place, usually before the gates of the treasury house (*bayt al-mal*). Whether the tax was collected with or without harshness, the open and public nature of the delivery was a central component of it. Bystanders who gathered to watch the ceremony could read in it messages about the ascendancy of Islam over the faith of the unbeliever and the relative social standing of the followers of each. Like the rituals associated with gift giving (the *hadiya*), the ceremony of the *jizya* was a theatrical performance filled with the rhetoric of power.[11] It transmitted forceful images of authority, it reproduced the social order in bold relief, and it made explicit the important message that even the lowly *dhimmi* could find a seat under the capacious umbrella of Islam.

For the Jewish minority, on the other hand, the *jizya* embodied the full meaning of exile, and popular literature presented it as one of the disabilities of living as a Jew in a non-Jewish land. Taxes were paid "to appease adversaries that oppress us . . . and who [aim to] destroy the heritage of the Lord, for when we give them taxes and extortion we close the mouths of the evil ones," according to one rabbinic commentator.[12] Jewish sources speak of fiscal obligations in tones of sorrow and suffering, and complaints about them "fill the prologues" of the collections of juridical literature.[13] Both Jew and Muslim agreed that the payment of the *jizya* was a corollary of a fundamental condition predicated on a disparity of power: they differed, however, in that for the Muslim it was a permanent and fixed disequilibrium, while for the Jew it was a temporary and transient one to be cast off with the coming of the Messiah and the return to Zion. A minor matter to Muslim officials, the *jizya* loomed large in the Jewish imagination as a critical benchmark for measuring the state of the Jewish community's relations with the Muslim authority. Now let us see how this event laden with cultural messages worked itself out in the local context of Tangier.

A CASE STUDY:
COLLECTING THE TAX IN TANGIER

After the Moroccan-Spanish War of 1859–60, Tangier became the main port of European commercial and political entry into Morocco. As the importance of the town grew and its elites prospered, the Jewish elders decided to form a community council, or *Junta,* which included representatives of the small yet powerful coterie of Jewish entrepreneurs who were acting as middlemen for European trading houses.[14] One reason behind its formation was to protect Jewish interests in the wildly burgeoning local economy. Another was to receive wealthy European Jews, who, after midcentury, became intensely curious about in their coreligionists in the "backward" East. The *Junta* played a principal role in hosting important European Jewish visitors like Sir Moses Montefiore, who arrived in Morocco in 1864 comfortably outfitted with ample funds and a surfeit of good will, anxious to spread the blanket of reform over his Oriental brethren.[15] The growing influence of the self-appointed *Junta* soon soon filled the pages of a Minute book, or *Libro de Actas;* reading this archive gives us a picture in miniature of the inner politics of the Jewish community at this moment in Tangier's history.

The *Junta* took on many tasks: it offered gifts to Muslim officials on special occasions and, at times of inner discord, solicited the *basha*'s mediation; it orchestrated dealings with the European consuls and promoted Jewish interests in the diplomatic arena; it acted as spokesman to the outside world for the Jews of Tangier and, occasionally, for the Jews of Morocco. But most of all, the *Junta* concerned itself with every detail of local Jewish life: policing public morality; ensuring ritual purity in the slaughtering of meat, the baking of bread, and the cleanliness of the bathhouse; extending charity to the less fortunate and shelter to travelers; offering dowries on behalf of needy brides and even providing a coach to carry them to their weddings; and of course, paying the *jizya*.

The collection and payment of the obligatory tax was a main preoccupation of the *Junta* in the period 1860–75, and from the Minute book we get a sharply etched picture of the part it played in the inner workings of communal life.[16] The question of the tax seized the *Junta*'s attention immediately after it was formed; the *basha* was asking for two payments at once, covering the years 1859–60 of the Spanish-Moroccan war. This came as a blow to the Jewish elders because the war had brought financial chaos not only to the *makhzan* but also to Tangier's 4,500 Jews, most of whom had fled to Gibraltar for the duration, where they had lived in misery off the charity of European Jews.[17] On their return, their first task was to repair relations with the *makhzan*, still smarting from its humiliating defeat at the hands of the Spanish forces. In November 1860, members of the *Junta* went to see Mawlay al-'Abbas, brother of the Sultan, hoping that his "influence over his Majesty" would win them time and even exempt them from paying the *jizya* for at least one of the two previous years.[18]

Despite a generous gift to Mawlay al-'Abbas, the negotiation failed, and the community had to meet a payment of 600 gold napoleons representing two years of taxes, a considerable sum.[19]

A list of "all those who are capable of paying" and their ability to pay was drawn up by Jewish assessors, with one full share set at twenty ducados. The rich members of the *Junta* made a special contribution of thirty-two ducados per share. On the appointed day the *shaykh al-yahud,* the official in charge of communal decorum, went from door to door collecting the tax, accompanied by a rabbi and two strong boys to carry the heavy sacks of coins. It was decided not to employ a soldier as a guard, a sure sign of the security that prevailed inside the town. Since announcement of the collection had been made in the synagogues, everyone assessed was expected to be at home, and if anyone should refuse to pay, a soldier would later visit him at home. In such cases, the person would not only pay his assigned share but also the commission (*sukhra*) for the soldier.[20] Despite careful planning, the capacity of the community to pay was miscalculated, and the amount gathered was about 300 ducados short of what was needed. Embarrassed to hand over an insufficient sum, the *Junta* requested to postpone the ceremony of the payment. But it became apparent that time was up when individual Jews began to receive threats (*amenazas*) from Muslim officials because the tax had not yet been paid. Under mounting pressure, the members of the *Junta* decided to make up the difference out their own pockets, and 500 ducados were finally handed over in April 1861.[21]

This episode revealed so many deficiencies in communal organization that the *Junta* decided to revise its system of collection. Moreover, in addition to the *jizya,* there were other gifts that had to be presented to the *makhzan* from time to time; although of lesser value than the *jizya,* they nevertheless constituted a significant expense. For example, the appointment of a new *basha* in June 1861 required a special gift of 736 ounces. Five rich men quickly banded together to pay the sum, but later they demanded a reimbursement from the communal funds.[22] Some regular form of taxation was needed in order to ensure that a tax-and-gift fund would always be at hand.

In 1863, the *Junta* took the unusual step of using part of the revenues from the sale of kosher meat to pay the *jizya*.[23] In Morocco, a tax (called in Tangier *tabahot*) was imposed on all animals slaughtered according to Jewish law. The meat tax was a guaranteed form of revenue collected from the butchers that went directly into the communal coffers, where it was supposed to be used for religiously sanctioned charities, such as aid to the poor and sick, help for indigent scholars, and assistance to wayfarers. Although technically it was the butchers who paid the meat tax, in reality, the tax was passed directly on to consumers in the form of higher prices. The *Junta* decided that seven of the twenty-five ounces collected on each head of cattle slaughtered would be set aside to pay the *jizya*, while the rest would go for other charities.

But paying the *jizya* out of the meat taxes was controversial for two reasons: first of all, in the popular mind, the obligation of the *jizya* was not a halakhic duty sanctioned by Jewish law but a practical necessity, carried out to ensure good relations with the temporal power. Many felt that meeting the tax obligation from the revenues on the sale of kosher meat was an incursion of the profane into the religious, for the proper slaughtering of animals, as well as dispensing the charity derived from it, was regarded as an act of piety. We hear echoes of this concern in the archives, when the secretary (*parnas*) of the poor fund complained that the meat tax was being used to pay the *jizya*, and as a result, "the poor were suffering."[24] Second, the meat tax was a regressive tax, falling equally on the poor as well as the rich; unlike the old method of apportioning shares of the *jizya* according to economic status, now everyone contributed the same. By raising the *jizya* from the meat tax, the men of the *Junta* hoped to distribute it more widely throughout the community and thus lighten the burden on themselves. How they managed to do this without raising a storm of protest is indeed a mystery; if there was any objection, it went unrecorded in the archives.

The treasurer put in charge of the new fund promptly announced that "no one will touch it for a purpose other than that for which it was intended, and it will stay under my hand like a sacred trust."[25] But when the special fund was opened for accounting the following year, the "sacred trust" had somehow melted away. Over a period of fourteen months, 22,942.50 ounces had been collected, of which more than half had been spent on items not connected with the *jizya* at all, such as paying the salary of the secretary of the *Junta* and buying him pens, candles, and paper. Not only had the *Junta* shifted the burden of the tax to the rank and file; it was also using the funds to cover its own running expenses.[26]

It took a full year for a tax revolt to erupt in this well-disciplined community. When the *jizya* once again came due in late 1865, the coffers were nearly empty. This time, funds had been used to cover the shortfall in the budget of a European-style school established in 1864 with the aid of European benefactors.[27] A thunderous confrontation between the *Junta* and the rest of the community ensued. Told that there was no money in the cash box to pay the *jizya*, members of the community rebelled, saying that they "would not consent to touching the money destined for the *jizya*, not for the school, nor any other purpose." The payment of the *jizya* was to take precedence over all other communal obligations. Rejecting the failed leadership of the *Junta*, a group of concerned citizens vowed to raise the rest of the *jizya* themselves and, as a sign of their seemingly successful revolt, signed the minutes of the meeting.[28]

When the *jizya* was finally paid, nearly a year late, 11,000 ounces were handed over, but not by the rebels. Moses Pariente, the richest Jew of Tangier, banker, interpreter, friend of European diplomats and Muslim officials, paid the tax. A contemporary sketch of Pariente shows a modest man in a plain frock coat, wholly unremarkable in appearance. More revealing of his personality, perhaps, is the setting of his family bank, which still presides over the old Jewish quarter of Tangier. The palatial structure faced, on one side, the street of the gold merchants and money changers and, on the other, the street of the synagogues.[29] Moses Pariente operated comfortably on the uneven terrain demarcated by the paired obligations of high finance and sacred duty. In this moment of crisis, he came forward to "rescue" the community, reconstructing the familiar paradigm of the very rich as protectors of the rest. His act was a reminder that authority in the Jewish community resided in a combination of political shrewdness, economic expertise, and religious piety.[30] The ability of one person to come up with the entire *jizya* was bound to affect intercommunal relations, for to hold such wealth within the confines of the community raised the status of all. Jews of the modest class forgot their anger against the so-called big men (*pudientes*) and returned to business as usual, allowing the *Junta* to reassert its control over communal affairs.

The next crisis regarding the *jizya* came about because the butchers who collected the tax went on strike. Most of the Jewish butchers were natives of Fez, migrants who sought to profit from Tangier's booming postwar economy. The *Junta* discriminated against migrant Jews from the interior, labeling them as *forasteros* (strangers), blaming them for their "lax morals," refusing them charity, and even banishing them from the town.[31] Made to feel like outsiders, the Fasi butchers now got their revenge by refusing to help collect the *jizya,* seeing it as a strictly Tangier affair. This was the last straw, and in 1867, the meat tax was eliminated as a source of the *jizya,* the method of collection reverting to the old one of assigning shares directly to individuals.[32]

The years 1868 and 1869 were a period of severe famine and disease in Morocco and the Maghrib. Hordes of outsiders flocked into Tangier, seeking relief in its relative safety and creating a host of social problems. Entries in the archives outline the dimensions of the crisis; the charity rolls swelled as the number of families requesting aid more than doubled.[33] In January 1868, at the height of the troubles, the chief rabbi implored the rich men of the *Junta* to adopt special measures to "alleviate the calamities our brothers are suffering." Led by the wealthiest, the *Junta* held a special subscription for charitable purposes that in one day collected 28,719.25 ounces, almost three times the amount of the previous year's *jizya*. Meanwhile, the *basha* of the

Tangier generously excused the Jews from paying the *jizya* while the crisis continued.[34]

In 1870, the crisis subsided and the *jizya* was again collected. In that year, 143 persons contributed to a total payment of 306 napoleons. Table 6.1 distributes the payment by economic grouping. If we consider rows 1 and 2 as representing the most wealthy, rows 3 to 5 as the middle-income group, and rows 6 and 7 as representing the least affluent, we see that 45 percent of the tax was paid by less than 17 percent of the contributors (rows 1 and 2). At the other end of the scale, 46 percent of the contributors (rows 6 and 7) paid only 18 percent of the tax. In other words, almost half of the *jizya* was paid by a handful of the very rich. The predominance of the very wealthy becomes even more dramatic when we consider that the total number of all contributors was only 143, whereas the total Jewish population of Tangier was between 4,000 and 4,500.[35] From the Minute book we know that "more than 300 families" were on the charity rolls. If we use the figure of an average of seven members per family, we get the following social pyramid: wealthy (168 persons), upper middle class (357), lower middle class (476),

Table 6.1 Collection of the *Jizya* of 1870

	Contributors	Share per Contributor[a]	Total Shares	Total Value	Percent of Contributors	Percent of *Jizya*
1	19	1	19	114	13.29	37.25
2	5	3/4	3.75	22.5	3.50	7.35
3	23	1/2	11.5	69	16.08	22.55
4	12	1/3	3.96	24	8.39	7.84
5	16	1/4	4	24	11.19	7.84
6	37	1/6	0[b]	37	25.87	12.09
7	31	1/12	0[b]	15.5	21.68	5.07
	143		42 1/5	306	100	100

Source: Actas I, #242, 3 Tebet 5631/27 December 1870.
a. 1 share = 6 napoleons.
b. Not counted as shares.

poor (2,100), subtotal (3,101 persons).[36] This leaves approximately 900 to 1,400 persons at the very bottom of the social ladder, forming a lumpen proletariat that not only did not contribute to the *jizya* but were absent from the charity rolls altogether. These data suggest that the Jewish community was not divided into simple categories of rich and poor but was highly stratified into at least five social classes, defined at the upper end by one's ability to contribute to the *jizya* and at the lower end by whether one shared in the communal dole. In other words, participation in tithing, whether as a giver or receiver, was a key measure of one's social standing.

TAXES AND COMMUNAL HARMONY

The *Junta* records show that the collection and payment of the *jizya* took place more in an atmosphere of negotiation than in one of coercion. As we have seen, the request from the sultan for payment often went unanswered for months on end while the Jewish community mulled over how to amass the necessary funds.[37] In the terrible plague years of 1868 and 1869, Muslim officials demonstrated lenience, and the tax was completely forgiven. Moreover, in a fifteen-year period from 1860 to 1875 in which Morocco suffered serious inflation, the amount of tax remained more or less fixed at about 300 napoleons. The stability in the amount levied and paid suggests that the tax was not used as a punitive measure but rather as a means of confirming the status quo.

Moreover, the description of the manner in which the tax was collected suggests a friendly transaction rather than a humiliating concession. The Minutes tell how Moses Pariente, who was president of the *Junta* in 1871, personally delivered the *jizya* to the *basha,* accompanied by the chief rabbi, Mordechai Bengio, whose reputation verged on the saintly.[38] There is nothing in the records to suggest that the two most important Jews in Tangier attended a ceremony of abasement. On the contrary, they appear to have been received with honor, as much as their presence conferred it. In sum, economic motives may have played a part in the affair, but if they did, they were not uppermost. Other factors came into play that made the collection of the *jizya* an important benchmark for measuring the tenor of Muslim-Jewish relations in Tangier.

Among these factors were the symbolic and subtle gestures of command and submission that were evident in the ceremony: in the slow, arduous climb of the Jewish elders up the steep path leading from the Jewish quarter at the lower end of the town to the casbah at its heights; in the somber appearance of the patricians in their long black coats, contrasting with the the multicolored uniforms of the *makhzan* troops and the spotless white of the *makhzan* officials; in the heavy sacks of gold, always the medium of payment, offered to the *basha* in the open space of the *mashwar*, amidst the exuberant, mixed crowd of Muslim and Jewish onlookers. All these gestures recalled an earlier time when Jews were tributaries par excellence and the prestige of the *makhzan* was unblemished. The ceremony of the *jizya* was a morality play that reaffirmed the imaginary idea of an immutable social order in which ruler and ruled, Muslim and *dhimmi*, each knew his place.

For the Jewish community, payment of the tax was also the opportunity for a public display of a different sort—a display of capable leadership and inner solidarity. The elite who orchestrated the payment were regarded as the trustees of the community, responsible for its physical and moral well-being. It is not surprising that three of the members of the *Junta* in this period were also builders of synagogues. Wealth, charity, and patronage went hand in hand as measures of social standing. These same men also monopolized relations with the European consuls and *makhzan* officials, cultivating their relations with them in the pursuit of commercial and social advantages. For them, paying the tax was a sign of superiority, setting them apart from other Jews by dint of their wealth, their competence, and their rapport with the sources of authority.

It has been commonly assumed that wealthy Jews who acquired foreign protection quickly opted out of paying the *jizya*, further weakening the prestige of the *makhzan* in the eyes of its subjects.[39] But in Tangier, Morocco's most visible Jewish community, this was clearly not the case. The 1870 *jizya* includes names of persons who could have been exempted from the tax because they enjoyed consular protection. Prominent Jews such as Moses Pariente, Aaron Abensur, Haim Benchimol, Haim Bendelac, and Abraham Laredo were protégés of foreign powers and employed in the foreign legations. Yet each contributed generously to the tax and were found in the highest categories of payment.[40] These holders of foreign passports belonged to the small circle of elite Jewish families linked together by ties of marriage, profession, and special interests who formed a distinct oligarchic class. Serving as an interpreter was a small part of one's public life that combined well with the roles of businessman, property owner, or banker. Many of the business operations of the more enterprising Jews involved Muslims; all of their business depended on good relations with the authorities. For them, paying the *jizya* was a form of personal insurance, a guarantee of access to power, a kind of civic responsibility.

The defection of the Fasi butchers is also significant. Although their contribution was only pro forma, they wished to abstain from paying the tax to avoid any hint that they were identifying with the Jews of Tangier. Identities were defined in local terms, Fasis were Fasis, and even a long residence in the coastal town did not confer on them membership in the Tangier community. For the ordinary Jews of Tangier, it was precisely this participation in a corporate identity conferred by payment that mattered most. Even though as individuals their contribution to the *jizya* was small, as members of the Jewish community they had to be taken seriously. Poor Jews did not benefit from the paying of the *jizya* in the same way rich Jews did, but there were still advantages to be gained. For the modest shopkeeper, the symbolic contribution of one napoleon or less meant a kind of rough parity with the wealthy, a sharing in whatever prestige Jews as a group could muster. Paying the tax in the assigned amount consolidated one's place in the social hierarchy and offered a stable mechanism for measuring one's self-worth.

A SOCIETY IN TRANSITION

In a world made coherent through the prism of faith, minority claims to membership in the wider collectivity are often mediated through participation in rituals based on the religious beliefs of the other. The *jizya* was one such ritual, designed to demonstrate permanent truths about the Muslim universe and the place of minorities in it. Jews who wanted to be part of the larger Muslim world—and there were many who did—were required to take part in ceremonies whose symbolic content may have been at odds with their own inner faith. The ability to make a distinction between outward display and inner sensibility is a critical skill for minority survival, practiced at every time and in every culture.

It is also important to remember that symbolic performances generate multiple referents that can be interpreted in a variety of ways. In examining the theater of the *jizya*, we come to understand that subordination was only one aspect of the Jewish-Muslim relationship and that the ceremony of tax paying invoked various other affective means that worked to accommodate Jews within the larger Muslim society. Paying the *jizya* with dignity allowed the Jewish minority to engage in reciprocal, if unequal, exchanges with the political authority on a variety of levels. In so doing, the Jews of Tangier were pursuing a strategy that promoted social integration without violating the terms of the *dhimmi* contract.

Finally, we should keep in mind the fact that *subordination* is a relative term whose meaning changes with time and place. By 1875, many Jews of Tangier had achieved a de facto parity with their Muslim counterparts, at least in terms of their economic well-being. Although legally still *ahl al-dhimma*, in fact they were moving rapidly out of a subordinate status to a superior one, marked by greater collective wealth, better education, more social mobility, and improved health standards in comparison with their Muslim neighbors. In sum, they were moving swiftly down the path to modernity.[41] Throughout this process of transformation, communal records show that the tax was still paid, albeit sporadically, until the coming of the protectorate in 1912, when it was finally abolished.[42] By the end of the nineteenth century, the *jizya* had become a ceremony in which Jewish and Muslim elites in Tangier colluded for the sake of social tranquillity, keeping formal appearances intact, while making room for the many changes that were taking place in fact.

NOTES

1. Eugène Aubin, *Le Maroc d'aujourd'hui* (Paris, 1904), trans. *Morocco of Today* (London, 1906), 116. 'Id al-Kabir is called 'Id al-Adhha elsewhere in the Arab world. For further studies of ritual performances in Morocco see R. Bourqia, "Don et théatralité: réflexion sur le rituel du don (*hadiyya*) offert au Sultan au xixe siècle," *Hespéris-Tamuda* 31 (1993): 61–75; M. E. Combs-Schilling, *Sacred Performances: Islam, Sexuality, and Sacrifice* (New York: Columbia University Press, 1989). See also C. Geertz, "Centers, Kings, and Charisma: Reflections on the Symbolics of Power," in *Local Knowledge: Further Essays in Interpretive Anthropology* (New York, 1983), 121–46.
2. P. Sanders, *Ritual, Politics, and the City in Fatimid Cairo* (Albany: SUNY Press, 1994), 7. Research on ritual in European historical studies is mentioned in the notes to Sanders's Introduction. Of special interest for the Middle East is R. P. Mottahedeh, *Loyalty and Leadership in Medieval Islamic Society* (Princeton: Princeton University Press, 1980), a discussion of the codes governing interpersonal relations in medieval Islam.
3. E. Hobsbawm and T. Ranger, *The Invention of Tradition* (Cambridge: Cambridge University Press, 1989), 3.
4. See, for example, N. A. Stillman, *The Jews of Arab Lands: A History and Source Book* (Philadelphia, 1979), 76–87 and especially 84; B. Lewis, *The Jews of Islam* (Princeton: Princeton University Press, 1984), 148–50.

5. E. W. Lane, *An Arabic-English Lexicon,* a reprint of the London, 1863 edition in 2 vols. (Cambridge, 1984), 1:422b.
6. The literature on the theory and practice of *jizya* is vast. Sources I found helpful were A. Fattal, *Le Statut légal des non musulmans en pays d'Islam* (Beirut, 1958), chap. 7; J. R. Willis, "Jihad and the Ideology of Enslavement," in J. R. Willis, ed., *Slaves and Slavery in Muslim Africa,* 2 vols. (London, 1985), 1:16–17; B. Lewis, "L'Islam et les non-musulmans," *Annales: ESC* 35 (1980): 784–98; *Encyclopedia of Islam* (new edition), s.v. "Djizya." For discussion of *jizya* in the Maghrib, see the excellent article by J. O. Hunwick, "Al-Mahili and the Jews of Tuwat: The Demise of a Community," *Studia Islamica* 61 (1985): 155–83; also R. Brunschvig, *La Bérbérie orientale sous les Hafsides: des origines à la fin du XVe siècle,* 2 vols. (Paris, 1940–7), 1:402–3. On taxation in Morocco in general, see the fundamental article by E. Michaux-Bellaire, "Les Impôts marocaines," *Archives Marocaines* 1 (1904): 56–96.
7. See S. D. Goitein, *A Mediterranean Society: The Jewish Communities of the Arab World as Portrayed in the Documents of the Cairo Geniza,* 5 vols. (Berkeley: University of California Press, 1967–88), 2:381; also his article "Evidence on the Muslim Poll Tax from Non-Muslim Sources: A Geniza Study," *Journal of the Economic and Social History of the Orient* 6, no. 3 (1963): 278–95.
8. The Koranic text usually cited in this regard is 9:29, which says: "Fight them that believe not in God and the last day and who hold not as forbidden what God and his apostle have forbidden, and do not profess the true religion, those that have scripture, until they pay the *jizya* in person and in subjection (*'an yadin wahum saghirun*)." This text has been subject to a variety of translations and interpretations. G. Vajda cites the extreme point of view of the sixteenth-century jurist al-Maghili in "Un Traité maghrébin 'Adversus judæos': Ahkam ahl al-dhimmi du Shaykh Muhammad b. 'Abd al-Karim al-Maghili," in *Etudes d'orientalisme dédiées à la mémoire de Lévi-Provençal,* 2 vols. (Paris, 1962) 2:805–13. For additional references, see Lewis, "L'Islam et les non-musulmans," 799 n. 5; J. Gerber, *Jewish Society in Fez, 1450–1700* (Leiden, 1980), 188.
9. James Riley, *An Authentic Narrative of the Loss of the American Brig Commerce, Wrecked on the Western Coast of Africa, in the*

Month of August 1815 (Hartford, 1847), 198–200; quoted also in Stillman, *Jews of Arab Lands,* 368–9.
10. Fattal, *Le Statut,* 286–7.
11. Bourqia, "Don et théatralité," 64.
12. S. Deshen, *The Mellah Society* (Chicago: University of Chicago Press, 1989), 46. Pragmatically speaking, the *jizya* was only one among many taxes and probably one of the least onerous because of its predictability. It was the more frequent and unexpected special taxes that created genuine chaos in the Jewish communities. See Gerber, *Fez,* 186.
13. H. Zafrani, *Etudes et recherches sur la vie intellectuelle juive au Maroc de la fin du 15e au début du 20e siècle,* vol. 1, *Pensée juridique et environnement social, économique et religieux* (Paris, 1972), 130.
14. On the phenomenon of Jewish "compradorship," see J.-L. Miège, *Le Maroc et l'Europe (1830–1894),* 4 vols. (Rabat, 1989), 2:549–73. Biographies of members of the *Junta* are found in A. I. Laredo, *Les Noms des juifs du Maroc: essai d'onomastique judeo-marocaine* (Madrid, 1978). They include David Sicsu, from a family that supplied shaykhs of the community (899); Mesod Abecasis, interpreter of the American consulate (210); Yusuf Eshriki, from an Essaouira family of merchants, interpreter for the Swedish consulate and the French legation (390); Yusuf Toledano and Yaakov Toledano, from a family of Meknessi rabbis, enjoying prestige but no financial power (607 ff.); Moses Nahon, banker, property owner (862); Yehuda Assayagh, from a rich Tetuani family (361); Moses Pariente, founder of the Banque Pariente (980); Aaron Abensur, banker and interpreter at the British legation (1025); and Yehuda Azancot (248).
15. While the visit of Sir Moses was the most celebrated of these delegations, it was not unique; Moses H. Picciotto, representing the British Board of Deputies, came in 1860, as did Albert Cohn, head of the newly formed Alliance Israélite Universelle. Each promised donations for schools, hospitals, and other good works, but only Montefiore actually distributed money in the streets, scattering handfuls of silver coins to eager onlookers, according to local oral history. See Dr. Louis Loewe, ed., *Diaries of Sir Moses and Lady Montefiore, a Facsimile of the 1890 Edition* (London,

1983), 145–61; M. H. Picciotto, *Jews of Morocco* (London, 1860), and A. Cohn, "Voyage de M. Albert Cohn," *L'Univers Israélite*, 15 (1859–60): 699–701.

16. Archives of the Jewish Community of Tangier, hereafter indicated as "Actas." See "Indice, Libro de Actas," transcribed by Sidney Salomón Pimienta (Paris, 1992), photocopy; see also S. Pimienta, "'Actas' de la communauté juive de Tanger: réflexion autour de la transcription du texte, tenu en solitreo, de 1860 à 1875," unpublished manuscript, n.d. These archives have been summarized in two articles: J. Bengio and J.-L. Miège, "La Communauté juive de Tanger dans les années 1860, 'Les Actas'," *Maroc-Europe* 6 (1994): 151–65, and in the same journal, J. Bengio, "La Junta selecta: le comité de la communauté juive de Tanger," 167–214.

17. On the financial crisis in Morocco following the 1859–60 war, see Miège, *Le Maroc*, 2:349–93; G. Ayache, "Aspects de la crise financière au Maroc après l'expédition espagnole de 1860," *Revue Historique* 220 (1958): 3–41. For its effect on the the Jews of Northern Morocco, see Picciotto, *Jews of Morocco, passim*. The population figure of 4,500 comes from Picciotto, 36. Miège gives the total population of Jewish Tangier in 1866 as 3,500 (3:26) but does not cite his source. Picciotto's statistic most certainly came from the *Junta*, who may have inflated it to give numerical superiority to their town over their rival, Tetuan, also a candidate for European charity.

18. Actas I, #5, 16 Heshvan 5621 (1 November 1860); #12, 14 Tebet 5621 (12 December 1860).

19. Moroccan and European coins were used interchangeably in nineteenth-century Tangier. In the 1860s, thirty-five ounces (*wuqiya-s*, a Moroccan bronze coin) equaled one Spanish dollar (*duro*) or one gold napoleon; a ducado was equivalent to ten ounces and a napoleon was 3.3 ducados. See Bengio and Miège, "La Communauté juive," 191; on the complex historical issue of the Moroccan currency, see 'Umar Afa, *Mas'ala al-nuqud fi tarikh al-maghrib* (Agadir: Faculté des Lettres et Sciences Humaines, 1988), and the review by A. Sebti in *Annales: ESC* 43 (1988): 1399–1402.

20. Actas I, #13, 18 Tebet 5621 (12 December 1860); #14, 29 Tebet 5621 (7 January 1861). The *shaykh al-yahud* (in Hebrew, the *nagid*) acted as a liaison between the Jewish community and the

basha. See Zafrani, *Etudes*, 106–9. In Tangier the shaykh was gradually relieved of his authority as the *Junta* took over the conduct of communal affairs.
21. Actas I, #22, 16 Iyar 5621 (12 April 1861). It should be noted that this sum (the equivalent of 166 napoleons) was far less than the original demand.
22. Actas 1, #25, Tamuz 5621 (June 1861).
23. Gerber notes that the Jews of Fez occasionally resorted to the same expediency. See her *Fez*, 188.
24. Actas 1, #176, 6 Tebet 5627 (13 December 1866).
25. Actas 1, #76, 24 Ab 5623 (9 August 1863).
26. Actas 1, #144, 15 Kislev 5625 (14 December 1864); #145, 21 Kislev 5625 (20 December 1864).
27. Establishment of the school, generally attributed to the Alliance Israélite Universelle (AIU) was seen by the *Junta* as its own project, with the AIU and the British Board of Deputies merely offering assistance. The *Junta* archives provide a perspective on the school—as well as on many other matters—that differs from that of the AIU archives.
28. Actas 1, #157, 13 Heshvan 5626 (2 November 1865); #158, no date.
29. Actas 1, #166, 14 Tebet 5626 (31 December 1865).
30. Pariente's payment was in the form of a commercial loan, guaranteed by a mortgage on community property for 400 napoleons to be repaid over time with revenues accrued from the meat tax. Actas I #166, 14 Tebet 5626 (31 December 1865).
31. Actas 1, #166, 14 Tebet 5626 (31 December 1865); for the exclusion of foreigners from the charity rolls, see Actas 1, #189, 19 Ab 5627 (20 August 1867), and Actas 1, #222, 10 Iyar 5630 (11 May 1870).
32. Actas 1, #176, 6 Tebet 5627 (13 December 1866).
33. Actas 1, #180, 12 Ve-Adar 5627 (19 March 1867); Actas 1, #185, 5 Iyar 5627 (9 May 1867); Actas 1, #193, 24 Elul 5627 (23 September 1867).
34. Actas I, #204, 27 Tebet 5628 (21 January 1868); Actas I, #205, 9 Shevat 5628 (2 February 1868); Actas I, #206 18 Adar 5628 (11 March 1868).
35. This was Moses H. Picciotto's estimate. See his *Jews of Morocco*, 36.

36. This figure does not include the twenty persons, or 12.3 percent of the 163 actually tithed, who desisted from payment, although they were judged capable by the assessors. Most of those who did not pay had been assessed at the rate of one-half or one napoleon, although three were asked for a hefty three napoleons, putting them firmly in the upper middle class. The amount they withheld as a group represented only 6 percent of the total.
37. How much did the payment of the *jizya* actually strain community finances? Calculating the *jizya* at the rate of about 10,000 ounces each year, and comparing it to the communal budgets of 1868, 1869, and 1870 as reported in the Actas, which averaged around 70,000 ounces, it seems that the *jizya* represented one-seventh to one-eighth of total revenue, not counting the regular and special subscriptions (*nedabot*), which were not reported in the Actas but which must have been also considerable. Thus the tax was only a small portion of the total budget handled by the *Junta* each year.
38. Actas, 5 January 1871.
39. In his comprehensive *Juifs et musulmans au Maroc, 1859–1948* (Rabat: Mohammed V University, 1994), M. Kenbib makes the assertion that the Jews of Tangier evaded the tax (463).
40. Among the subscribers were Aaron Abensur (six napoleons), interpreter of the British legation; Haim Benchimol (three napoleons), interpreter of the French legation; Haim Bendelac (three napoleons), interpreter of the Portuguese consulate; Moses Eshriki (three napoleons), interpreter of the Swedish consulate; and Moses Pariente (six napoleons), interpreter of the consulate-general of the United States. See *Bulletin* of the AIU 89 (January 1865).
41. Jewish migration from northern Morocco to Latin America began in the 1860s and became a mass movement by the 1880s. Emigrant remittances helped to dramatically change the living standards of Tangier's Jews. For a study of this phenomenon and its effect on local society, see S. G. Miller, "Kippur on the Amazon: Jewish Migration from Northern Morocco in the Late Nineteenth Century," in H. A. Goldberg, ed., *Sephardi and Middle Eastern Jewries: History and Culture in the Modern Era* (Bloomington: University of Indiana Press, 1996), 190–212.
42. In 1893, the Jews of Essaouira were ordered to pay arrears for eighteen years of *jizya*, and they continued to pay the tax "until the twentieth century," according to D. Schroeter, *Merchants of*

Essaouira: Urban Society and Imperialism in Southwestern Morocco, 1844–1886 (Cambridge: Cambridge University Press, 1988), 290 n. 46. However, Moise Nahon wrote in 1909 that the collecting of the *jizya* was "much relaxed" in the majority of Moroccan towns. See his "Les Israélites au Maroc," *Revue des études ethnographiques et sociologiques* (1909): 266.

Part Three
CENTERS

· SEVEN ·

The Reinvention of Dar al-mulk: *The Moroccan Political System and Its Legitimation*

Abdellah Hammoudi

Why do I choose to center my analysis of power in Morocco around the *dar al-mulk*? Other concepts have been used to describe the organization of the Moroccan government and the institutions that, over centuries, have lent Morocco its distinct political character. *Makhzan*,[1] central power, and the state are three concepts that immediately come to mind, though the list could certainly be longer. The justification for the choice made here will become increasingly apparent as the concept of *dar al-mulk* is elaborated. For the moment, we should note that those analyses carried out in terms of *makhzan* and central power have tended overwhelmingly to favor questions of organization, hierarchy, and control and their main correlate, the mobilization of resources and the collection of taxes. Questions of legitimacy and the capability of Moroccans to reflect on their own system have either been reduced to insignificance because of the emphasis placed on describing the *makhzan* as an "organism" or as a structure or, alternatively, have been treated according to canonical formulas of the *imama* and a formalized local custom. Without minimizing the contributions of these approaches, we should turn our attention instead to the forms in which power and domination have become embedded and to the symbolic constructions in which they are active. In so doing, our analytical categories are not just a set of interrelated categories but also describe concrete forms (ritual, aesthetic, etc.) that induce moods, thoughts, and changes.

I likewise avoid, at least at the outset, making use of the concept of the state. Beside the fact that its invocation often leads to the same descriptive and analytical difficulties as *makhzan* and central power, the forms it takes in its European variation (first in the sixteenth century and later during the English and French revolutions) run the risk of seriously distorting our image of the Moroccan reality and blurring its specifics. This is not to say that the Moroccan system should not be subsumed under the concept of the state; rather, I intend to analyze the components and the functioning of the *dar al-mulk* as a concept of politics before determining what kind of state it is.

Clearly, *dar al-mulk* exists as a permanent entity, distinct from the groups through whose daily activity the relations of sociability, work, and religious life are reproduced. Like other forms of political regulation, its task is to influence these interactions without becoming enmeshed in the social frameworks in which they play themselves out. Moreover, it claims a communal (Islamic) reason, which is universally applied to rulers as well as ruled.

The nation-state, as it developed in Western Europe, makes claim to no particular rights but rather to reason itself. The integration and interaction it seeks to promote are not founded on an association whose primary objective is to limit individual appetites but rather on an association of rational individuals or individuals made rational by the action of the state. (I am not advocating the idea that the European nation-state is rational; I am simply summarizing, all too quickly, one of its claims.) For purposes of explanation, we could place the two images in opposition. *Dar al-mulk* presents itself as "the house of power," making a claim on a communal purpose whose guarantor is

God. It is not the state in the definition we have just put forth. Nor is it a "being there" kind of state claiming to stand for the rational criteria for directing human groups.

An elaboration of the concept of *dar al-mulk* allows us to better account for the relationships of power in Moroccan society, both past and present. The process of renovating *dar al-mulk* links these two moments, not by offering the illusion of an exceptional historical continuity but by showing that in the twentieth century this renewal appeared simultaneously with a kind of modern authoritarianism that it has adapted to its own needs. This renewal is based on particular elements in the political process, the most important being the gift, the favor, and the notion of proximity molded after kinship proximity. Sociologically, this reconstruction articulates itself in the patriarchal relationship of subordination. Symbolically, its foundations are in the paradigm of the master-disciple relationship, which is acutely present in the practices of learned and popular Sufism diffused throughout the Moroccan social body in the fifteenth century.[2] In this symbolic construction, terror and grace are so inseparable that one could be inferred from the other.

Sanctification of the person of the monarch and the modernization of infrastructure and of the systems of management and coercion were completed under colonization and came into full flower after independence. They consolidated the ascendancy of forms of power relationships that rested on the dissemination and reappropriation of the style of subordination characteristic of the master-disciple dialectics. This process was achieved in a novel situation in which the new state gained control over the religious domain, after it had imposed its will in the economic and the social spheres and had achieved a monopoly over all the instruments of violence. These factors allow us to trace the shape of this specific state and to isolate the characteristics that differentiate it from other authoritarian systems.

This chapter is divided into five sections. First I describe *dar al-mulk* as it appears on the eve of the French protectorate, a political society and a field of power relations structured by personal service. As such it exerts a visible social and moral impact, thanks to gift, grace, and terror combined. In the second section, I try to show how sainthood came to anchor this combination symbolically, something that constituted a historical break with the political system that preceded it. Specifically, I outline the main aspect of the master-disciple relationship in Sufi initiation—the primacy of the knower (here, the master) over all other principles in the generation of knowledge and in the definition of power relations. Following Foucault, I call this the diagram of knowledge and power,[3] a diagram that became hegemonic in Morocco after the fifteenth century. At the end of the nineteenth century, immediately before the French intervention, the master-disciple relationship, with its characteristic gender reversal as a condition of access to power, was generalized. It was transferred from Sufi circles to the main spheres of cognitive, social, and political life.

In the third section, I analyze the Muslim annual sacrifice and the masquerades that often follow it as they can be observed today, in order to test my central claim that gender reversal in important rites of passage both recognizes and circumvents the vital role of woman as the matrix of reproduction. Gender reversal in mystical initiation as well as in the current rituals is a specifically Moroccan interpretation of how reproduction occurs, constituting a violent confiscation by men of the reproductive powers of women.

In the fourth section, I examine *dar al-mulk* as a modern authoritarianism and as a reinvention of the precolonial *dar al-mulk*—first as a colonial, then as a postcolonial system. The diagram already identified, and the social and moral forms reelaborated in colonial practice and discourse, are shown to contribute to the genealogy of the postcolonial *dar al-mulk*. However, the line of argument insists on the constant struggle to define reality and stresses the changes that have produced both the reassertion of the formula and its precariousness. The conclusion restates the main claim and anticipates future forms of political interaction beyond authoritarian rule.

ON THE EVE OF THE COLONIAL UPHEAVAL: *DAR AL-MULK* AS A CONCEPT OF POLITICS

The presence of a monarch in any given space creates an "exemplary center,"[4] where the form and rhetoric of domination are intensified. *Dar al-mulk,* despite its appearance, must not be confused with a particular residence of the sultan. As a central category defining the distribution of resources and the classification of persons and things, *dar al-mulk* moves about with the palace and imposes itself within its variable forms, whether a fortress, an encampment, or a procession. It also appears in the disposition of human groups, of animals, and of equipment for travel and combat. This is not to say, however, that the cities themselves mean nothing; without their recognition, *dar al-mulk* could not exist as such.

The Power Center as a Society Structured by Personal Service

Although *dar al-mulk* should not be confused with a particular place any more than with the person of the prince, it is true that some types of institutions, such as the palace or the *mhalla,* correspond more closely to *dar al-mulk* than others. But if such institutions, as well as the presence of the prince, define its conditions, they do not necessarily prescribe its manner of functioning. We must go beyond the titles and the juridical and ideal attributes that endow *dar al-mulk* with its permanent, institutional character—*imama, khilafa,* or sometimes, *imara 'uzma*—for once the latter are proclaimed, titles, ranks, and responsibilities often evade the law, and the exercise of power tends to follow personalized styles and to fuse with local customs. For example, presents vary according to the situation and the venalities of officeholders, as do various non-Koranic taxes over and above the Koranic obligations.

Full power of command is accorded to the monarch once he is recognized. (Under Islamic law, there can be no *she* in this instance.) But even after his accession, achieved through fierce competition and violence, the candidate thus imposed must constantly renew the efforts that allowed him either to win over his competitors or to reduce them to impotence. In other words, *dar al-mulk* is distinguished by its decisiveness and the respect that it inspires (*'azima* and *hayba*). It follows that movement and war (*harka*) constitute two vital functions of this type of government.[5] There is no split between ideological, moral, and religious legitimacy, on the one hand, and armed force, power, and domination, on the other. The latter is symbolic of the former, which in turn defines the cultural competency that power can exercise. Such a monopoly of control in which grace and violence are indistinguishable is not exercised free of consultation. In fact, the prince seeks out the opinions and advice of the representatives of the population: the ulama, the *shurafa'*, the notables, and the pious. Although this kind of consultation has always remained within a vaguely institutional framework, these groups are approached on an ad hoc basis and usually at the initiative of the prince. In any case, the role played by these groups that mediate between the people and the center of power is derived from their position in society, without their capacity to represent being in any way called into question. While the exercise of authority is translated into concrete reality through *dar al-mulk*, the function of consultation has never been put into concrete form—in a *dar al-shura* (house of consultation), for example. In the imperial capitals, the encounter between the people and their ruler takes place in the courtyard of the palace, called the *mashwar*. The house of power therefore includes both the space for and the function of consultation.

In the encampment, *dar al-mulk* has a spatial-political geography that can be deciphered easily. The groupings that distinguish it are: at the center the royal household, then the army quarter with its tents arranged in a hierarchy reaching outward from the center according to degrees of professionalism and seniority, next the secretaryships and the lodgings of the domes-

The Reinvention of Dar al-mulk 135

tic servants, then the auxiliary tribes, and beyond them the multitudes that provide service to this city on the move (the *mhalla*). In the urban setting, the geography of *dar al-mulk* is well known, and I do not discuss it here. But whether it is in movement or at rest, the specialization of its functions is not clearly defined. The preference is to delegate by task and by circumstance, the clearest line of division being that between the secretaries (*kuttab*) and members of *dar al-mulk* serving in other capacities. Beyond its prerogatives and functions, what is important to recognize is that *dar al-mulk* appears to be an effort to represent society as a whole. If a group remains on the margins, it means either that it lacks political influence or that it is in a state of rebellion. It could also imply a mutual reduction to insignificance of the *dar al-mulk* and the marginal group.

Dar al-mulk is more than a group of people bound to its tasks. It is a society in which one can distinguish different guilds (associated with the upkeep of property and the organization of daily life) and a multitude of persons whose presence is indispensable for religious life, for work, for leisure, or simply for rounding out the "exemplary center." This explains the coexistence of people of religion, companions in play and pleasure, those endowed with *baraka*, and guests enjoying the hospitality or good will of the prince.

Participation in this society is justified by a connection with the prince that is seen as natural (or quasi-natural), coupled with a vague set of duties. This is the case with relatives, allies, and friends whose primary task is simply to be there. At any given moment they might be called on to deal with some matter, their choice being made according to their reputation and circumstances. Participation in this society called *dar al-mulk* is also justified by a precise function coupled with a vague natural relationship (natural in the sense of a relation perceived as natural and expressed as such). Such is the case, for example, with certain army commanders who were raised with that function in mind and attached to the sultan by quasi-filial ties. A natural relationship reinforced by a vague official one, and a precise functional tie linked with a vague natural one, together define the privilege of belonging to the house of power.[6]

In the first case, the tie of kinship is important. All who claim it serve the prince but often without a well-defined or permanent function. According to this logic, the monarch must expect to face certain risks related to the pairing of these two precepts. This is a potentially explosive pairing; a system based on kinship assumes that the monarchy is a common heritage, and rebellion is not quite considered a crime. In the second case, the prince must agree to delegate his powers to actors whose fidelity must be guaranteed by other means (honor, concessions of wealth, coercion, threat, etc.). Finally, the efficacy of both arrangements is proportional to the simultaneity of their applications. Whatever may be the relationship between the sultan and the persons admitted into his service or his court, their success and careers depend on royal patronage. Relatives take advantage of a domestic code of honor, while nonrelatives make claim to attachments and services rendered whose ethos and rhetoric is not much different from those established by kinship. Both groups set themselves apart from the rest of the population and regard this rupture as a privilege, a norm, and a necessity.

How is power realized and recognized? In order to bring together the means to control or consolidate the political capital already acquired, it is necessary to gain an introduction to the prince. One must arrange to be in close proximity to his person and to his closest associates. *Dar al-mulk* works to increase these ties by eliminating competing centers of power or, at the very least, by making them subordinate. Particular attention must be paid to centers of moral authority (*zawaya*).[7] In every case, in order to enter into proximity with *dar al-mulk*, influence and prestige are necessary, meaning that one should already have accrued authority of one's own—in short, a symbolic capital that awaits sanction and legitimation thanks to this crucial contact. This is because proximity, except perhaps for members of a closely allied family, does not confer power *ex nihilo*. To achieve power one must belong to the elite (*khassa*)—that is, to a recognized social category. But this recognition in itself is insufficient. Power is constructed through entry into a particular elite, which is itself the result of work that is essentially political. The *khassa* constructed in this narrow sense of the term is defined by access to the prince. In this respect, it remains inseparable from his personal service (*khidma*), which is the guiding principle of political relations and all other activity within the framework of *dar al-mulk*.

One could argue that proximity and personal service enter as agents in all political relations, regardless of the type of state under consideration: democratic, authoritarian, or totalitarian. However, *dar al-mulk* distinguishes itself from other systems by the fact that it elevates these agents to the level of an ethic by according them decisive influence in directing affairs, especially considering the rudimentary division of tasks and the relative lack of distinction among them in terms of competence. Nothing illustrates this relation between proximity and service better than the attitude toward what we call nowadays professional error. The guilty party must face punishment that issues forth directly from the prince's anger (*sukht*),[8] and it can be erased only through his pardon and satisfaction (*al-afwu, al-rida*).

Personal service is not compensated by salary. Its counterpart is the gift. In *dar al-mulk* the salary is of small importance. It is subordinate to the gift, which is not clearly differentiated from generosity. As for taxes, they are clearly distinct from the gift, a distinction marked by a precise terminology and a rigorous explication in the Sharia. However, theoretical rigor accommodates itself in practice to the widespread coexistence of salary and taxation, on the one hand, and the exchange of presents and favors, on the other. Someday it would be worthwhile to determine more precisely the respective shares of canonical and statutory taxes and of the presents freely circulating within the confines of *dar al-mulk*. In the absence of study, a good bet would be that the latter is more substantial. At any rate, the widespread circulation of gifts bears witness once again to the characteristic accommodation between legal practice and the customary exercise of power. All this takes place as if authority had to be expressed and sanctioned through the transgression of the law (Sharia). Better still, the *dar al-mulk* had to demonstrate its paramount authority by transgressing the very law it was charged to uphold. In violating the boundaries of the law, the *dar al-mulk* claimed a monopoly of defining and redefining its limits. This trespassing represents a central feature of the *dar al-mulk* that makes it different from patrimonialism. The Sharia, although reappropriated, maintains the utopia of the contractual nature of power (as another limit), pointing up the transgressions that take place through proximity, kinship, and coercive relations.

Gift, Grace, and Terror Combined

In any case, the gift as the visible exchange of gestures and objects constantly reaffirms the obligation of service and obedience, on the one hand, and the patronage and favor of the prince, on the other. Through specific signs, such as the difference between the objects and gestures exchanged (fine horses, rare cloth, silver, the kissing of hands on one side, and words of welcome or benediction on the another), the two parties demonstrate their consent to the terms of authority that confirm the inequality of their status. The process also allows for an increase in rank and subsequent modifications in status.

The circulation of gifts is marked by this stratification, which is always in flux, so much so that the inequality of status must be periodically reviewed and reasserted. Between *dar al-mulk* and those desiring its favors, this inequality is in principle absolute. But, in practice, each encounter has to affirm it in some of its forms because the attributes of the exemplary center are not completely fixed and, most important, the signs by which these attributes make themselves known are never the object of a total consensus. On the contrary, they provide a fertile ground for contestation. For example, the conduct of the commander of the faithful is the subject of heated debate, as is also the well-known obligation "to promote good and to forbid evil." The defense of the community against external danger is another subject of polemics and recurrent confrontation, as are controversies concerning the relative worth of genealogies (sharifian genealogies in particular), of personal merit in the determination of rank, and of claims to honors and positions. Because every candidate for supreme power has to bolster his hereditary status with an individual effort to personify the Sharia and the customary norms and ideals, questions raised in the debate over the definition of legitimacy have never been fully answered.

Each time a center appears, terror appears along with it. The center makes itself present through a physical threat reaching even to family and personal wealth. A house standing in ruins, its occupants now vanished, constitutes the well-known sign of this threat. In this domain as well, *dar al-mulk* has gained control over a specificity. At the outset, it attempts to justify the use of terror by invoking the law: according to the usual justification, the disobedient ones undergo punishment, death, or torture because they have placed themselves outside the law and threatened the *umma* by breaking with the communal consensus (*shaqqu 'asa al-jama'a*). Even while invoking the law, *dar al-mulk*'s uses of terror are often justified in terms of patriarchal custom, which is precisely the domain that the Sharia cannot strictly limit. Custom stresses the patriarch's right of life and death over the members of the group he has fathered. No doubt it is to these customary practices that certain memorable cases of torture can be readily ascribed, as well as the ritualized procedures of decapitation. As they appear frequently in the chronicles, they posit *dar al-mulk* as the house that administers death, and in this sense, the radical difference between it and any other house becomes clear. In such a system of governance, unlike any other, terror meets the sacred in the figure of the prince as saint and executor. At this level there is no distinction between sainthood and violence, in contrast to what advocates of the theory of segmentation would claim.

We must go beyond the Khaldunian model[9] if we are to grasp the composition and functioning of *dar al-mulk* in the post-

Marinid period. With the Saʻdi and ʻAlawi dynasties, a third basis of power is at work. In addition to *ʻasabiya* and the defense of Islam, there is a sacralization, either by genealogy or by direct contact with the source of charisma. This goes beyond both sociological reason and the well-being of an *umma* that limits individual appetite. It is a concept that has progressively taken root for reasons that historiography has not yet been able to explain. Whatever interpretation we may give to this new phenomenon, the perception of terror as a sign of transcendence underscores a very distinct difference between terror sanctioned by the Sharia, which is the prerogative of the caliph, and the terror resulting from alliances cemented by *ʻasabiya* and put forward to defend personal interests or the interests of a community of allies.

Hereafter, whoever achieves power raises himself above others since prevalence is a sign of charisma. Moreover, he will be in a position to appear both in battle and in ritual as the manifestation of the mystical body of the Prophet.[10] Such an ascendance is amply illustrated in the major rituals, such as the Feast of the Mouloud, which is always celebrated with unsurpassed splendor. Establishing order and representing the charismatic source with regularity (that is, presenting it once again) converts violence into benediction. And therein lies the innovative basis of *dar al-mulk*, which seems to go beyond *ʻasabiya* and the *bayʻa* contract. Sainthood underlies the violence of the specific state that is *dar al-mulk*.

SAINTHOOD AND THE MASTER-DISCIPLE RELATIONSHIP AS SYMBOLIC ANCHOR

According to its profile on the eve of colonial conquest, *dar al-mulk* was a specific historical concentration that slowly came into being after the Almohad decline and the restructuring of the state under the Marinids. The universalizing synthesis of the *khilafa* was succeeded by narrow and particularizing structures. Universalism was not abandoned but was henceforward translated into local figures of charisma and authority. It was made manifest in the synthesis between *'ilm* (exoteric sciences) and gnosis, a synthesis that led the ulama to mystical awareness and the Sufis toward the acquisition of *'ilm*. To make sense of this new situation, the contrast between *'ilm* and gnosis (doctor and saint), as Gellner and others put it, is not relevant. On the contrary, the effort to create new forms reconciling the two is what characterizes the era. This is also the case with another supposed opposition, that of saint and chief, that some believe to be exclusive. In fact, *dar al-mulk* is the embodiment of the fusion of these two functions.

At the local level, the two functions remain distinct. However, as soon as the authority of the chief tries to go beyond the restricted circle of the family, it has to find justification through the moral ascendancy of the saint. It is as though the image of the father, in order to impose itself outside restricted social circles, has to be magnified and anchored in the powerful figure of the servant of God. This figure is not only one of the transmitters of doctrine and law; he is also the concrete manifestation of the mystical body of the Prophet, which confers on law and doctrine a fleshly existence that is both active and present.

At this stage, it is possible to see how some of the major forms of the power relationship, as they are practiced in the work of *dar al-mulk*, are identical with those that animate the master-disciple relationship. In fact, a process of initiation produces the new master. Only through an extended stay in the company of a shaykh and through submission to his discipline can a disciple hope for success. Success is concretized by gaining access to mastery—that is, by having the power to found a new community and initiate other candidates. Certainly, this path toward God has always been the subject of bitter disputation, and the need to follow an initiating master has never been generally conceded. Likewise, many illuminated ones (*majadhib, bahalil*) found their way without initiation or master. For others, the process was often not a protracted one. In spite of exceptions, the fact remains that the masters of initiation preserved their hegemony.[11] Whatever controversies may have arisen around the issue of sainthood and the various means of accession to it, authority and its related powers always possessed some form of sanctification.

The initiation process implies a transgression of the norms on which the foundations of the whole community rest. As we read in the biographies of saints, initiation requires the temporary inversion of the disciple, who becomes female before he can recover the marks of his manliness. Why are power and authority rooted in the transgression of the norm and in the image of femininity, usually the figure of submission par excellence? How is it that access to power requires passing through this stage of nonpower, which is also a counterpower so totally different in nature from the former, as well as its radical opposite? As I try to show, the stable source of the new sociopolitical equilibrium established in the fifteenth century lies in the identification between saint and sultan. The effort, and the difficult path, by which an exemplary center is created and sustained runs parallel to, and is identified with, the path toward sainthood and the foundation of a brotherhood (*zawiya*) that purports to replicate the exemplary community founded by the Prophet Muhammad. If such is the case, the sultan, as a synthetic figure of charismatic force, founds *dar al-mulk* as a replica of the Prophet's exemplary center. His own center then becomes the paramount one insofar as he succeeds in subduing all rivals. Being at the heart of that center, the sultan manifests the mystical body of the Prophet through his reenactment of the foundation of the Muslim community.

If we accept the notion that the driving metaphor of power is the saint, then a consideration of the path to sainthood will give us insight into the path to power. Hence ordeal and initiation will appear as the central cultural agents by which all the exemplary centers are constructed.

The Call to the Way: The Apprentice Saint and the Ordinary Man

I should emphasize from the outset the difficulty of this enterprise. The lives of the saints are numerous, and within the limited scope of this study I mention only a few: M'hammad b. Nasir (1603–1717); his disciple al-Yusi (1631–91); Ibn 'Ajiba (1747–1809); and, closer to our time, al-Hajj 'Ali al-Darqawi.[12] The choice is complicated by the abundance of the material. On the other hand, these are not biographies of ordinary men. The idea would have scandalized specialists of the genre. We find ourselves reduced to a reconstruction beginning in the present, running the risk of abusing the past by projecting onto it contemporary categories of analysis. Happily, the hagiographic texts themselves, along with historiography and belles-lettres, insist on certain norms and usage when defining a good man's life: *rujula* (male being, manliness), *himma 'azima* (noble ambition, resoluteness), *haya* (modesty), *khudu* and *inqiyad* (submission and submissiveness), and *hayba* (inspiring fear in others), to name just a few.

In Morocco and the Maghrib, the main stages of life are marked by rituals and special codes defining social interaction. The newborn and the adolescent in particular have to be surrounded by precautionary measures in proportion to the dangers that threaten the integrity of body and spirit. During adolescence, an occult violence threatens the virility of young males and the sexuality and honor of young females. Girls must show themselves to be modest, while boys are subject to a twofold code of behavior: reserved in the presence of elders, particularly the father, and virile and ambitious in the company of their peers. At this coming of age (*sawma, rushd*), boys are engaged in the practice of daily life and often attend Koranic school. They are preparing for adulthood, and their energy must constantly be displayed in defense of honor and space (of the family, of the lineage, or of the Muslim community). However, at this point paths of development begin to diverge. Some will show greater assiduity in learning the Koran, while the majority will devote their energies to earning a living. Thereafter, the first group will distinguish itself more and more from the other, and soon the quest for knowledge and the sacred text will absorb them entirely. Before long, this quest will take them to places and people distant from the group and the space in which they belong.

This is the primary separation between those who will carry the book "in their stomachs"—as it is often described in literary parlance—and those who will remain in the routine of daily life. The search for knowledge induces a separation from the ordinary that intensifies the pursuit of charisma. We should note, however, that movement in pursuit of *'ilm* introduces the seeker into the ranks of a minority (even without an overt refusal of the world), and an initiation into mysticism uproots countrymen, artisans, and even tradesmen from their normal work. M'Hammad b. Nasir, for example, left his village against his father's will and quit the entourage of the governor of the Draa Valley in order to find *'ilm* and initiation of the *zawiya* of Tamgrout. His disciple al-Yusi also fled, traveling southward from the Middle Atlas to seek the company of his master in the Draa Valley. Finally, Ibn 'Ajiba and 'Ali al-Darqawi threw their families into disarray when they decided to reject the career of *'alim* in favor of an initiation that forced them to "violate custom." Many *majadhib* and other saints were seized by their callings while in the field or the workplace, and some were already at an advanced age when the call came. Whether it comes in adolescence or at another time, the call constitutes a new beginning that sweeps away all past memory.

When the call imposes itself on the will, it leads a person toward a master. It orders the youth to abandon all hope of founding a family (unlike others of his age) and the married man to abandon his marriage. He who seeks initiation separates himself from the mass and becomes a knight errant. Four stages are distinguishable in this new life, each marked by its own rules and dangers: pilgrimage and wandering, long maturation under the watchful and enigmatic authority of a guide, the revelation of *baraka* in an atmosphere of drama and turmoil, and finally, induction into the spiritual order and to the power of protecting others, especially the person's own disciples. M'hammad b. Nasir starts out by taking the road leading to Dadès, where he profits from the virtues of a famous master. Then he settles down in Tamgrout. He will not return to visit his family or his native village for fifteen years, not until 1645. Al-Yusi wanders around Morocco in all directions, first to Fez and then to Marrakesh, before he crosses the Atlas mountains to receive initiation from M'hammad b. Nasir, who has become the undisputed guide of a whole generation of disciples after taking charge of the *zawiya* of Tamgrout in 1646. Ibn 'Ajiba leaves his birthplace in the Anjera, between Tangier and Tetuan, attends the *madrasa* of Tetuan for a short time, and receives the title of *'alim,* which he promptly rejects in order to put himself into the hands of the shaykh of the Darqawa. Finally, Hajj 'Ali leaves his village in the Sous and does the same.[13] To everyone's surprise, he abandons the "exoteric sciences" in which he excels, causing his family great pain, and runs away to his master, al-Madari. After that, he goes to Fez and wanders throughout the north, where he obtains the *wird* from the Darqawa and has a mysterious and portentous encounter. To wander is an obligatory stage and standard practice; it is also a topos dear to hagiographic literature. Al-Yusi, Ibn 'Ajiba, and 'Ali al-Darqawi spend a good part of their lives on the road and have to wait many years for the authorization of their masters—that is, for their consecration as shaykhs with an acknowledged *baraka* who are authorized to guide *murid*s. It is not necessary to expand on these examples, for most initiations follow this same well-worn path.

The refusal of power goes hand in hand with the refusal to become rooted in any space other than that in which *baraka* is located—that is, where it has shown its impact. To wander, as we have seen, is to forego the space of family, lineage, tribe, urban quarter, and ultimately, civic space. These are the territories of socialization, of political authority, and of identification with the norm. The initiate rejects this territoriality, whose coercive functions are known to all, in order to attach himself to the only true anchor between the earth and heavens: to the master who is the vessel of active and contagious *baraka* or to the sign of an ancient irruption of it, which is the sanctuary.

Let us consider this aversion to ordinary spaces. It is a decision heavy with consequences, for territories thus transcended also mean relationships that have been foregone. The *hurm* of the family and the lineage are inviolate and off limits. In order to maintain its exclusivity it must be defended by men in arms. These are places of purity and defilement, and any threat to them has to be repulsed or ignored while the *hurm* itself has to be kept in a state of inviolability. Its defense justifies the flow of blood. Its exclusivity constitutes a conceptual link between group and territory, thus defining the conditions for the daily reproduction of social relations. The youth must either invest in that reproduction or suspend his investment (albeit temporarily) and pursue the path of initiation in order to begin again the moral reproduction of the group.

The negation of space is also a negation of time, for the stages marking the ordinary life span do not make any sense to those intoxicated by God. We understand that for them everything is inverted. Instead of public demonstrations of energy and manliness, the *murid* joins a society that submits to rules of modesty, humility, and isolation that impose extreme constraints on all the desires: for food, comfort, love, and the power of speech. Such is the censorship that governs the initiate, in a space beyond authority where the shaykh is the only master on board.

The Violation of Custom and the Obligatory Passage through Womanhood

The human drama that begins with the quest for a spiritual guide can be measured by the disruption within the family. The father vainly attempts to keep his son at home, while the mother's suffering is echoed in the hagiography. We have already mentioned the thwarted will of M'hammad b. Nasir's father. We know nothing about this period in al-Yusi's life, but we do know that the loss of Ibn 'Ajiba was intolerable for his family and that al-Hajj 'Ali's parents put their son in irons in an attempt to overcome his enthusiasm for his shaykh. Their renouncement, which for those two *murids* begins with obeying the rule known as breaking with tradition (*kharq al-'ada*), as it was codified by the Darqawa, fills their relatives with shame. Here are two successful young men, their comfortable future assured, who suddenly don patched garments (*muraqqa'a*), go begging in the streets, and humiliate themselves by accepting the most menial tasks. The rupture with the ordinary, according to the order of the master, requires that one should break the cutting edge of his psyche (*taksir hidda al-nafs*). The shaykh steps in for the father and, in reality, replaces him in matters concerning the *murid*'s education (*tarbiya*). The turn the *murid*'s life takes seems extraordinary, striking the ordinary man as a loss. When we look closely at the relationship with the shaykh, we see that this choice requires an inversion of norms and ordinary behavior.

What does the *murid* do during this long association (*suhba*) with the shaykh? He has to place himself at the shaykh's beck and call and at his service (*khidma*); he tries to pick up his secret (*al-sirr*) through proximity. His responsibilities might include work in the fields, the *zawiya,* or the household, producing goods and filling domestic tasks. For the Darqawa, they also include the four famous rules (*shurut*) of silence, hunger, *dhikr,* and isolation. The absolute submission that this work requires means that the disciple must observe restraint and modesty in the presence of the master. When the master eats, he takes up a position somewhere nearby, ready to respond to his orders. A sense of extreme modesty and respect (*haya*) show themselves by his blushing when the shaykh looks at him. Here we touch on characteristics usually associated with female behavior.

This inversion is even more apparent in certain activities: the disciple fetches wood for the master, heats water for his ablutions, prepares his meals, makes his bed, and even washes his undergarments. It seems that at a certain stage of initiation, the feminization of the disciple and a strong emotional bonding (translated by the expressions *musahaba* and *istimata fi al-khidma,* companionship and self-abnegation) are as indispensable to the transmission of *baraka* as are study, prayer, and asceticism.

One might protest that some of these attitudes are not specific either to *murids* or to women. Servants, slaves, and all "people of a lowly condition" are required to show submission to their masters. To this lack of specificity something else should be added: during the mystical initiation and the passage of the *murid* from man into woman, the *murid* retains some male characteristics such as dress, a manner of doing things, segregation from women, and the respect demanded from women by the men. In spite of this, there is a feminization of the *murid* in regard to other activities and attributes. With few exceptions, men do not normally cook, wash, heat water, or gather wood. To ask a man to perform these chores would be taken as a provocation and an insult. Furthermore, we should note that the tradition recounts that celebrated initiates have, on occasion, assumed the dress and appearance of women. Finally, we should realize that the affective relationship between master and disciple can also be revealed through a love that is both symbolic and occasionally physical.

Ritualized expressions and procedures in the elaboration of a new personality, as they are presented in the hagiographic literature, shape a new field of synecdoches that overturn the ordinary (reduced to a state of mere appearances). This new field favors inversion and transgression as much as it is conditioned by it. It creates an opening through which the invention of meaning passes freely. Nothing is more instructive in this regard than the final acts of transmission and the manifestation of *baraka*.

At a certain moment, something has to pass from the master to the disciple. Just before dying, the master of M'hammad b. Nasir offers his wife to his *murid* and orders him to marry her; later he comes to him in a dream and gives him explicit instructions about leading the prayer. M'hammad b. Nasir himself gave his pants to an incontinent student, and between him and al-Yusi there was a sharing of food and even more. A tradition recounts how one day the disciple al-Yusi went to wash the shirt of his shaykh. The shaykh was ill at the time and his body had suppurated onto his clothing. Al-Yusi soaked the shirt in water, wrung it out, and drank. His eyes blazing, he went into the presence of the shaykh, who anointed him with this famous blessing: "May God make you the source from which East and West shall drink!" Like al-Yusi, Ibn 'Ajiba and 'Ali al-Darqawi are the recipients of meaningful words. In the liminality of the moment and in the midst of this rite of passage, it should be obvious, we ought not to be surprised to find unexpected forms and gestures alongside the traditional ones. Jacques Berque points to several astonishing events that marked the conclusion of some initiations: a horselike neighing of the master, a sudden dash, a few enigmatic words.[14] Transmission by mouth, saliva, and the tongue is also practiced. Martin Lings writes:

> Strictly speaking, the rite of transmission of the *baraka* from one vessel to another cannot be confined to any particular set of forms. Its form may depend, in exceptional cases, on the inspiration of the moment. For example, in addition to the Shadili initiation which the Shaykh al-Darqawi received from his master Shaykh 'Ali al-Jamal, he also received one from an aged saint at the point of death who made him spiritual heir by the ritually unprecedented yet highly significant act of placing his tongue in the Shaykh al-Darqawi's mouth and telling him to suck.[15]

Westermarck, in the course of his research in northern Morocco at the beginning of this century, tells of still other mannerisms, such as spitting in the mouth of the one seeking *baraka* or transmitting it through sexual contact.[16]

At the close of al-Yusi's initiation, drinking was the principal metaphor. The consumption of something that was part of the master inhabits the hagiographic writings. In its most acute forms, it involves the absorption of the master's body (saliva, pus, and even vomit), as we witness in the culmination of the spiritual itineraries of two noted disciples of a celebrated saint of Tadla.[17] The process itself resembles an act of impregnation, a familiar theme in Sufi circles.

Contradiction and Accommodation: The Metaphor of Procreation

The young man (or the head of the family lately come to his vocation) who, in search of *baraka,* abandons his family and his group adopts a radical stance of refusal. The patriarchal virtues, coterminous with social cohesion and authority, are for the time being placed between parentheses. Sexual ambiguity, a partial inversion, and the love for the master, in certain cases to the point of ingesting his bodily fluids, situate the *murid* in stark contrast to the ordinary man.

The feminization is not total: the *murid* is both man and woman. He is between the two, in the undefined place that is opened by the rite of passage. The master, however severe he might be, exercises a paternal authority over this son/daughter/woman, all the while lavishing on him the attention of a mother. What is surprising here is not only the presence of these transformations but also the fact that society reveres them. How is it that society accommodates them and even places them at the very center of its values?

The saint intercedes with God in favor of men and women. Everyone looks to him or to his memory for guidance in everyday life and, at the level of authority and power, for some principle of legitimacy. The masses stand behind the one who has the power to contest, admonish, and even more, by his withdrawal from the world, to call into question the powers that be. All the personalities evoked here have been cast in this role at one time or another. These roles were still active at the beginning of this century, their energy sustaining a living *baraka* transmitted through modalities both codified and unpredictable.

The itinerary of sainthood opens up paths of subversion. Certain great figures deploy this subversion through a ritualized procedure. At the same time, even while circumscribed in time and space, sainthood has lost none of its incandescence. Ever present as a potential for upheaval, for *baraka* incites a permanent rejection of values corrupted by history. The disciples of Sidi Haddi, little studied even to this day, still manifest this option and echo ancient themes through their refusal to live in a fixed place and by their extreme mendicancy and marginality.

This two-sided character of living *baraka*, open to institutionalization but at the same time subversive, explains its paradoxical ability to animate divergent currents. Since it is at the origin of all categories, it threatens their specific sociohistorical incarnations. In reality, sainthood questions neither the patriarchal system, the father-son relationship, the relation between man and woman, nor the relation between rulers and ruled. But without changing anything in the relation of subordination, it claims to be at its foundation, therefore making such relations subject to the renewed claims of religiously and ethically superior elaboration made by any exemplary center regarding the organization of its own moral basis. As a result, it opens the way to both criticism and further elaboration. It follows that *baraka* can strike down any impious act not justified by revelation. Hence the danger of sainthood to the structures of everyday life does not reside in its ability to overthrow the normalcy that guarantees their permanence but rather in the voice of revelation that can, at any moment, point out an injustice or an impiety to be annihilated. This potential for revolt corresponds to the inexhaustible nature of great ideals, such as the ideal of man and woman, of father and son, and, finally, of the king, which exists only in an embodiment continually subjected to the fires of criticism. From this come the endless uprisings, especially in times of crisis, against leaders who stand for aborted ideals.

At every stage dissidence is radical, but in destroying the accursed incarnations of the categories of man, ancestor, father, sultan, and so on, it imposes them even more as specific categories sanctified in the name of venerable figures known to signify the continuity of the group. The legitimation of these categories proceeds from an initial indeterminacy that has every appearance of an absolute origin—so absolute, in fact, that creation of the community cannot do without it, either at the local or global levels. In these conditions, it is not in the least surprising that father, saint, and sultan demand identical attitudes of loyalty and submission, all of which require a feminization that denies the signs of manhood usually seen at work at different levels of subordination. These are the same notions of shame, restraint, and modesty that regulate the behavior of the disciple on the path to initiation, the son preparing to assume the paternal legacy, the apprentice seeking the approval of his master, and the candidate for investiture to political and bureaucratic power: all proceed from the critical acceptance of service (*khidma*).

Let us sum up, then. Sainthood, at its critical stage of development, deploys a constellation of practices that seem to infuse society as a whole. This hegemony, deeply anchored in the moral life of society, shows itself in the symbolic power of the saint that always surpasses the power of the *'alim* and the sultan. It does this to such an extent that it is widely understood that the existence of a political center and the guarantee of *'ilm* are not sufficient to breathe life into the community. In order to do that, every creator of cohesion, the sultan included, has to associate himself with *baraka* as a life source. Judging from its creative breakthroughs, marked by the founding of settlements, markets, and agricultural developments around the site of a new brotherhood, *baraka* cannot be reduced to a pious deception whose *raison d'être* derives from a simple structural function. A reading of the accounts produced by society about itself, often neglected by the anthropologists of the Maghrib,[18] reveals the lack of definition at the source of both function and structure. This indeterminacy is embodied in the shaykh-initiator, who requires his disciple to submit to the iron-clad will of the father, even while he comforts him and enfolds him in a warmth that is quasi-maternal. In so doing, he replaces both father and mother; by synthesizing their respective positions, he assumes the role of procreating the disciple as a future master. The symbolic anchor of this power, realized in the indeterminacy and inversion characteristic of the making of a saint, is so crucial that we can see it come into play not only in the hagiographic writing but also in the most important rites of passage. I limit myself here to a discussion of those that mark the end of the Muslim (lunar) year.

THE RITE OF PASSAGE AS TEST[19]

The Muslim Feast of the Sacrifice that ends the old lunar year and inaugurates the new one is celebrated everywhere in Morocco. To satisfy the need of a universal practice, every family has to have a victim: a sacrificial animal or the animal of the feast (*bhim't l'id*). The Word *'id* (feast) carries in its root the idea of renewal and repetition. In places where I observed this feast celebrated, the choice would fall on a goat or a sheep from the herd of the sacrificer. This is the practice in the rural setting. In the city, the victim is usually purchased. Often it is kept in the house during the weeks prior to the feast and is treated with special care, almost as if it were a person.

Power and Gender: Sacrifice as Founding Drama, Inversion as Circumvention of the Woman

On the tenth day of the month of Dhu al-Hijja, sacrifice takes place. On this day, as the sacrifier and sacrificer knows,[20] every Muslim is taking part in the same ritual, including pilgrims in Mecca. On radio and television, loudspeakers blare forth the prayer preceding the sacrifice and the ceremony during which the Moroccan sovereign slaughters the first victim, which is a privilege accorded only to him as the "commander of the faithful and protector of the religion and the *umma*."

In 1984, I found myself in the High Atlas during the holiday. My host, the head of the household, woke up early. He performed the first prayer of the morning, and after a quick breakfast he readied himself for the prayer held *extra muros* (*salat al-'id*). He joined the men already assembled at the edge of the cemetery. A married son living with him inspected the two rams to be sacrificed. In the name of the two adult males, father and son, the family was offering two victims, as was proper. The son and the mother cleaned the animals' bedding and spent some time remarking on their beauty. The night before, the women had decorated the victims' foreheads with henna.

At the *msalla*, the men, clothed in white, carried out the canonical prostrations and listened to the sermon. After the prayer, they kissed each other's hands and wished each other good health and prosperity before heading homeward. My host tells me that "on this blessed occasion, the *faqih* reminds us what is ahead and that we are walking in the steps of Buna Ibrahim [our father Abraham]." On their return to the village, the men recognized as heads of household gathered in front of the Koranic school and breakfasted together. Each family sent a dish of bread, pancakes, or rice cooked in milk accompanied by butter, honey, and olive oil. After the meal, there was a discussion with the schoolmaster about accounts, including the budget for his salary and the annual expenses for communal institutions. Then everyone went home.

The sacrifice of the two victims was the climax of the feast, called *tfaska* in Berber, which was the language of my hosts. All the members of the family gathered around the bodies of the victims, even women whom I now saw for the first time. Behind the "mother" (the wife of the head of household), they readied themselves for the tasks assigned to each. The married son turned the victims to the east and cut their throats with a sharp blade. Just before the fatal blow was struck, the mother forced the animals to swallow a mixture of salt, barley, and henna, to the great displeasure of her younger son, a student of the *lycée* in Marrakesh. One of the women then collected a bit of the blood, still warm, in a ladle. The student protested vigorously: "It's paganism, paganism. . . . Isn't this paganism!" but in vain. His remarks seemed to be primarily directed at me. His mother whispered something I did not hear, and his father did nothing to interfere. "At least I did not allow them put kohl [on the animals' eyes]," the student told me. The rest of the ceremony unfolded without incident. The gall bladder was removed by the mother and the feces were collected by the other women and thrown into the nearby stable.

To simplify to the extreme, one can say that the sacrifice sets the boundaries of the family and reaffirms the father's authority as it is instituted by the community of men, which places the social order under the law of the father—that is, the law that forbids woman from being the sacrifier or sacrificer. Those who take the place of God on earth by meting out death are the father (who acts on behalf of the family) and the king (who acts on behalf of the *umma*). In the Abrahamic saga, the mother does not disappear completely; the patriarch separates himself from her and from all human habitation, using the pretext of gathering wood, in order to carry out the divine order. The order is imposed on a submissive son who, by renouncing his life, renounces his function as a man, which, in theory, is the continuation of the agnatic line—that is, the recreation of civilization in the sense imposed and defended by men, a patriarchal system. The concern to avoid the mother announces the gap between the actual motive and the motive invoked at the very heart of the primal scene, which all subsequent sacrifices refer to as a theme to be repeated and replayed as if it were a living drama.

The miraculous apparition of the ram as victim replaces and rescues the son, who will soon assume the paternal function with the inevitable disappearance of the father (Abraham is old and suffering). The presence of the woman works the saga from within, since she gives the patriarch the pretext of performing the domestic chores that are usually the province of women. Because it is impossible to get rid of the woman, one must find a way to go around her: in a word, the abdication by the son of all that defines manhood. By accepting to be killed, he abandons his right to be genealogical procreator—that is, his place as "father" sanctioning the symbolic transfer. Instead, he legitimates his own "father" when he obeys his father's order. Father and son perform this symbolic circumvention that allows reproduction to take place exclusively among men and through them, which is the goal of the fundamental law of the group. However, this circumvention does not take place without problems. Breaks and compromises with history are introduced in the space that separates the given pretext from the received order. In the practice of the sacrifice, they arise from the tension between the woman's active presence and the masculine power that attempts to circumscribe it.

In ritual as it is practiced with all its particularities in Morocco, the actions of the woman and the affirmation of the son's future powers as opposed to those of the father are played out with a particular intensity. In fact, a reverse perspective appears in the second part of the feast, which is habitually and incorrectly (by anthropologists and Islamic purists alike) separated from the first. The feast of the sacrifice and the other ceremonies marking the end of the old year and the beginning of the new one also have a burlesque and blasphemous component in addition to the solemn and ceremonial one. This is exemplified by the various masquerades and games that took place in the village where I observed the sacrifice, of which I mention only one.

Circumventing Women: Power as the Capability of Defining Limits through Transgression

This masquerade lasts between three and eight days, depending on the region and the circumstances. Among Berber-speaking people it is called Bilmaun, and among Arabophones, Bujlud (that is, "the man in skins"). It is an old ceremony that was described by ethnographers of the nineteenth and early twentieth centuries and probably is the same as those condemned in the writings of the *fuqaha'*. In the case I observed, the village was given over to the young people. The old folks left the place, and the only ones allowed to stay at home were the women and the young girls. Toward late morning, a two-legged being emerged from the room next to the prayer hall reserved for ablutions and the washing of the dead. It was clad in skins and wore the head of a goat. It was followed by four other figures called the Jews (*yudayan*), one of whom answered to the title of rabbi. He was preceded by a black person called a slave (*ismagh*). All the young people, both boys and girls, followed this procession with music and dancing. Anyone who left the procession became the object of blows from the slave and the Jews until they consented to return to the group. The party proceeded in this manner through all the houses, making as if they would turn them upside down. The Jews chased the women in a way that was both playful and obscene, and before they left, they demanded and received gifts, mainly consisting of flour and eggs. The slave kept running after the children and the young people who followed the man in skins, as they jostled, insulted, and rained blows on him. Meanwhile, obscenities flowed from the Jews' lips.

In the center of the village, a stage was improvised where scenes of plowing, harvesting, and marriage took place. The man in skins kept on changing his identity. First he was a blacksmith's bellow that blew air through his anus onto a fire where the plowshare was being repaired for the coming season; next he was a cow pulling on a yoke while being ill-treated, insulted, and impaled through the anus; then he was the wife of the rabbi (who was also the landowner) preparing couscous for the fieldworkers of the master. The slave, the Jews, and the rabbi joined her in turns, with each character invariably leaving the stage under the blows of the others.

The man in skins had male organs on his behind, and only one breast in the middle of his chest. He was, as they say, topsy-turvy (*maqlub*). Every now and then he emitted a scream that could not be categorized as either human or that of any known zoological species. It was the "cry of Bilmaun." He would also strike out with his paws, touching sick children, an act that I was told was charged with benediction and virtuous qualities. Neither the slave nor the man in skins spoke. The procession always followed the same order: first the slave, then Bilmaun, and finally the Jews bringing up the rear. These last were the only ones who talked, pouring invectives and obscenities on everyone and even uninhibitedly miming lovemaking between men.

The masquerade is the reverse of the sacrifice. But this reversal, which is relatively weak in respect to the male-female relationship, becomes radical with regard to the father-son relationship. Women and young girls are in fact at the center of the feast and do not allow themselves to be taken for granted. They negotiate the gifts, they fight, and they even advance the play, taking part in it with an obvious relish that clearly violates traditional bounds of modesty. Meanwhile, it is the class of young unmarried men who chase away the heads of households and take over the village. Those who make the sacrifice and lay the foundations of the patriarchal social order are set apart and reduced to performing feminine tasks (herding the cows, cutting the grass to feed them). A fundamental tension is thus played out, delineated in the youthful conquest of power that is paralleled by the father's obliteration.

This conquest has an effect on the home and the women. From their initial position as outsiders and inferiors, the Jews are transformed into masters capable of breaking with tradition, hoarding all the wealth (as gifts), and achieving a total monopoly on sexuality, including that acted out between men, which leaves the women out. This is the second tension that is publicly displayed. On the one hand, one has to struggle against the father who monopolizes sexuality and procreation with the women. On the other hand, one makes every effort to ensure that the children being produced belong without question to the men (patrilineal filiation). The avoidance of the woman, like the elimination of the father, is performed under the guidance and authority of an ambiguous being who, through a series of mutations, imposes himself as a vital link in the configuration of the activities that make up a normal existence. By inverting the hero of the sacrifice according to the parodic mode, the hero of the masquerade lays the basis for everyday life, with its incongruities, contradictions, ambiguities, and necessary transgressions. It is not purely by chance that at the end of each scene, the four Jews shout in unison: "May the year be a favorable one!" (*açuggas bikhir!*)

This ambiguous being breaks the law by instigating insubordination and disorder. He inverts the hero of the sacrifice, who himself was ordered to transgress the law (Thou shalt not kill!) for the sake of forcing submission. All of this occurs as if the crossing of these two limits constitutes a supreme power that consists in defining and giving shape to individual and collective identities. These powers are embodied by Bilmaun, with his much sought-after benediction, his inversions, the absurdity of his ritual, and finally, the bullying behavior of his cortège.

Therefore, in sacrifice and the masquerade, as well as in the initiation to sainthood, the same ambivalent schema seems to be at work, an outcome of the turning of submission/revolt/ambivalence into mastery and into the conquest of the position of father and of saint. Therein lies the paradigm—or to use Foucault's word, the diagram—for access to authority, which informs all relationships of precedence and especially the relationship to the leader. In both cases, the symbolic mooring of the patriarchal powers is realized by a saintliness that transgresses the limit. This diagram functions at the heart of the *dar al-mulk,* as it was renewed in the colonial and postcolonial dynamics.

DAR AL-MULK REINVENTED: REELABORATING AND DISSEMINATING THE MASTER-DISCIPLE RELATIONSHIP BY MEANS OF A NEW AUTHORITARIANISM

Rather than simply assuming either a transhistorical legitimacy or an arbitrative function as the essence of the monarchic system, I propose instead to sketch out the evolution of *dar al-mulk* into an authoritarian modern state. First, let us define this authoritarian structure before proceeding to an analysis of the processes of its colonial and postcolonial institutionalization.

The Authoritarian Structure: The Chief and the Closed Circles of Disciples

The definition of this structure can be made by highlighting relationships among the principal elements of the regime, which may be summarized as follows:

- Restriction of the power of decision to a small group of men, of whom only one truly emerges onto the public scene;
- Absence of social control over the apparatus of state and, instead, a society that is controlled by a highly ramified and repressive bureaucratic apparatus;

- A need to conform to what the state defines as popular tradition, which need goes hand in hand with a loyalty-based ideology that is defined largely on ethnic or theological grounds or both and then endorsed by nationalist ideals;
- Nontolerance of public expressions of political pluralism, regardless of what that pluralism may be, and a state that seeks to arbitrate conflicts of interest through its own means (this limited pluralism is upheld by some as a fundamental characteristic of all authoritarian governments);[21]
- Obedience and the fulfillment of duty in the form of ostentatious submission to the leader's authority (all bureaucratic behavior is modeled after the relationship to the leader: at every rank, passivity is required from the subaltern who must react to the leader's actions and authority).

The two basic problems that the relationship to the leader present (see the first and last points above) are summed up in a fundamental ambivalence and by the violence of the succession. The leader has to control the apparatus of the state. He achieves this by means of his small but faithful group of friends. Rarely does he intervene publicly in specific matters. Rather, he asserts his presence by correcting his disciples' errors in dramatic ways. Master and disciple live in an ambivalent relationship, and since there are few formalized rules of succession, one can pass quickly from absolute obedience to the chief to plotting his assassination in a period of crisis. The tension between these two attitudes may be momentarily resolved, but then a new cycle begins, reproducing the dialectic of passivity and activity, authority and submission. The two attempted coups d'état in 1971 and 1972 illustrate this point.

Authority thus exercised does not mean that the authoritarian state lives a life of its own outside the bounds of society. The ambivalence of the relationship—chief-subaltern, master-disciple, father-son—functions at its very heart. Still, the state must look to elites to direct its affairs. The colonial and postcolonial development of the state apparatus and its unprecedented ramification into various organs contrast sharply with the simplicity of the precolonial apparatus. A situation of this kind implies great social mobility. Changes in status and class follow two main paths: the school and the army. Elites are coopted and success comes quickly because latent rivalries among leaders and ties of personal loyalty take precedence over the acquisition (inevitably slow) of technical skills. The intelligentsia is digested en masse by the apparatus of the state, is reclassified, becomes *declassé,* or is physically eliminated. In this context, the coopting of the elite facilitates the insertion of centralized power at the local level through its social, familial, and ethnic origins. However, this insertion is short-lived due to the factional nature of politics at the local level. Three levers of control remain: accelerated economic development, ideology, corruption and repression. Economic development is limited from within by the prebendal character of the groups in power, a feature that is linked logically to the mode of cooptation and the rules concerning loyalty. It is also limited by an unequal exchange and a dependence on external economic powers. Consequently, social explosions and their repression occur with regularity.

So the army finds itself at the center of national life. The chief must emerge from its ranks or show evidence of martial distinction. The army becomes the royal path to social mobility. However, given the absence of a true civilian base, the leader is confronted by the perils inherent in the support provided by the army, so the governing group is caught in a contradictory game. The army is used to win over public opinion, while at the same time an alliance is sought with civilian forces to avoid a fatal dependence on the army. Also entering into the process are the politics of regional, confessional, or ethnic diversity. The chief embodies the unity of the nation, and destruction awaits those who threaten his life or career. The authoritative state is caught between its desire to level and homogenize national life totally, on the one hand, and its need to encourage the diversity required by the game of leader, on the other.

Two means are employed, if not to resolve the contradiction, at least to diminish its acuteness. The army can be used to defend the nation or some other cause that brings legitimacy to the leader, an enterprise that necessitates dependence on what is appropriately called the popular masses. Therein lies the role of ideology. External conflicts, either with non-Arab states or with Arab states accused of betraying the pan-Arab ideal, justify an internal authoritarianism. At this crossroads, the state establishes itself as the exclusive producer of ideology. Affiliation with its ideology is made explicit by visible signs, the mystique of a cultural heritage in its broadest sense constituting one striking example. The fundamental requirements are that ideology belongs to the people, is derived from the people, and is not alien. An ideology stamped with the stigma of foreign is what the state defines as such. It could as easily be a liberal ideology as a socialist one or indeed both at once.

The authoritarian state, with the characteristics outlined above, was slowly put into place. It perfected a reelaboration of precolonial *dar al-mulk* into colonial forms between 1912 and 1956 and reached a classical maturity between 1965 and 1975. Subsequently, limits placed on the political socialization of the youthful masses imposed by economic inefficiency (itself linked to the prebendal character of the state) and by the state's own interpretation of the Islamic foundations of the social order—to which competing interpretations (liberal or fundamentalist) could be opposed—revealed the growing precariousness of the situation, hence the need for a redefinition of political participation. Since 1975, social participation has, in effect, brought about great changes. But the new constitutionalism and the liberties conceded by it have left intact the kernel of the authoritarian structure. In fact, it is as if the institutions having elective powers (from the communal level up to the parliament) and the government both exist on the margins of a central decision-making process that maintains supreme control over the main political and economic levers. *Dar al-mulk,* with its power base modeled on the master-disciple relationship, has spread throughout the key structures of the technobureaucracy. With its system of patronage deeply entrenched in economic life, it keeps for itself the essential decision-making powers. Now let us examine the process of its construction as a modern political concept within the context of a society modernized under colonial oppression.

The Integration of Ritual and Violence: Dar al-mulk as Colonial and Postcolonial Construction

Reforming the mechanisms of command, defense, and governance preoccupied Moroccan rulers and thinkers throughout the nineteenth century. Some measures were adopted during the second half of the nineteenth century that had as their priority military reform. This movement of reform[22] was part of a larger logic of action that seized Mediterranean Muslim societies in general. A sense of profound change and the perception of crisis deepened with the affirmation of Europe's economic and military superiority. By the end of the century, the failure of reforms and a growing foreign penetration had greatly weakened *dar al-mulk,* so that between 1900 and 1927 its hold over society and politics was reduced even further. An ever-expanding social and political rebellion and the unceasing pressure from imperialist powers culminated in the establishment of the French protectorate. This decisive event sanctioned the temporary eclipse of the exemplary center.

But *dar al-mulk* did not entirely disappear. Between 1912 and 1930, and especially under Lyautey's leadership (up to 1925),[23] a new hybrid system was elaborated that has to be defined in its specificity. It was not a traditional sharifian government collaborating with, manipulated by, or even resisting a modern apparatus. Instead of adhering to this largely illusory dichotomy, we should try to understand the system of colonial rule as a specific totality. If the new technocracy compartmentalized space, people, and resources, we could also say that it compartmentalized culture. It introduced new ways of managing humans and material: work in the mines, work in industry, the cantonment of tribes, and military conscription are but a few examples. All operated through the geographical redefinition of space and its administrative organization. This new technocratic governance appeared first in the colonies where it developed rapidly, finding its center in cultural reproduction, as Lyautey well understood—that is, in the creation of social and moral forms that transcended the individual. These forms were to take over the process and to function as a kind of rhetorical space for new modes of control; in short, as a condition for the production of new categories at work in the definition and transformation of society.

These new forms would constitute the articulation between what is discursive (the immense body of knowledge generated in a dominated society and culture) and what is visible; between the institutions producing knowledge and its practical applications in the creation of new cities, infrastructures, and bureaucracies; between the reorganization of rural spaces and the resources that gear them toward capitalist enterprises of the large towns; between the redefinition of sacred space and religion and the borders between religions and confessional groups; between the redefinition of contacts and borders between languages; and between the redefinition of education and procedures of transmission and allegiance. This rearticulation was so effective that the living moral forms, once they were absorbed into a technocratic elaboration, became frozen and reduced to univocal signs and orientations. Thus, for example, the *qa'id* tended to be redefined as an autonomous chief, summing up the wisdom of the group and entrusted with leading it toward modernity. The tribe, meanwhile, tended to be identified as a discrete entity tied to a particular territory and to a chief and consultative council (collective land and *jama'a*).

Meanwhile, the central power, pushing to the limit the previously fluid definition of *umma*, became the owner of land, forests, and river basins, while monopolizing the use of arms. To be sure, alternative redefinitions were possible. For example, the *jama'a* could have easily been redefined as an elected rural and municipal council and *umma* as a parliament. However, rather than eliciting this democratic potential of the so-called traditional Moroccan institutions, the colonial system made other choices; it tapped the autocratic potential of these institutions within a new integration of forms and categories. This is how specific affinities came about between the colonial technocracy, charged with administering a process of civilization, and the authoritarian-based chieftaincy, benevolently mediating the passage toward modernity. The main form in which the two are articulated in this dynamic of change—which is also a dynamic of instruction and initiation—is naturally that of the master and the disciple. Putting aside differences, the common diagram that constructs this Janus-like head is one of submission and an attentive silence that the newly reformed and civilized society is forced to observe.

This colonial interpretation of cultural forms and categories renewed archaic relationships of power and modernized the means of their generalization—through infrastructures, communications, the army, the police, administrative redistricting, a prison system, and a national marketplace of goods and ideas. Before long, this archaization became the target of a civil society born in the interstices of the grid, most notably in the cities, where the politics of colonialism favored such a development. A civil society with restricted freedoms gave birth to a powerful nationalist movement that took the form of parties, unions, and associations. Thus we witness a paradox: the colonial party continually consigned Moroccans to a cultural past it carefully redefined, while the nationalist movement (between 1930 and 1956) fought for a redefinition of this same heritage by reappropriating the past of the colonial power whose claims it opposed. Thus, the French protectors identified themselves with a Moroccan tradition, while the anticolonialist leaders looked for renewal to the Enlightenment tradition in support of their call for liberation and democratic reform. While the colonial party became increasingly archaic, the national party became more modern—hence its denunciation of native chiefs (*quwwad*), of *contrôle civil*, marabouts, superstition, and authoritarianism. From this also came a call for the restoration of a legitimate monarchy, with its powers limited by an organic law derived from popular consensus.

The final manifestation of *dar al-mulk* as a gathering of discrete segments having a certain level of structural and ideological autonomy was organized by Resident General Juin together with the powerful native chieftains following the coup of 1953 that ousted the legitimate king (Mohammed V) and installed a pretender in his place. The immediate failure of this effort indicates the breadth of the change Moroccan society had undergone. Between 1930 and 1950, the majority refused colonial oppression and alienation and was mobilized into new structures, parties, unions, secret associations, networks of martyrs (*al-fida'* or terrorists in the colonial discourse), as well as an army of liberation. While earlier forms did not entirely disappear, they were pushed into the background. Subtle relationships were established between them and the new organizations. Tribes, *hanta* (corporations), groups of *shurafa'*, and networks of *zawaya* were denounced as social structures manipulated by the colonialists. But once the members of these cadres declared their loyalty to nationalism, it was decided not to dismantle them but rather to coopt them. Mutual transfers traditionalized the new forms, while the brotherhoods provided a model for the structuring of the nationalist movement. Indeed, many of the most prominent nationalist leaders, including Allal al-Fasi, were educated in the *zawiya* and in the *madrasa*.

Within this context of colonial dynamics, of exchanges between archaic structures and new structures of mobilization, of battles fought by nationalist forces to counter colonialism to bring about the renewal of political and religious life, the figure of the king imposed itself as a rallying point for the social movement out of which independence emerged. The discrediting of the regional chiefs and the heads of the brotherhoods as a result of their collaboration with the apparatus of colonial oppression helped to centralize the attributes and power of sainthood in his person. In this highly charged context, and in the face of ideals of equality and liberation, the master-disciple relationship became generalized and legitimated as the form in which political interactions were articulated and given symbolic intensity.

Now that the process of reconstructing *dar al-mulk* in the colonial system has been outlined, we can turn to the main phases that led to the establishment of a renewed *dar al-mulk* after independence. The essential facts have already been described by others.[24] Here it suffices to recall a few important elements whose chronology traces the reinforcement of *dar al-mulk* to the detriment of other political, syndicalist, and associative formations that might have evolved into a civil society counterbalancing its powers. Three periods can be distinguished: that of the rearrangement of power relations, that of the consolidation and maturation of a new system, and finally, the present one of a gradual and hesitant opening. Since this last phase has already been mentioned, only the first two remain to be described.

The rearrangement of power relations came about between 1956 and 1965. This was a period of competition, struggle, and readjustment marked by social upheaval in the towns and dissidence in the rural areas, especially in the Rif and in Central Atlas. It set in train the gradual weakening of the national party by a fission that produced new parties. Other political formations were also suppressed, and there was a return in force of regional alliances and notables after the brief interim of the Abdellah Ibrahim cabinet (1958–60). The army, the security services, and the apparatus of the Ministry of the Interior were taken over by the monarchy and its faithful. The first constitution was promulgated in 1962, with elections that were marked by the intervention of the new regime, which opposed the nationalist parties with a coalition created under the patronage of the monarchy (FDIC). In 1965, the parliamentary defeat of this large but shaky coalition and serious riots in Casablanca led to the establishment of a state of emergency.

A second period with its own distinct characteristics extended from 1965 to 1975. A political opening on the ground was not truly initiated until after 1975, although the new constitution was promulgated in 1972. However, the modalities of "the concession" of a constitution belong to the specific political culture of the 1956–65 era, represented by a new relationship of forces. Between 1965 and 1975, a sharp repression of political parties, unions, and associations took place. Disturbances, most notably in the educational sector, resulted in a confrontation between the regime and the popular student union (UNEM), in which the latter was violently eliminated by a series of administrative measures and the dismantling of its leadership. This was also a period of merciless confrontation with groups on the left and the extreme left, made up of intellectuals and students, which led to the elimination of their leaders or their incarceration.

It was not only the weakening of the parties that distinguished this period; even more, it was their proliferation at the instigation of the political center and the continual efforts devoted to their domestication. Repression and negotiation also led to the widening of the field of action of yet a third factor: cooptation. Once institutions were suspended, compromise and secret negotiation settled in, and various forms of cooptation made conditions favorable for corruption. In this climate, partisan structures and even the unions were won over by the system of patronage. The syndrome of the notable, signifying the return to the countryside, won over the towns as well, and its practices spread to the so-called modern sector, as well as to industry and business. With the help of a measure of economic success, especially in agriculture, agroindustry, and light industries, *dar al-mulk* reestablished itself as a center of patronage and hegemonic promotion controlling the economy in both the public and private sectors.

The program of development, the recuperation of colonial lands, the Moroccanization of the tertiary sector, and the development of public administration rapidly changed the face of the country, especially with regard to an unprecedented urban expansion and the development of a middle class. A general improvement in the conditions of life went hand in hand with an increase in inequity and a rise in the unemployment of youth. The resources available for the cooptation of elites and the networks of patronage shrank, while the same groups that profited from this policy knew how to take advantage of the movement for privatization that accompanied structural readjustment. Thus limits were placed on the expansion of a market capable of generating employment.

The new institutions that came into being on the heels of the promulgation of the 1972 constitution confirmed the integration of this unprecedented configuration of power. They legitimated the arbitrative role of *dar al-mulk* as a means of managing disparities and differences but not as a means of modulating the inequality of opportunity. They legitimated a situation whereby patronage became as widespread within the institutions of the state as it was in the syndicates and party structures. This outcome was not fated to be inscribed by some inexorable historical logic. Rather it was the product of struggles and sacrifices whose importance should not be underestimated and whose consequences were not easily foreseen. Any description that presents them as "destined to be" would be making the error of excessive hindsight.

CONCLUSION: THE FOUNDATION OF *DAR AL-MULK* AS AUTHORITARIAN RULE

Approaching *dar al-mulk* as a specifically Moroccan political concept, not unlike other Arab and Mediterranean authoritarianisms, allows us to redefine the political system and to grasp more firmly the conditions of its success. At the outset, we must rid ourselves of all assumptions of continuity—not that there is no continuity but that we must learn to see changes within continuity itself. In this sense, *dar al-mulk* benefits from ideological and formal continuities that, when seen as configurations endlessly criss-crossed by contradictory currents, show themselves to be new constructions. From this point of view, it seems unreasonable to continue to force *dar al-mulk* into the habitual typologies, such as the semitraditional monarchy, neopatrimonialism, or some other neopatriarchal form of government.[25] By the same token, continuities of structure and legitimacy are genuine, insofar as we may understand them as reinventions.

The new specificity of *dar al-mulk* consists in the legitimation of a modern authoritative structure. It relies on the fact that it is no longer dependent on local formations (tribes, chiefdoms, *zawaya*, etc.) that negotiate their autonomy at the same time as they support a more powerful center benefiting from a broad consensus. These local formations are either dead or are coopted and subjugated into the functioning of the new state. The new specificity of *dar al-mulk* as a field of power relations consists in the generalization of the practice of service, of the gift, and of sacralized terror, not only through the new technobureaucratic apparatus but also through anticolonial and postcolonial structures of mobilization. The demand for equality at the local level has grown more vigorous thanks to the battles fought for national freedom. However, the power relations specific to these new political formations struggling for their own freedom were not well elaborated beyond the ideals of constitutionalism, and a redefinition of everyday political interactions between men and women and between generations was conspicuously absent. The articulation of political interactions took on a revived form of the master-disciple relationship, buttressed by the reemergence of the mystical sharifian body. This reemergence is demonstrated with increasing splendor in the feasts and the holidays of *dar al-mulk,* which have been vigorously reinstated since the 1960s.

At this point we should recall that the paradigm of sainthood, at work in all the trajectories and foundations of power since the fifteenth century, is actualized through the striking modalities of the renewed *dar al-mulk* as creative and procreative center. Comparing the head and embodiment of *dar al-mulk* as father of the nation with the father of the household, who is the repository of authority and the guarantor and symbol of the law (as sacrificer), we can see it is an error to believe that we have a metaphor on one side and reality on the other. Both are in fact metaphors. And both are also symbols of the continuity of a group or of an identity. There is also a third metaphor—that of the body of the Prophet who transcends death, to which the first two metaphors owe their emotional energy. The charisma that each saint manifests transcends the law (of the *faqih* and of the father) to make concrete through his body the uninterrupted presence of the Prophet. Here is the continuity of all creation and procreation that the hagiography returned to its place of honor after the so-called maraboutic crisis that so intrigued colonial historians. Coexisting alongside the *faqih* and the law and in tension with them, this new condition tends to strip the woman of the privilege of reproduction and of the sharing of wealth and honors at the time of the patriarch's death (inheritance). In other words, the monopoly of creation and procreation as a condition of preeminence and power occults the mother (matrix of continuity). Inasmuch as the disciple is feminized before attaining mastery—that is, a position of authority and power—he incorporates this other principle of reproduction, which is well hidden though always there, as if it were meant to introduce inconsistency into the patriarchal myth.

This process of incorporation acknowledges and manifests the feminine even while designating its limits. Enormous changes in the condition of women under the protectorate and after independence have caused an upheaval in their daily lives and in their juridical status. But for the most part, these changes have been reformulated and sanctioned on the normative level by men. Through a constant transgression of the law, some women have managed to radicalize them by putting patriarchal power on the defensive. One might wager that decisive innovations in the future will come from a cultural revolution in the relations of power between the sexes, the generations, and other as yet unquestioned hierarchies. The incorporation of the feminine could allow for a renegotiation of the very forms of political interaction and of the qualifications of the people in charge of defining them. This concerns no less than a debate focusing on the basic relations of command, consent, and refusal in the *dar al-mulk*, as well as in the parties, unions, and associative structures, not to mention family and educational structures. The master-disciple paradigm would be pushed aside and replaced by this debate; it would then return to the passionate pursuit of a relationship with God (which is its point of origin and its chosen arena), ceding the ground in everyday matters to an open discussion of differences and of conflicting identities.

NOTES

The author wishes to thank Mohamed Kably, Abdelfattah Kilito, Susan Gilson Miller, and Edmund Burke III for their excellent remarks and suggestions. He also wishes to thank Roger Owen very warmly for taking time to read this chapter and helping him to clarify and revise it.

1. There is a very extensive literature on this ancient word and institution. Both are mentioned in the Arabic sources: see, for example, E. Lévi-Provençal, *Documents inédits d'histoire almohade* (Paris, 1928), Text 71 and glossary, and Abu al-Qasim Ahmad al-Zayani, *Al-turjaman al-muʻrib ʻan duwal al-Mashriq wa-al-Maghrib*, ed. and trans. O. Houdas, *Le Maroc de 1631 à 1812* (Paris, 1886). An example from the nineteenth century can be provided by M. Akansus, *Al-jaysh al-ʻaramram* (Fez, 1918). See also Charles de Foucault, *Reconnaissance du Maroc* (Paris, 1888); E. Aubin, *Le Maroc d'aujourd'hui* (Paris, 1904), chaps. 10–12; R. Montagne, *Les Berbères et le makhzen dans le sud du Maroc* (Paris, 1930). For an overview, see E. Michaux-Bellaire, s.v. "Makhzan," *Encyclopaedia of Islam* (old edition). Reformulated as a descriptive or interpretive concept by colonial historiography, political science, and anthropology, *makhzan* is still used uncritically by many authors: for example, A. Laroui, *L'Idéologie arabe contemporaine* (Paris, 1967), 131; idem, *Les Origines sociales et culturelles du nationalisme marocain (1830–1912)* (Paris, 1977), 67, 81 ff, and 160; idem, *Esquisses Historiques* (Casablanca, 1992), 50 ff, 180 n. 10.
2. G. Drague, *Esquisse d'histoire religieuse du Maroc* (Paris, 1951);

J. Brignon et al., *Histoire du Maroc* (Paris, 1967); M. Kably, *Société, pouvoir et religion au Maroc à la fin du moyen âge* (Paris, 1986).

3. M. Foucault, *Surveiller et punir* (Paris, 1975), 207; G. Deleuze, *Foucault* (Paris, 1986), 42 ff.
4. C. Geertz, *Islam Observed* (New Haven: Yale University Press, 1968), 36.
5. C. Geertz, *Local Knowledge* (New York, 1983), 138 ff. Mohamed Afif, "Les Harkas hassaniennes d'après l'oeuvre d'A. Ibn Zidane," *Hespéris-Tamuda* 19 (1980–81): 153–68; D. Nordman, "Les Expéditions de Moulay Hassan," *Hespéris-Tamuda* 19 (1980–1): 123–52; Abdellah Hammoudi, *Master and Disciple: The Cultural Foundations of Moroccan Authoritarianism* (Chicago: University of Chicago Press, 1997), chap. 2 and p. 170 n. 15.
6. Hammoudi, *Master and Disciple*, chap. 2.
7. Ibid.; idem, "Segmentarity, Social Stratification, Political Power and Sainthood: Reflections on Gellner's Thesis," *Economy and Society* 9 (1980): 279–303; idem, "The Path to Sainthood: Structure and Danger," *Princeton Papers* 3 (1994): 71–88.
8. This seems to have been a widespread practice. For example, see Hammoudi, *Master and Disciple*, chap. 2, and 168 n. 3.
9. Kably stresses the need to go beyond Ibn Khaldun and to describe what he could not see or did not live to see; see his *Société, pouvoir et religion*.
10. I borrowed this notion of mystical body from Ernst H. Kantorowicz, *The King's Two Bodies: A Study in Medieval Political Theology* (Princeton: Princeton University Press, 1957).
11. Hammoudi, "The Path to Sainthood"; idem, *Master and Disciple*, chap. 3.
12. Abdellah Hammoudi, "Sainteté, pouvoir et société: Tamgrout au XVIIe et XVIIIe siècles," *Annales; E. S. C.* no. 3–4 (1980): 615–41; idem, "The Path to Sainthood: On al-Hajj 'Ali (1850–1910)," see idem, *Master and Disciple*, 86.
13. Muhammad al-Mukhtar al-Susi, *Al-tiryaq al-mudawi fi akhbar al-shaykh sayyidi al-Hajj 'Ali al-Susi al-Darqawi* (Tetuan, 1960) and his *Al-mas'ul*, 20 vols. (Rabat, 1960–3), especially vols. 1, 3, and 5; Hammoudi, *Master and Disciple*, chaps. 3 and 5. On the process of initiation see Hammoudi, "Segmentarity," and "The Path to Sainthood"; A. L. de Premare, *Sidi Abd-er-Rahman el-*

Mejdub: mysticisme populaire, société et pouvoir au Maroc au 16ème siècle (Paris, 1985).

14. J. Berque, *Ulemas, fondateurs et insurgés du Maghreb* (Paris, 1982), 50, 89.
15. Martin Lings, *A Moslem Saint of the Twentieth Century: Shaikh Ahmad al-'Alawi, His Spiritual Heritage and Legacy* (London, 1961), 72.
16. E. Westermarck, *Ritual and Belief in Morocco*, 2 vols. (London, 1926), 1:198.
17. V. Crapanzano, *The Hamadsha* (Chicago: University of Chicago Press, 1973).
18. See in particular E. Gellner's theory of the saint's election in *Saints of the Atlas* (London, 1969), 150–2; idem, "Concept and Community" in Hollis and Lukes, eds., *Rationality and Relativism*, 43–6; idem, "Pouvoir politique et fonction religieuse dans l'Islam marocain," *Annales; E. S. C.* (1970): 699–713; idem, *Muslim Society* (Cambridge, 1981), chaps. 1, 4.
19. I describe and interpret the sacrifice and masquerades in *The Victim and Its Masks* (Chicago: University of Chicago Press, 1993), first published as *La Victime et ses masques* (Paris, 1989).
20. The sacrifier is the one who makes the offering to God, while the sacrificer is the person who actually performs the immolation. These terms are used by Henri Hubert and Marcel Mauss in their classic *Essai sur la nature et la fonction du sacrifice* (n.p., n.d.). For an English translation, see *Sacrifice: Its Nature and Function* (Chicago: University of Chicago Press, 1964).
21. J. Linz, "An Authoritarian Regime, Spain," in E. Allard and S. Rokkan, eds., *Mass Politics: Studies in Political Sociology* (New York, 1970), 255. Also J. Linz, "Totalitarian and Authoritarian Regimes," in F. Greenstein and N. Polsby, eds., *Handbook of Political Science*, 9 vols. (Reading, Mass., 1975) 3, 255–9.
22. The reform of the state bureaucracy and the army and the creation of new institutions was in no small measure a reaction to the growing encroachment of Europe after the conquest of Algiers in 1830. For information on the reforms, see Brignon et al., *Histoire du Maroc*, 314–20; E. Burke III, *Prelude to Protectorate* (Chicago: University of Chicago Press, 1976), 31–8; J.-L. Miège, *Le Maroc et l'Europe*, 4 vols. (Paris, 1961–63), 3:224–34, 4:106ff.; M. Lahbabi, *Le Gouvernement marocain a l'aube du XXe siècle*

(Rabat, 1958); Laroui, *Les Origines;* W. Rollman, "The 'New Order' in a Pre-colonial Muslim Society: Military Reforms in Morocco 1844–1904" (Ph.D. diss., University of Michigan, 1983); T. Berrada, "The Moroccan Army and Its Evolution in the Nineteenth Century" (in Arabic) (Ph.D. diss., Mohammed V University, 1984); M. Kenbib, *Juifs et musulmans au Maroc, 1859–1948* (Rabat: Mohammed V University, 1994); Bahija Smimou, *Les Reformes militaires au Maroc de 1844 à 1912* (Rabat: Faculté des Lettres, 1995); M. al-Manuni, *Madhahir yaqaza al-Maghrib al-hadith,* 2 vols. (Beirut, 1985).
23. D. Rivet, *Lyautey et l'institution du Protectorat au Maroc, 1912–1925,* 3 vols. (Paris, 1988), and Hammoudi, *Master and Disciple,* chap. 4
24. In particular, J. Waterbury, *The Commander of the Faithful: The Moroccan Political Elite—a Study in Segmented Politics* (New York: Columbia University Press, 1970); R. Leveau, *Le Fellah marocain, défenseur du trône,* 2nd ed. (Paris, 1976); O. Bendourou, *Le Pouvoir executif au Maroc depuis l'indépendence* (Aix-en-Provence, 1986). See my account in *Master and Disciple,* chap. 1 and bibliographical notes.
25. E. Hermassi, *Etat et société au Maghreb; Etude comparative* (Paris, 1975); Hisham Sharabi, *Neopatriarchy: A Theory of Distorted Change in Arab Society* (New York, 1992); and my reservations vis-à-vis the concept of neopatriarchy and the views of Sharabi in *Master and Disciple,* chap. 6.

· EIGHT ·

Performing Monarchy, Staging Nation

M. Elaine Combs-Schilling

Popular performances of the Moroccan monarchy create and revalidate the white-robed ruler as the emblem of the nation, the icon on which the whole gazes and constructs and experiences their commonality, even when the gazing is made in critique. I want to address this articulation of nation and then turn to a crucial moment of its transition, a national reenactment that took place on the night of 30 August 1993.[1]

Morocco's emblematic and performative construction of nation stands in sharp contrast to Benedict Anderson's articulations. Anderson portrays national unity as a post-1700s Eurocentered phenomenon that he associates with standardized print culture. In Anderson's depictions, nationalism emerges "in common reading and speaking in common territories," through which "imagined communities" of "nation" are born, communities that are dispersed, fluid, nonsubstantive, and yet unequivocally existing.[2]

Great collective performances can serve this same generative role, centering, substantiating, and dispersing popular experience and imagination so that a sense of nation is born. In Morocco, national unity has been performatively staged through common looking on the white-robed king. The dazzling center has been a formidable nationalist construction, effective in mobilizing the technologies of power that Foucault has emphasized as crucial to effective regimes—that is, having available effective means of embedding models of authority within the intimate lives of everyday people so that exterior power and interior passion in some arenas converge.[3] In Morocco, popular performances inscribe the regime's legitimacy on individual bodies in local spaces so that many within the population actively are drawn to the paradigms and practices that simultaneously reconstitute the nation, themselves, and the king.[4]

Yet Foucault, in his analytical work, like Anderson, insists on unequivocal difference when it comes to post-1700s European nationalism. Foucault contends that "from the seventeenth and eighteenth centuries onwards" there was in Europe "a veritable technological take-off in the productivity of power . . . a new 'economy' of power . . . new techniques much more efficient and much less wasteful."[5] Foucault goes on to say, "It's the body of society which becomes the new principle in the nineteenth century," contrasting this with earlier monarchical forms where, he argues, the king's body was singularly fundamental.[6]

But when we look at the political-cultural constructions of post-1500s Morocco, the distinctions are not so clear. Morocco's political order was enormously effective in mobilizing productive technologies of the body. Through performative techniques, including mimesis, the king's body became Everyman's body, the body of society. There are more parallels than Anderson or Foucault imagined, making their insights useful in other places and to other forms.

Morocco's Nation

Morocco is an old and durable nation, one that constantly has transformed itself in addressing an ever-changing world but also one that has maintained domains of continuity so that, to some degree, it has met transformations on its own terms. Islam and monarchy have been essential to the Moroccan nation since its beginning but have been articulated in different ways. An Islamically legitimated monarchy was established in Morocco in 789 by an Arab descendent of the Prophet Muhammad, a sharif.[7] Morocco's first dynasty lasted until 959. The next two dynasties (that ruled 1069–1147 and 1147–1269, respectively) consolidated central power and in many ways made Morocco a nation. These two dynasties, both local Berber in origin, legitimated their right to rule through the Islamic jihad, as Kably shows.[8] Ideologically dogmatic and violently coercive, they periodically resorted to killing the faithful in order to establish the faith, killing citizens in order to establish the nation.[9]

By the fourth dynasty, the Banu Marin (1258–1420), Kably argues, ideologically exclusivity and physical coercion had largely (though not entirely) been set aside. Rigid dogmas and military repression were used less often, while shared practices and common understandings tying monarchy and population were relied on to a greater extent.[10] The fourth dynasty was able to make this turn, according to Kably, because an ever-expanding repertoire of political and cultural supports had been built over the centuries that linked monarchy and population, a veritable "arsenal of legitimizing means which . . . represented an embarrassment of riches" on which the fourth dynasty as well as the two that followed relied in "polyvalent and pragmatic ways." Hence by the time of the Banu Marin, the monarchy came to abandon violence and dogmatic exclusivity in favor of more supple means of connection with the population.[11]

My own interests concern the era that followed the Banu Marin—namely, the 1500s to the present—during which time two sharifian dynasties (that claimed direct lineal descent from Muhammad) have ruled: the Sa'di (1548–1641) and the 'Alawi (1666–present), the fifth and sixth dynasties. How was the "arsenal of legitimizing means" expanded during this era of economic and military assault from southern and western Europe?[12]

I contend that great orienting rituals of faith were the sharifian monarchy's crucial addition to the arsenal. Other foundations remained important and were mobilized on occasion, but the staging of great performances of culture, in which monarch and population actively participated, were the sharifian monarchy's most innovative and enduring elaboration. The productions—simultaneously personal, political, and religious events—placed the monarchy at the center of popular experience and consciousness. Because of their generalized credibility, the rituals helped embed the monarchy in the population's heartfelt longings, sensual desires, and sacred imaginations. The performances validated the monarchy and gave it a means of access to taxes and conscripts, legal arguments, personal potency, Islamic images of justice and authority, the loyalty of administrators.[13]

Great orienting rituals are not always effective foundations of political regimes, but they can be.[14] In post-1500 Morocco, they were potently developed, were persuasively staged, and became convincing regenerative means of linking the population and the king through productive common experience. The collective performances did not blind people to what the king did elsewhere. But for many people they became part of the repertoire of experience through which they evaluated themselves and their system of rule, making for complicated and multifaceted reads, as exemplified in el-Zerhouni's poignant lamentations about the Moroccan monarchy made in the early 1700s after his father's religious lodge had been burned by the king's order and by the king's men.[15] El-Zerhouni's laments include a reaffirmation of the monarchy; since God created that institution as well as the inherently fragile humans beings that inhabit it, el-Zerhouni reasons, there must be some overriding purpose in it.

The performative elaboration of the Moroccan monarchy and the Moroccan nation were by no means inevitable. Like other supports or underminings of political regimes, these foundations of the Moroccan monarchy were created in specific times and places and had to be continually revitalized in order to endure.

THE PROPHET'S BIRTHDAY, 1593–1992

In what follows, I briefly note the consequences of an innovative performance of the Prophet's Birthday that took place in 1593 that made it a national ritual that continued to be reperformed over the next 400 years. The elaborator of the performance was the king, al-Mansur (the Victorious One); the place was Marrakesh. As I argue at length elsewhere, al-Mansur's performative staging was crucial in establishing descent from the Prophet Muhammad as a criterion of rule and in articulating the white-robed monarchy as an orienting emblem of the nation.[16] Descent from Muhammad, sharifian descent, was by no means taken for granted by the population as the legitimating foundation of rule. At the time that the rite was performed, the new dynasty, claiming superiority on the basis of this descent, had been in place for only forty-five years, and the claim of lineal descent from Muhammad had not been a definitive criterion for monarchical rule in the previous 646 years (since the end of the Idrisi dynasty in 959). To be an effective foundation for political rule, the excellency of sharifian descent needed cultivation within popular experience and consciousness.[17] The popular performance of the Prophet's Birthday became that. Through song, dance, and the sound of trumpets, through plays of sacred words and glittering light, people's own bodies seemingly demonstrated the natural hierarchy that elevates men over women and that elevates the white-robed ruler, the descendant of the Prophet, over all the rest as the best-of-case representative, the man par excellence.

Al-Mansur invited representatives from the whole of the nation to Marrakesh for the performance he designed, which took place in the spectacular palace of al-Badia (the Incomparable), which he had built over the previous fifteen years. The 1593 celebration of the Prophet's Birthday served as its gala opening.

In elaborating the national ceremony, al-Mansur drew on local performances of the Prophet's Birthday that were held in certain parts of the land. He combined those elements with other symbols and significations that the population deeply valued (the Prophet, holy words, white light), orchestrating them into a single performance that was sensually vivid and conceptually persuasive. There—in the fragrant palace gardens on the balmy night in Marrakesh—sat the descendant of Muhammad, the ruler, dressed in robes of pure white, the mantle of the Prophet on him, radiance surrounding him, words lifted toward him, the nation gathered in gazing at the central king, the material signifier of the whole, the nodal point of the festivities, and the emblem of the nation.[18] As described in their own words, people who witnessed the event found it vital and persuasive and easy to remember.[19] It combined vivid sensate experiences in sound, sight, touch, taste, and fragrance into a performative score that the population carried back with them to the countryside and revitalized in their own local celebrations of the Prophet Muhammad's Birthday.

The 1593 performance crystallized a vision and version of nation that was to endure. On that fragrant night in Marrakesh, al-Mansur established the white-robed ruler, descendant of Muhammad, as the emblem of the nation, provided a way to merge everyday men into that image—by donning the white robes—and distinguished the commonly cloaked men from all women. The 1593 performance depicted women as valued and valorized but unequivocally different, the complementary other to the white-cloaked men, separate from the national performance and its emblematic space. Actual women did not attend the festivities in Marrakesh that night. Imaginatively, they were called forward in poetry where they were celebrated as the icon of passion and sensuality, dressed in multicolored and glimmering garments that shimmered with golden and silver threads, like brides on their way to marriage. Women were included in this imagined community of nation as the valued other, physically absent from the central political and religious scene but linked in intimate ways.

This version of rulership, nation, and Prophet's Birthday performance came to be repeated through much of the land. Through time it became one of the three most important annual celebrations in Morocco. In most of the countryside, it came to center on white-cloaked men gathered in holy places lit by candlelight, singing words of evocative passion for the female and then praise for the holy Prophet and the reigning king.[20] Through the local repetitions, in ways that echo the galactic polity of Thai monarchy elucidated by Tambiah,[21] the white-cloaked ruler was brought to much of Morocco as the central orienting icon, the material signifier on which diverse hopes, dreams, and historicities of the nation's population could converge. This is the magic of effective emblems; they mobilize multiple sentiments, diverse perspectives, and channel them onto a common physical signifier, in this case, the white-cloaked king, designating an imagined community of formidable and fluid dimensions.

MIMESIS We see in al-Mansur's 1593 ritual staging of the Prophet's Birthday and in its repetition through the land the play of the mimetic capacity, the drawing on and channeling of what Benjamin calls the "powerful compulsion . . . to become and behave like something else," what Michael Taussig describes as the "soulful, willful" desire to imitate the other, "the compulsion to become the Other," especially the desire to imitate those in power.[22] Taussig suggests that a part of the desire to imitate power comes from a desire to gain control over it, to protect oneself from it: "The mimetic faculty carries out its honest labor, suturing nature to artifice and bringing sensuousness to sense . . . granting the copy the character and power of the original, the representations the power of the represented."[23]

In the Prophet's Birthday performance, al-Mansur drew together in mimicry the men of the nation. Through common action, common space, and collective performance, a fraternity of men mimetically converged onto the Prophet and king and were distinguished from all women.[24] Dress is the material carrier of culture that as Buck-Morss states, "presses closest the skin. . . . Clothing is quite literally at the borderline between subject and object, the individual and the cosmos. Its position surely accounts for its emblematic significance throughout history."[25] As the Prophet's Birthday came to be performed in Morocco, the men of the nation, again and again, have been mimetically brought together into a fraternity of cloak, performance, and gazing. The same white robes that touch their skin, touch the skin of the king, the descendant of Muhammad. Through words and dress, Muhammad is brought to and embodied in the king. Those gathered are brought to and embodied in the king also, making the white-cloaked ruler the point of convergence, the mediating link between past and present, between Muhammad and all men, between the habitat of the living and the domain of God, an empowered, in-between place-to-be.

Since Sa'di times, the nation's rulers have worn these simple white robes on high religious and political occasions. The robes have a white hood that is drawn over the head and covers part of the face, blurring distinctions between men so that each man becomes an Everyman, formed through gazing and mimicking the king. The king wears no crown, no jewels, nothing to distinguish him. Of all the garbs the king wears, this performative dress most unites him with other men and unites all men with each other. This common visual and tactile experience has made for the kind of homosocial bonding of which Anderson speaks as being so important to the construction of nation, an image and experience of Everyman as a part of the whole.[26] The white-hooded robes visually obliterate distinctions between men allowing the suggestion of egalitarianism in the dramatic construction of vertical hierarchy. It has been precisely through this icon of commonality that the male hierarchy in sharifian Morocco has been built. The image is one of the king as the first among equals, like other men but chosen by God to uphold the rest. The practice is one of dramatic rank and distinction.

How different are the robes worn by England's monarchs in the same era (the late 1500s to the present)? England's kings and queens have worn ceremonial robes that distinguished the ruler from all the rest. Imperial authority there has been built on elaborate visual and material distinctions, not on imagined convergences. In England, the monarch was the multicolored, shimmering one, cloaked in brightly colored silken brocades that caught the light.[27] In England, brocade legitimated the monarchy's right to the central throne, while in Morocco the same texture was used to keep Moroccan women away.

The mimetic process cuts a number of ways. By imitating power, by visually and performatively allying oneself with it, men in Morocco can participate in that power, can gain a degree of felt control over that power. Through that same process, the men also make these constructions of power intrinsic to themselves, obfuscating and complicating the boundaries between self and monarch, individual and ruler, for the two—in some domains—become fused. This process of mimicry, of mimesis, of repetitive likeness, reduces and sometimes obliterates the alterity, the outsideness of domination. Constructions of power reside within the self, making them much more difficult to move away from, for one's own definition is in part configured through and in opposition to them. Self-definition is not simply wrapped up in the imperial definition; self is fabricated from imperial cloth. The experience of self is in part created from the sacred white robes that the monarch wears and the sensate occasions when he wears them. Thus a dependency is born, a bodily identity between subject and monarch that makes the monarchy extremely difficult to move away from, through processes Foucault has highlighted.[28] In Morocco, one's definition as a man is in part configured through active engagement with the corporality of the king, so that to undercut the monarchy is in part to undercut the self, making for an enormously complicated personal-political process. There is critique. There is collusion and mimicry as well.

EMBLEMS Durkheim argues that "in general a collective sentiment can become conscious of itself only by being fixed upon some material object."[29] As Taussig says: "the image here is an image of the need for images."[30] Both highlight the ways in which graphic icons can focus sentiment, rally reservoirs of individual and collective meaning, and orient them to common forms (as do the emblems of the Black Madonna for many Poles and Our Lady of Guadalupe for many indigenous peoples of Mexico). Morocco's monarchical emblem—the white-robed sharifian king—is a richly laden material object that is brought into play in the lives of everyday Moroccans.[31] On it, the Moroccan population has been able to focus its extremely rich, diversified constituency through common gaze and common cloaking and has been able to construct and consolidate unifying collective sentiment in an environment of considerable diversity, fluidity, and contest.

Yet the way the emblem works is by a process very different than the one Durkheim envisioned; the Moroccan rituals and the common icon do not produce a singular isomorphic collective consciousness. Quite the contrary, the material signifier brings into sensate contact a great multiplicity of languages, ideas, images, and people who share only "partial connections."[32] The diverse constituencies are linked through the mediation of the national emblem itself. The content of the emblem, the white-robed ruler, can vary from person to person, from time to time, but its concrete physicality remains the same—the white robes—allowing for the experience of continuity and commonality in the midst of enormous diversity, contest, and change. The Moroccan population speaks different languages, dresses, sings, dances, holds land, and constructs houses in very different ways. Yet in donning the white garments and gazing on the white-cloaked king, the population has been able to experience itself as interwoven in a distinct political-cultural entity, a nation.

Durkheim goes on to claim that the emblem itself, the material center, "is not merely a convenient process for clarifying the sentiment society has of itself; it also serves to create this sentiment; it is one of its constituent elements."[33] The representation acquires not just the power of the represented "but the power over it, as well."[34] The material signifier comes in some ways to dominate the signified.[35] There are some limits in the degree to which the material signifier (the white-robed ruler) can dominate the signified (the nation), some boundaries that cannot be crossed without risking the monarchy's role as orienting icon. Still the limits are broad, and in Morocco, when something goes wrong, those surrounding the king are blamed more often than is the white-robed monarch himself.

As a national emblem, the white-robed monarch is a potent signifier that traverses, mobilizes, accents, and conflates the multiple referents that it signifies, drawing power from the diverse significations and having power over them as well. The registers of power in sharifian Morocco to which the king has preferential access are many. They include the state apparatus, the system of gender asymmetry, the military, the economy, sensate profusion (fine fragrances, sumptuous feasts, exquisite textiles, passion, and poetry), the power of mysticism, sufism, *baraka* and sharifian descent, the power of Arabic speech, the importance of genealogy, the potency of Islamic law and its undergirding in justice, the success of achievement, of being the one who wins, and the power of links to local groups and families, including links through multiple women.[36]

There is enormous diversity in Morocco and in the registers of power to which the monarchy lays claim at any given instance. Yet there are limits also. The maleness of the sharifian monarchy has been absolute. No daughter has ever held the throne. There have been no independent, ruling queens, only kings, and sharifian kings have been linked to numerous women. Power and ultimate authority in sharifian Morocco have been configured on the material constancy of the orienting emblem in the midst of ideational and practical multiplicity. Included in that constancy has been the maleness of the unifying image.

There remains a prominent notion in scholarship that political dominance rests on direct access to dominant narrations and to dominant administrative, military, and economic structures. Even the emphasis on resistance ("slippages, ruptures, disjunctures") often tends to assume a coherence of dominant forms from which alternatives and resistances are presumed to derive.[37] Certainly preferential access to dominant structures including dominant narrations is an important component of political authority, and the Moroccan king has access to many of these. But the point I am stressing here is that much of the potency of this national consolidation lies in the monarch's access to peripheral peoples, discourses, and symbols; that is, his access—as popularly valued bridging emblem—to the outlying, the marginal, and the aberrant as well as the mainstream. The monarch as white-robed emblem can traverse the multiple registers of power and mobilize them for his purposes by playing different subsectors of the population off of each other—sometimes mobilizing the subordinated in order to circumscribe the power of the ruling elite, thereby maintaining the monarchy's own monopoly of dominion. Uniting in icon while subdividing in practice is part of how the Moroccan monarchy rules.

I contend that in Morocco diversity, ruptures, and multiplicity are a part of dominance itself, which the king as orienting emblem can traverse and use for his purposes.[38] The white robes give him a point of entry into the sensate labyrinth of self and the sensate labyrinth of community. In at least some cases of political dominance, authority seems to depend on preferential access to multiple narrations and practices, an ability to physically, tactilely, iconically consolidate them on oneself while differentially mobilizing them. Here diversity is not endless but sufficiently complicated and broad so that vital human beings with their own perspectives and degrees of independent individual agency can convincingly participate in them.

In terms of post-1500 Moroccan monarchy, I suggest that dominance comes not from ideational coherency but rather from effective *emblematic constancy* in the midst of considerable ideational and organizational flux. The pivotal question of political affiliation here is not "Does this ideology hold?" (the sharifian monarchy tapped numerous ideologies) but rather "Does this image fit?" which allowed for enormous diversity to be channeled through and mediated on the white-cloaked reigning king. The emblematic center, the white-cloaked monarchy, has remained materially constant, while the ideational content with which the monarchy is endowed at any moment by any given constituency, such as military conqueror or persona of justice, has been subject to considerable alteration. The magic of this notion is that the emblematic position of the monarchy (vitally renewed in popular performances) gives the ruler preferential access to multiple peoples and multiple registers of power that he can pragmatically mobilize for his own purposes.

The ability to unify a diverse and sometimes oppositional

population on itself as common emblem is part of the reason the Moroccan monarchy survived the centuries that followed. Al-Mansur died in a wave of bubonic plague that struck Marrakesh in 1603. The Sa'di dynasty itself did not last, nor did al-Mansur's magnificent stage. The Incomparable Palace so lavishly built was destroyed, its stones used for other palaces and places. What remained was the performance. The Prophet's Birthday continued to be held in varied and converging forms in the national center and in its galactic sites throughout the land. The performance recreated, through people's own bodies, a benevolent image of the white-cloaked monarchy, dispersing and diffusing that image in ways, as Foucault has powerfully argued, that undergird central authority by making it no longer simply exterior and coercive but interior, intimate, and productive as well.[39]

Another sharifian dynasty, the 'Alawi, with even stronger claims to descent from the Prophet Muhammad, came to the fore in 1666 and remains in power to this day. The 'Alawis continued the national celebrations of the Prophet's Birthday, recreating and revitalizing the performative mechanism of renewal that al-Mansur so effectively had built. The 'Alawis also elaborated a second national performance, the Great Sacrifice, which made the monarch's reenactment of Abraham's sacrifice essential to the good of the nation. Again the performance was held at the national center and at local sites throughout the land, again the performance pivoted around the king and men dressed like him in the simple white robes of honor and faith.[40]

The symbolic strength of the monarchy and its ability to mobilize a diversified population around itself and to set different constituencies against each other have helped it to survive and were crucial factors in Morocco's ability to resist western assault. Morocco was the last North African country to be colonized by the French (eighty-two years after Algeria, thirty-one years after Tunisia) and the first to receive its independence. Morocco became a French protectorate in 1912, but parts of the countryside remained outside of French control until 1933. Morocco gained its independence in 1956. The early postcolonial era was characterized by the interplay of a population pulled apart by practical, ideological, and institutional diversity and a nation held together by the emblematic potency of its white-robed king. I set this complicated history aside and jump to a dramatic reenactment of the nation.

THE 1993 PROPHET'S BIRTHDAY CELEBRATION

On the eve of 30 August 1993, Hasan II, the current king of Morocco, held so monumental a reenactment of the Prophet's Birthday in such a spectacular place that al-Mansur's celebration 400 years earlier provides a ready comparison. Like al-Mansur, Hasan II was trying—in performance—to restage the nation, to revise the constituency directly covered by the white robes of authority and faith. He was also, like al-Mansur, inaugurating the new national stage he proudly had built. It is important to distinguish alterations in the performance itself from the space where it occurred, the lavish mosque in Casablanca bay. In 1993, Hasan II, like al-Mansur in 1593, implemented an innovative performance of the Prophet's Birthday to try to reconfigure the vision and version of nation (and thereby resecure his own place in it). It was also an occasion to inaugurate a distinctive building that he had made in his own honor, like the Incomparable Palace—the Hasan II Mosque. First we look at the stage, the new mosque, and then at the performative reconfiguration itself.[41]

The Hasan II Mosque

The new mosque can be seen as a monument built by the people of the Moroccan nation through the demands and the auspices of the reigning king to honor the Prophet Muhammad and Islam. And to some degree it is that. But the mosque is also a marker of Hasan II. It carries his name, and the king oversaw every detail of its building. The mosque was in part an attempt to spatially affect the king's place in history, by breaking with history. Mosques in Morocco do not, as a rule, carry an individual king's name. The king is an aging man who is concerned about his historical legacy.[42]

The mosque was also an attempt to address three points of strain in Morocco: (1) the unemployed and the economically and politically dislocated, especially those in the major cities, the greatest number of whom live in Casablanca, a commercial and industrial city; (2) the *ikhwan,* the brothers, as they are typically called in Morocco (or *ikhwan al-muslimin,* the Muslim Brothers), people who emphasize a return to what they regard as Muslim essentials (most members of the *ikhwan* tend to regard dominant forms of faith and politics in Morocco as spurious and seek to change them);[43] (3) women and men in Morocco's cities and rural areas who are pressing for systematic changes in the legal and cultural renderings of the female in Morocco, specifically, for transformations in the family code of law written in 1957 to bring it more in line with what they understand as the basic guarantee of equality for male and female existing in the Koran and in the 1961 Moroccan Constitution. These three categories of people represent different constituencies whose support for and critique of the political system stretch across different ranges. But in some ways, the king's building of the mosque and performative innovation were designed to address all three.

Soliciting Hasan II inaugurated the mosque on 8 July 1988 by calling for a forty-day popular subscription drive (which actually lasted for over five years). On national television, the king delivered a poignant speech inviting everyone to participate in the building of a great mosque in the waters of Casablanca that would be one of the wonders of the world. Such participation, he assured, would allow every Moroccan to fulfill the *hadith:* "For he who builds a mosque where the name of God is called on, the Most High will build for him a place in paradise." Every contribution would be accepted, the king announced, "even if only a dirham," and would help build for oneself a place in paradise.[44]

The call was noble, the perspective of "even a dirham" (about thirteen cents, at that time) was laudable, but the organizational tactics of collection were in some cases severe. During the first forty days' subscription, people were often strong-armed into making donations. With obvious pressure from above, people at different levels of the Ministry of Interior sometimes overstepped their bounds in persuading people to give voluntary donations. I was in Morocco during this period and know of representatives of foreign corporations who found themselves in jail because their corporations had not yet contributed.[45]

Moroccans too were pushed. This was one gift tax from which Morocco's powerful families were not excluded. On the contrary, they were expected to contribute a fair share. The zeal of collection in some sectors seemed to push the monarchy's credibility to the point of danger. A number of people inside and outside the system expressed the notion that "this time he has gone too far."[46] But a year later, when I returned to Morocco, some of the resentment had eased. Some Moroccans seemed to be taking a more wait-and-see attitude; others, including a few who, the year earlier, had described themselves as having been coerced into giving, now began to look on the mosque and their gift with a certain amount of pride. Not everyone participated in the reversal, just as not everyone had participated in the initial critique, but there was a change.

Over the years, the mosque was built in stops and starts. Apparently no one in the king's entourage had realized just how expensive the construction was going to be, and the call for contributions continued. Still, the mosque began to go up in the bay of Casablanca. It was huge. It was riveting.

CONSTRUCTION, ECONOMY, AND HOPED-FOR RECUPERATIVE SPACE While the king phrased the choice of Casablanca in terms of the Koranic image that the "throne of God is on the water," the choice was economic as well. Casablanca is the industrial, commercial, banking, and transportation center of the nation, where the largest number of employed and unemployed live, a huge teeming city with most of the population under the age of twenty. Except for a few areas of the Rif,

Casablanca may well be the place where the king has access to the least intrinsic credit, especially among certain subsectors of youth who in the practice of their everyday lives are confronted with the hardship of unemployment. Major bread riots broke out in Casablanca in the 1980s when the price of bread was increased.[47] The selection of Casablanca was an attempt to create jobs and bolster the economy as well as an attempt to create an icon and a place of systematic experience that could make for more recuperative connections between the monarch and Casablanca's population.

For five years the mosque provided jobs and income. Approximately 35,000 people were employed in the building (25,000 laborers and 10,000 artisans). The marble and stonework alone took 16 million workhours to complete. The mosque required basic unskilled labor—old men pushing wheelbarrows back and forth—as well as fine artisans who carried out the work of *zillij* (mosaic tilework) and stucco. Many hoped that the international publicity about the mosque (including the opening night gala) would serve as an advertisement for the skill of Moroccan workers and bring them employment elsewhere in the burgeoning international market in mosque building.[48] That employment was hoped for because when the mosque was finished, the employment it had provided also stopped.

Increased tourist trade, international and national, was another goal of the mosque builders. Previously, Casablanca had nothing distinctly its own to captivate tourists. While Fez, Rabat, and Marrakesh are ancient cities with a plethora of exquisite sites, Casablanca is mostly a twentieth-century colonial creation, an industrial commercial center with few distinctive aesthetic markers. Tourists are often disappointed; many have seen the Bogart and Bergman film and expect to find something of that world in Casablanca but do not.[49]

The king hoped that the mosque would provide Casablanca with a monumental place for enchanted gazing and that the people who run hotels, restaurants, and grocery stores in Casablanca would feel its impact. He also hoped to create a benevolent national and sacred space in his name in Casablanca. The king could hardly build another palace; seventeen palaces distributed around the countryside are quite enough, one would suppose, for any man. And although the king sometimes uses the palaces as national gathering places, those occasions are not many.[50] Morocco's population, especially in Casablanca, is becoming ever younger and has a shorter-term memory than of old. The king needed a more regenerative national space to which the people of Casablanca could connect. He hoped the mosque would be that space—that it would become a source of pride, income, and collective identity for Casablancans, as the Eiffel Tower is for Parisians and the Statue of Liberty for New Yorkers. He hoped that people would be drawn to it, that they would come to use it as a place for picnics and prayers, a place in which they would see something of themselves and what they most valued.

But, of course, popular resonance was precisely the dimension of the Casablanca mosque that the king could least control. He could build the mosque, orchestrate the initial performance in it, bus people to it, and hope that he had constructed performance and place in ways that the population found compelling. But he could not determine the resonance of the space within the interior lives of individuals. That was for them to decide.

MONUMENTAL SPACE In terms of size, the mosque competes for aggrandized place in the international arena. The main floor covers 20,000 square meters.[51] Combining the main floor with mezzanines and adjoining courtyards, over 100,000 people can gather there for prayer. From the beginning, the mosque was advertised as the biggest mosque outside the Muslim holy places of the Hijaz. Casablanca's mosque ranks second in size only to the Great Mosque of Mecca, the center of worldwide prayer and pilgrimage, the center of the Muslim faith. It would have been vastly inappropriate, indeed somewhat blasphemous (as well as incredibly expensive), to even have considered building the Casablanca mosque larger than that of Mecca and apparently that possibility was not put forward.

But the Casablanca mosque is higher than the Great Mosque of Mecca. The Hasan II minaret reaches 190.5 meters into the sky (625 feet), which is twice as high as the minaret of the Great Mosque of Mecca (89 meters high, 292 feet). Indeed it is higher than any other religious edifice in the world (higher than the Basilica of Rome, the spires of Chartres cathedral, the Taj Mahal). This was no accident. Hasan II intentionally competed for celestial space in order to validate his religious and worldly regime.

In Morocco, the height comparison with the Great Mosque of Mecca received little play. It was not much publicized and certainly there was no gloating that "we beat Mecca by 333 feet (101.5 meters)," which would have been inappropriate for Moroccan Muslims (98 percent of the population). The king did not publicize this comparison in Morocco, yet he did choose to make his minaret higher than that of Mecca and all other religious structures in the world.[52]

AESTHETICS The mosque literally rises from Moroccan soil. The king used a build-and-buy-at-home economic policy so that almost all of the materials and the workers came from Morocco.[53] Moroccan marble and granite weighing 25,000 tons cover the mosque's floors, wall facings, and 2,500 columns. In the search for marble and granite of sufficient quality, 300,000 tons were gathered and then discarded to glean the 65,000 tons of superior stone from which the 25,000 tons of finished work for the mosque were carved.

Magnificent arches, adorned with *zillij,* carvings, and silver inlays, grace the interiors. Water abounds. The bay of Casablanca surrounds much of the outside, while 124 fountains are found within. Moreover, outside and inside can be brought together: the central part of the main roof of the mosque (a mass weighing 1,100 tons) can be opened in five minutes to let the sea air and sunlight envelop the 4,200 square meters of interior, transforming the central part of the mosque into a huge open-air courtyard, truly a celestial space.

Light from the outside is echoed by lighting within. Fifty

chandeliers of Venetian glass grace the mosque interior (one of the few imported items). The seven largest chandeliers each measure thirty feet in height and eighteen feet in width and weigh over a ton (ten meters by six meters weighing 1,200 kilograms each). The mosque glitters with their bright white light.

The minaret of the Hasan II mosque is built along classical lines. Its shape resembles the 800-year-old Koutoubia of Marrakesh. But beyond that, it vastly differs. A shiny all-glass elevator is mounted on the outside of the Hasan II minaret and speedily shimmers up and down. The mosque is run from a computer center housed inside the minaret, which is topped by a laser beam. For opening night, the laser shot its 30 kilometer ray of bright linear light steadily toward Mecca. The color was green that night, the color of the Prophet Muhammad.

INVITATIONS AND GATHERING Like al-Mansur, Hasan II invited representatives from the whole nation to come to the opening of the monumental place he had built: small-scale farmers, tradesmen, and religious teachers from Morocco's outback, as well as representatives of top international corporations, members of the cabinet, ambassadors, and prominent religious leaders. Most came. I was in the home of a religious teacher in the high mountains when the invitation came from the king for him to come and pray with the Prince of the Faithful, the chosen one of God, in the nation's new mosque in Casablanca on the occasion of the Prophet's Birthday. A messenger sent by the local *qa'id* knocked on the door (the message had been radioed to the nearest post; the messenger had ridden on muleback from there). He announced the news to Si Abdalatif.[54] A man of good-hearted faith and few material belongings, Si Abdalatif teaches the Koran to the children of this high mountain village. In the dark winter months, candles illuminate the slates on which these *tashilhit*-speaking children write and recite Arabic verses from the Koran in mimicry of Si Abdalatif.[55] There is no electricity anywhere near here.

Si Abdalatif's family and the village were awhirl with the

news. His eldest daughter rewashed the white robe that Si Abdalatif wears on all major religious occasions—the Great Sacrifice, the Prophet's Birthday, the Night of Revelation, the feast that ends the fast of Ramadan—the robe that he wore when he was married and for those moments was transformed (figuratively) into the reigning king.[56] The daughter washed the robe in the mountain stream, using extra Clorox, and hung it on the bushes nearby to dry. It became a center of conversation about Si Abdalatif's prospective journey for those passing to and from their fields. Si Abdalatif's wife baked special sweets and packed them along with almonds, bread, and cans of sardines for him to take on the trip.

The day of his departure, family and neighbors came to wish him well. He bundled his belongings into a folded cloth and set off down the mountain. He trekked four hours down the steep trails until he reached the paved road where he hitched a ride on the back of a truck to the provincial capital. There he found the bus, arranged by the Ministry of Interior, for the local invitees from his area. The bus set out for Casablanca. The men got little sleep for the bus kept stopping at improvised checkpoints. Never had Si Abdalatif seen so many gendarmes, the king's own gray-cloaked guard, who used their sleek black motorcycles as barriers, stopping travelers in order to make sure that those on their way to the king's festival were the ones he wanted to have there.

I heard Si Abdalatif's reactions when he returned to the village. Like many Moroccans, Si Abdalatif is a pragmatist and realist as well as a good-natured man of faith. The bus drive was long, he admitted, many of the evening's events were boring, the mosque was hot; yet there were moments of splendor when he felt transported to an incomparable place. "I have never seen such beauty, such grandeur, so many people praying together to God. It was an honor to be in that place on the night our Prophet was born and to be praying with *sidna* [Our Lord, one of the appellations of the king]."

The old *faqih* and the village talked of the performance for weeks. The event was not monolithically perfect, but it was singular, an event of a lifetime, an occasion of orienting significance. The villagers' talking about it, their praising it and critiquing it, was a way of making it their own. A number of people in the village had seen the ceremony on al-Hajj Umar's battery-run television (al-Hajj Umar is the village headman). Many were sure they had spotted Si Abdalatif. I wasn't. Since almost all of the tens of thousands of men gathered on the mosque floor were cloaked in the same white robes with white hoods pulled over their heads, partly covering their faces, I found it hard to distinguish anyone, much less be certain that the tiny figure that people pointed out toward the back left of the screen was Si Abdalatif. But it didn't matter. The point was that Si Abdalatif *was there praying* in the mosque with the whole of the nation in the presence of the king. Many people in the village *saw* him there and *saw* themselves through him there.

Performance

Representatives of the nation gathered and, through the use of television, the king effectively drew the eyes of the rest of the nation onto the event.[57] Men of the nation sat in the main space, on the mosque floor, wearing the white-hooded robes of national integration, looking very much like each other and like the king who sat in front, visually similar and yet spatially separate from all the rest. Moroccan women sat above in a balcony designated for them. Foreign diplomats (mostly non-Muslim) sat in a second woman's balcony, but there was no screen separating them from a full view of the mosque floor.[58] Some said the screen had been removed, others said it had not yet been built; in any event, the diplomats had an unrestricted view of the evening festivities, the mosque gleaming, the lights glittering, the king in front, the focal point of the national gaze. There was spectacular beauty, but not as in 1593 from multicolored candles; the Casablanca mosque shone with electric light.

Once the huge crowd had gathered, the performances began. There was collective reading of the poetry in praise of Muhammad, ancient verses, poignantly chanted and sung. There were speeches, readings, and recitations from the Koran and the

Hadith. Then finally came the selected poets. One after another three men stepped forward who had competed and won in the poetry competition sponsored by His Majesty Hasan II. One by one, each chanted evocative poetry that sung of the majesty of the Prophet Muhammad, his bloodline, and his descendant on the throne. Then the ceremony drew to a close. A fourth figure, draped in white, walked to the front of the mosque through the crowd of tens of thousands of men and stood beside the king. There were audible gasps; it was a woman.

A friend of mine, a highly educated Moroccan woman who was watching the ceremony on television at home, gasped as the woman began to speak. (Women do not speak in front of mosques filled with men in Morocco.) What was the king doing? What would the fundamentalists in Morocco and in Algeria do and say? Would there be a backlash? My friend could not bear the tension as the poet continued to speak and turned off the television. She went to bed and tried to sleep, deciding to wait until morning to see what the repercussions had been.[59]

A high official in the audience told me that his first reaction was: "His Majesty has lost his senses." But as the exquisite words about the Prophet began to fill the air, he sat back thinking, "His Majesty is very, very smart." And the white-cloaked woman, on whom the whole of the nation was gazing, recited in strong voice the beautiful words she had written of faith in Muhammad, Islam, and the Prophet's blood descendant ruler who occupied the central throne. Then the king took the floor and brought the evening's festivities to an end.

This momentous event, this high occasion of the nation gathered in glittering unity had as its penultimate event a white-cloaked woman taking center stage and focusing national attention on the Prophet through her image and her words. She wore white cloaks, not precisely the robes of the men and the king, but sufficiently close so that the message was clear. She too was a part of faith and citizenry. She too was a part of the white-robed body of nation.

MUSLIM BROTHERS In attempting to reform the national body the king is trying, I believe, to rally broad-reaching popular sentiment for an expansive form of Islam in order to counter Islamic fundamentalists who claim a single pathway, a cornered truth. The *ikhwan* (brothers) are striving to implement their version of nation, which puts them at the center. They call for a political configuration of justice in which there would be no monarch, no single man who would be superior a priori to all others. Rather, all men who hold the truth, the brothers, would be equal and would make decisions in compliance with the edicts of Islam (as if there were no ambiguity there). In the *ikhwan* national system, all men would be equal, although women would not be. Women in this ideology and practice are highly valued; they have their proper fields of operation, particularly in the birthing of children and the care of the family. But they are to be circumscribed from other domains, especially from the centers of public politics and the collective sacred. Moroccan *ikhwan* seek to occupy nationalist space, and in this quest they have two main foci of attack: the space of the monarch and the space of women.

The *ikhwan* in Morocco do not have the widespread popularity or credibility that they have in some other places in the North Africa and the Middle East. Certainly, there are active participants in the movement, people who find within it compelling models of Islam, justice, personal identity, and national participation, especially certain sectors of educated youth. But widescale popular sentiment is not allied with it. In Morocco, those who call themselves the *ikhwan* comprise small, relatively dispersed, and for the most part noncoordinated groups.

Part of the explanation for this lack of a reservoir of popular credit comes from the regularity with which the Moroccan monarchy has intertwined itself with popular expressions of Islam. For at least 400 years, sacred performances have been the most effective means of reweaving the popular-imperial connection. The performances have brought the image of the monarchy to local bodies, lives, and spaces. They have successfully entangled the image of ruler with the hopes, dreams, and longings of many of the individuals who are ruled.

In postindependence Morocco, Mohammed V and Hasan II

never forgot or forsook this basic connection. They continued to stage the postcolonial Moroccan nation in Islamic terms with themselves as central to it. The monarchy was made pivotal to the postcolonial legal constitution. But more important for popular opinion, the white-robed ruler remained central to the popular performances that circulated the image of benevolent monarchy throughout the land, an image that served as a counterpoint to some of the others that the population more practically experienced. Unlike Egypt, Tunisia, and Iran, the postcolonial Moroccan nation—while absorbing and utilizing all sorts of models and templates from all over the world—did not deny or forsake the essential framing and centering of its national identity in Islam or the essential occasions that bring Islam to the present through the joint celebrations of the Prince of the Faithful and the Community of Faith.[60]

One can argue that the political elite of Egypt, Iran, and Tunisia were so enchanted with secular modernist models that they gave the playing field of populist Islam to others who used it to rally popular opposition against them. But Morocco's monarchy never gave up popular Islamic space. Quite the contrary. For centuries the monarchy has been the central occupant and producer of it. As for the current king, one can argue that he was less effective in rallying Islamic space in the 1960s and 1970s and has been more effective 1980s and 1990s, but the issue is one of degree.[61]

The *ikhwan* seek to establish distinctive Islamic space, but the problem for them in Morocco is that the monarchy keeps visiting, occupying, and mobilizing popular Islamic space. The *ikhwan* therefore are unable to find a set of discourses and practices distinctly their own that unite them with the vast majority of the population and at the same time separate them from the monarchy, for the monarchy is embedded within those popular discourses and practices.

The 1993 reenactment of the Prophet's Birthday with its presentation of a female icon of Islamic merit and national significance was another move in the monarch's game of chess with the Islamic opposition and his game of using the threat of Islamic opposition, of fundamentalist chaos, to check other forms of dissent within the nation and to promote the playing of different subsectors of the population against each other, perhaps to the nation's, but certainly to the monarchy's benefit. Through the 1993 Prophet's Birthday performance, the king attempted to counter the brothers by rallying an increasing number of women and men to him, women and men who fear the excesses of Islamic fundamentalism.

In calling for a broad-reaching Islam, the king is rallying forms of faith that resonate with many within the population. In placing a woman at the center of the Prophet's Birthday, the king is staking the monarchy's durability on a flexible and inclusive form of Islam that has been a part of Morocco since the time of the Banu Marin, 700 years ago. Certainly there is opposition. But the question is, where does majority opinion in Morocco lie? It seems to lie with diversity and flexibility.

The threat of the *ikhwan* can be seen as the impetus that pushed the king toward an alliance with women's rights. For many who know the king personally, this alliance comes as a surprise. He has not—in many parts of his private life—been a great friend of the elevation of women. But one needs to see the move in terms of strategic power politics. The *ikhwan* wish to circumscribe women's domains as well as the king's domains. The king is in part protecting himself by attempting to maintain both, by stressing a form of Islam in which women's rights have a high priority.

POET, PARLIAMENT, AND WHITE CLOTHES 1993 was a banner year for this alliance. In early 1993, a popular petition amassed what is reputed to have been a million signatures. It called for changes in the Family Code written in 1957 to bring it in line with more egalitarian forms of Islam and with Morocco's 1961 constitution, where women and men are guaranteed equal rights. There is a large professional class of women in Morocco, including lawyers, judges, doctors, teachers, and businesswomen, who are pressing for greater rights and greater political, cultural, and religious say. They are increasingly joined by an ever-growing workforce of women. Garment manufacturing is the largest growth industry in Morocco; it employs almost exclusively women, many of whom are pressing for increased rights and representation. There are many others, women and men in urban as well as rural Morocco, who are supportive of women's rights. In some parts of Morocco women have long occupied crucial roles in the economy, and in some places they have held important roles in political and sacred life. For some of these women the 1957 codification of the Family Code of Law (a combination of Maliki and Napoleonic codes) took away rights that they had held for centuries.[62]

As of 1993, the national political system is responding in part. In the same year that the popular petition was submitted to the king calling for a change in the Family Code of Law, the first women were elected to Morocco's national parliament. It was the freest election to have taken place since independence. In it two women gained seats; they literally came to occupy some of the national space.

The relationship between national emblem (the white-robed monarch), the dress of men on key occasions (the white robes that visually unite them with the king), and the gendered construction of the citizenry was obvious in the postelection discourse. Part of that discourse seemed less concerned with the fact that women had been elected and more concerned with what clothes these two women would wear to the opening of parliament. Since parliament's inception, all parliamentarians have been men. At recent opening ceremonies, the men have worn the white robes that mimetically unite them with the king and with all other men. What would these women wear, as they entered what had for decades been an all-male national space? In the end they wore white garments but not quite the men's robes. Where women sit and what they wear has much to do with how people envision and construct the nation.

In the same year, a woman was chosen to speak publicly, sacredly, and centrally to the nation from the front of a mosque filled mostly with men on the occasion of the Prophet's Birthday. While these innovations, most likely, were not entirely controlled by the center, Morocco is a highly centralized and orchestrated system, and when changes of this proportion occur, one can be certain that they have at least been scrutinized by the monarch and most likely were set in motion by him.

The women who were elected to parliament and the woman who spoke in the mosque are exceedingly meritorious. Public discourse stresses their merit as the reason for their achievement (merit being the mode of access to sacred or political power that is least likely to offend those who have marked themselves off in the present as the "upholders of the tradition").[63] The two parliamentarians are highly educated women with years of experience in politics. The poet is wonderfully gifted.

Certainly these women are meritorious, but the problem with merit as an explanation for their 1993 achievements is that there have been highly skilled political women in Morocco since the inception of parliament and meritorious woman poets could have sung the Prophet's praises in central mosques on the Prophet's Birthday for centuries. The issue is not that these women had the merit necessary to occupy the positions they came to fill. The issue is why in the 1993 staging of nation these women of merit were allowed to hold the places that they deserved. It is the timing of the performance that is interesting and that I suggest is related to the influence of the *ikhwan* in Morocco, the Islamic Front's potency in Algeria, and the monarch's current understandings of where his base of cultural credit is most likely in the near future to lie.

CONCLUSION

In 1993, we saw an attempted reconfiguration of the nation with the expansion of central performative space to include women in it and the widening of the emblematic white robes to cover them also. Whether the alliance will work depends on coming events, staged and de facto. Change, like stasis, is always a gamble. But from my own limited understandings, I venture a few comments.

The opening of the mosque in Casablanca and the restaging of the Prophet's Birthday with a woman as central was yet another strategic move by a politically adept and culturally empowered monarch. As far as the performative innovation itself is concerned—that is, the direct inclusion of a woman in the white robes of community and faith—I suspect that it was a wise move in the current situation that potentially allies increasing numbers of people with the king, an act of mimesis writ larger. In some ways the innovation simply reconfirms—on the level of national high garb and national high drama—realities that are already in place. Women are crucial citizens of the Moroccan nation—its doctors, lawyers, mothers, line workers, accountants, scholars, air force pilots, agricultural workers, bankers, cooks, poets, parliamentarians, and maids. The performative innovation simply extends the unifying white material to an ever-larger number of people who already occupy the nation. The alteration in the national performance was new, but that change already has been accomplished in much of everyday life.

The forum that the king chose to manifest the change, the Prophet's Birthday, for centuries has been the most important mechanism of popular connection. The yearly performance—central and peripheral—has reproduced the dynasty's credit and the nation's consciousness in the individual bodies, minds, and lives of the population. Like reading a favorite novel, performing a valued national rite simultaneously disperses and unifies the Moroccan nation. The credit it produces is popular, portable, and unifying. Almost everyone in the nation participates in the Prophet's Birthday. It is performed everywhere in the land. A common thread runs through it that continues to reweave the nation, a nation that exists as Anderson has wisely observed nowhere and everywhere at once. In widening the spread of the national cloth, Hasan II has strengthened the nation.

But what of the mosque itself? Here I am less certain. What Hasan II has done with the mosque is establish a new national icon. Seven years of media attention and a billion-dollar fundraising effort have made it that.[64] Whether it will be a unificatory mechanism like the Prophet's Birthday and the emblematic white robes is less clear, for the mosque attempts to draw on very different kinds of credit than those that have sustained Morocco's nation and its monarchy in the past.

The Hasan II Mosque establishes a space of national separation and differentiation of the ruler. Instead of performatively merging the king into the image of Everyman, the mosque sets off the king as monumentally different. The mosque is singular, unparalleled, the highest. It is individually named, occupies a single stretch of ground, and cannot be transported to local peoples. They have to come to it. The mosque relies on heightened differences rather than obscuring likenesses to draw people to it. The mosque is an attempt to create a new kind of regenerative credit, a stable monumental marker in the name of an individual king. Foucauldian analysis would lead one to suspect that this kind of credit—nontransportable, stable, specialized, differentiated—will be less likely to produce popular connection and will be less likely to disperse, diffuse, and circulate a productive image of the monarchy throughout the land.

Still, new kinds of credit are always possible. They depend on popular reception. If the Moroccan population comes to frequent the mosque with enthusiasm and pleasure, if the mosque becomes effectively intertwined with people's most valued occasions, if Moroccans come there to pray, picnic, and celebrate and find it a compelling place in their lives that resonates with what they value as most important, then the national innovation of a monumental mosque in the ruler's name has the potential to become yet another element in the monarchy's rich "arsenal of legitimizing means."[65]

If, however, the affective connection between the Hasan II Mosque and the lives of individual Moroccans is not made, if the mosque stands frequently empty, if the population rarely and without much enthusiasm attends, if the population tends to evaluate the amount of money spent on the mosque over and against the amount of money needed to give jobs to the legions of Casablanca's unemployed youth, then a very different kind of popular evaluation could take place. The individually named national mosque—so clearly marked and materially differentiated from the everyday population—could become a ledger of accountability for the individual king, not, like the Prophet's Birthday, a mechanism for publicly dispersing a common image of rulership into people's everyday lives.

The Hasan II Mosque is a different kind of national signifier that reflects a different kind of national imagination than the simple white robes of national integration—robes that, to some degree on some occasions, have united everyday men of faith with the king and the nation, robes that through the king's own doing increasingly serve to unite women with him and the nation also. Whether the mosque, pouring its towering name over Casablanca, can become—like the simple white robes—a fount of popular credit or whether it will deepen into a whirlpool of popular critique, only the future and the Moroccan population will determine.

NOTES

1. I am grateful to the National Endowment for the Humanities, the Social Science Research Council, and Columbia University's Council for the Research in the Social Sciences for the research grants that allowed me to undertake this study during the academic year of 1987–88 and the summers of 1990, 1991, 1992, 1993, and 1995.
2. Benedict Anderson, *Imagined Communities* (New York, 1991).
3. M. Foucault, *Power/Knowledge: Selected Interviews and Other Writings, 1972–1977,* ed. Colin Gordon (New York, 1980) and *The History of Sexuality,* vol. 1 (New York, 1990).
4. Of course there have been resistances but resistance in Morocco is a complicated issue that I address elsewhere ("Death and the Female Saint," Frank Tannenbaum Lecture presented at the Forty-ninth Annual Meeting of the University Seminars, Columbia University, New York, 1983). Resistances in Morocco often partake of as well as confront dominant forms.

5. Foucault, *Power/Knowledge*, 119.
6. Ibid., 55.
7. Most of Morocco's population at the time spoke one of several dialects of Berber.
8. See Chapter 2 in this book by Mohammed Kably, "Legitimacy of State Power and Socioreligious Variations in Medieval Morocco."
9. Ibid., 23. Violence is often a part of nationalist movements, as we have seen over the last century throughout the world and over the last years in post-Soviet constructions.
10. Ibid., 24.
11. Ibid., 25.
12. Morocco's relatively sophisticated economy, based in sugar production and long-distance commerce, in many ways collapsed after the bubonic plague first hit in 1350. The long-term repercussions of the plague in Europe were the opposite of those in North Africa. After the plague, Europe's relatively underdeveloped economy went spiraling upward and started to expand outward. Iberia began attacking Morocco in the late 1300s. Morocco did not pull out of the crisis until the 1500s with the emergence of a new dynasty that rallied its legitimacy on the basis of familial descent from the Prophet Muhammad. See M. E. Combs-Schilling, *Sacred Performances: Islam, Sexuality, and Sacrifice* (New York: Columbia University Press, 1989), 103–56; M. Dols, *The Black Death in the Middle East* (Princeton: Princeton University Press, 1977); P. Ziegler, *The Black Death* (London, 1969).
13. Combs-Schilling, *Sacred Performances*, 135–276.
14. F. de Boeck, "Of Trees and Kings," *American Ethnologist* 21 (1994): 451–73; G. Feeley-Harnik, "Issues in Divine Kinship," *Annual Review of Anthropology* 14 (1985): 273–313; C. Geertz, *Negara: The Theater State in Nineteenth Century Bali* (Princeton: Princeton University Press, 1980); S. J. Tambiah, *World Conqueror and World Renouncer: A Study of Buddhism and Polity in Thailand against a Historical Background* (Cambridge: Cambridge University Press, 1976).
15. Sidi Mohammed ez-Zerhouni, *La rihla du marabout de Tasaft, Sidi Mohammed ben el Haj Brahim ez-Zerhouni*, trans. Col. Justinard (Paris, 1940).
16. Combs-Schilling, *Sacred Performances*, 129–74. On the importance of the "sharifian stream" that consolidated other supports,

see Clifford Geertz's classic, *Islam Observed* (New Haven: Yale University Press, 1968).

17. When the Saʻdis came to the forefront, claims of descent from the Prophet carried a certain popular credibility as did other criteria (knowledge of the Koran, Hadith, scholarship, Koranic recitation, economic success). The Saʻdi national staging of the ritual of the Prophet's Birthday helped consolidate these diffuse sharifian sentiments and cluster them around the new ruler and new dynasty.
18. Combs-Schilling, *Sacred Performances,* 157–74.
19. al-Fishtali, in M. al-Ifrani, *Nozhet el-Hadi; Histoire de la dynastie saʻadienne au Maroc (1511–1670),* trans. O. Houdas (Paris, 1888–9), 237–57.
20. On the performances in the countryside, see P. Paquignon, "Les Moulouds au Maroc," *Revue du Monde Musulman* 14 (1911): 525–36; A. Salmi "Le Genre des poèmes de nativité (Mauludiyyas) dans le royaume de Grenade et au Maroc du XIIIe au XVIIe siècle," *Hespéris* 43 (1956): 335–435; P. Shinar, "Traditional and Reformist Mawlid Celebration in the Maghrib," in M. Rosen-Ayalon, ed., *Studies in Memory of Gaston Wiet* (Jerusalem: Hebrew University, 1977), 371–413.
21. Tambiah, *World Conqueror,* 102–31. As Tambiah observes, "Although the constituent units differ in size, nevertheless each lesser unit is a reproduction and imitation of the larger" (115).
22. W. Benjamin, "On the Mimetic Faculty," in *Reflections* (New York, 1986), 333; M. Taussig, *Mimesis and Alterity* (New York, 1993), xviii.
23. Taussig, *Mimesis,* xviii.
24. On the importance of the bipolar division in Islam, see A. Bouhdiba, *Sexuality in Islam* (London, 1985), 30–43. In the practice of daily life there are people in Morocco who cross over the bipolar division and somewhat mute it, for example, women who have made the pilgrimage to Mecca and on their return dress in the white garments of faith and boys who dress in multicolored garments and dance like women before men. It is common in many parts of the Islamic world for boys to be associated with the feminine.
25. S. Buck-Morss, *The Dialectics of Seeing* (Cambridge, Mass.: MIT Press, 1991), 97. See also T. Turner, "The Social Skin," in C. B. Burroughs and J. D. Ehrenreich, eds., *Reading the Social Body* (Iowa City: University of Iowa Press, 1993), 15–39.

26. The white robes accomplish something of the same process that Anderson highlights in his discussion of the Tomb of Unknown Soldier. The whole point of the tomb is that the individual identity of the man who lies buried therein is unmarked so that he can be Everyman. See Anderson, *Imagined Communities*, 9–12. The donning of common white robes in Morocco also blurs individual characteristics and helps consolidate the collective experience and imagination.
27. In England during this era, rigid sumptuary laws elaborated class distinctions among the population through the medium of dress. See M. Garber, *Vested Interests* (New York, 1991).
28. Foucault, *Power/Knowledge*, 146–65. In this article, Foucault stresses the eye of the overseer looking down. Here, I am stressing the eyes of the beholders looking up. Notions of the well-tempered self are well-developed in sharifian Morocco as Eickelman has elucidated. See D. Eickelman, *Moroccan Islam* (Austin: University of Texas Press, 1976), 126–54. The idea of being in control of self and gaze receive considerable praise in ideology and practice.
29. Durkheim cited in M. Taussig, *The Nervous System* (New York, 1992), 126. From E. Durkheim, *The Elementary Forms of Religious Life*, trans. J. W. Swain (London, 1915), 263.
30. Taussig, *Nervous System*, 125.
31. Until the colonial period, the image of the sharifian monarch was not individuated; his face was not represented; he was not epitomized in coins, paintings, or distinctive coats of arms. The image of the monarch was collective and portable, a white-cloaked sharifian king who could represent the monarchy, the nation, and every man in it. The lack of human representation in Morocco's graphic art over the last millennium represents a compliance with the formal Islamic injunction that only God can create humans and hence humans should not illustrate themselves. Historically, the injunction carried more weight in the far west of the Muslim world than elsewhere. For instance, in some regions of the east like Persia, some of the finest Muslim art appeared in miniatures that represented humans. As I have argued at length elsewhere, the sharifian emblem of ruler and nation, performatively produced, becomes for many Moroccans a source of personal intervention in the world, a means of survival and hope, a personal-political fusion that makes the emblem widely compelling and effective. See Combs-Schilling, *Sacred Performances*, 129–309.

32. The phrase "partial connections" comes from M. Strathern's book *Partial Connections* (Lanham, MD, 1991), which addresses the organizational importance of these links.
33. Taussig, *Nervous System,* 126.
34. Ibid., 128.
35. Ibid., 125.
36. In sharifian Morocco, no particular male child had preferential access to the throne. There was no rule of primogeniture or ultimogeniture. The one who won the throne occupied it, and fierce battles between brothers often determined occupancy.
37. See James Scott, *Domination and the Arts of Resistance* (New Haven: Yale University Press, 1990).
38. Stephen Greenblatt makes a similar suggestion in *Shakespearean Negotiations* (Berkeley: University of California Press, 1988), 21–65.
39. Foucault, *Power/Knowledge,* 119.
40. For an analysis of the Great Sacrifice in highland Sumatra, see J. R. Bowen, "On Scriptural Essentialism and Ritual Variation," *American Ethnologist* 19 (1992): 656–71. For Morocco, see Combs-Schilling, *Sacred Performances,* 221–74.
41. The research for this section of the chapter was carried out during 1987–88 and the summers of 1990, 1991, 1992, and 1993 as the mosque was being built. I visited the mosque, talked to workers and designers, gathered written material from national and international newspapers, videotaped the king's speeches on television, and conducted interviews with over sixty people in different parts of the country (Casablanca, Rabat, and two rural areas). I repeated most of the interviews in different years to get people's changing reactions as the mosque was going up.
42. In life cycle terms, it is no surprise that the king is drawn to this kind of staging at this point in his life. He is nearly seventy and was quite ill several years ago. In building the mosque, Hasan II is trying to establish a durable monument that will renew his worth and bolster his memory after he is gone.
43. Outsiders often call such people fundamentalists or scripturalists. Like any group that consolidates interpretations of a broad-reaching faith, the fundamentalists select certain dimensions of Islamic practice and faith that they emphasize and systematically disregard others. See L. Ahmed, *Women and Gender in Islam* (New Haven:

Yale University Press, 1992), 208–34; G. Kepel, *Muslim Extremism in Egypt* (Berkeley: University of California Press, 1993); F. Mernissi, *Beyond the Veil* (Bloomington: Indiana University Press, 1987), vii–xxx; H. Munson, Jr., *Islam and Revolution in the Middle East* (New Haven: Yale University Press, 1988); M. Tozy, "Champ et contre-champ politico-religieux au Maroc" (Ph.D. diss., University of Aix-Marseille, 1984).
44. Televised speech, 8 July 1988.
45. Ambassadors phoned, compromises were made, and donations were given. The men were quickly released.
46. Interviews, 1988.
47. D. Seddon, "Winter of Discontent, Economic Crisis in Tunisia and Morocco," *MERIP Reports* (October 1984): 23–51.
48. Many newspapers and magazines around the world carried glowing reports of the mosque's opening and the Prophet's Birthday celebration in the days that followed: for example, the Tunisian weekly *L'Observateur;* the Spanish magazine *Hola;* the Mexican Daily *Excelsior;* the Qatar daily *Al-Raya;* the Yemeni newspaper *Al-Thawra;* the Egyptian magazine *Al-Musawwar.* For detailed coverage of the mosque itself, see *Le Monde,* 30 August 1993, pp. 1, 6.
49. The movie was an entirely American production. Conceived, produced, and filmed in Hollywood, it holds no relationship to the Moroccan city.
50. The royal marriages of his daughters have been occasions when the king has invited representatives of the nation, young couples from every province, to be married in the royal palace along with his own children. The representative couples came to the palace; the king provided them with garments, had his picture taken with them, and gave them money for their honeymoons. The young couples brought along entourages from their local areas. In these elaborately televised ceremonies, the king performed the role of father of the nation, concerned about every one of his children. Many of those who were married, as well as those who came with them, were dazzled by the king's beneficence.
51. An underground motor route leads to an underground parking garage for a thousand cars and thirty-four buses.
52. *Le Monde,* 30 August 1993, pp. 1, 6.
53. Ibid. The architect, Michel Pinseau, is a hybrid product of the

Mediterranean world. He was born in Germany, claims French nationality, and has spent much of his adult life in Morocco, where he has the official title of Architect of His Majesty, the King of Morocco. He has designed and decorated many of the king's palaces. He was the architect of the Moroccan pavilion at the Universal Exposition in Seville.

54. *Si* is an honorific title, a shortened form of *Sidi,* meaning, "Master, Mister, My Lord."
55. Tashilhit is the local Berber dialect. Three distinct Berber dialects are spoken in Morocco, but Berber speech in Morocco is not a foundation for a separatist ethnic identity. On the complexity of intermingling of Berber and Arabic speech and identities, see E. Burke III, "The Image of the Moroccan State in French Ethnological Literature," in E. Gellner and C. Micaud, eds., *Arabs and Berbers* (Lexington, MA, 1974).
56. Combs-Schilling, *Sacred Performances,* 188–220.
57. As Rosalind Morris argues concerning the use of mass media in Thailand, far from diffusing power, mass media can serve to centralize it. "Conjured Nightmares, the Ephemeral Weight of Political Tragedy, Thailand 1992" (paper presented 9 February 1994, Columbia University), 17.
58. Many Moroccans hold to the view, articulated in formal Islam, that it is better for women to pray in the privacy of the home. If women attend mosques (a minority phenomenon in Morocco), they sit separated from the men, either behind the men or in balconies above them. Ideally, the women's section should be separated by a curtain or a screen. Unlike men, women are not to pray out loud. The justification given for this separation of females and the suppression of their voices is framed from a male perspective. It is commonly said (by men and women) that if men saw women or heard their voices in the mosque, they would be distracted from a focus on God, a bipolar image of the sexes that al-Mansur's 1593 celebration of the Prophet's Birthday helped elaborate.
59. For many Moroccan women who are profound and flexible Muslims, extremist attacks on women in Algeria are a real threat, a near nightmare that haunts them with increasing frequency. But Morocco is not Algeria. In the days that followed the woman's speech, much of the reaction in Morocco was positive; people tended to talk about the beauty of the poem, the wisdom and

knowledge of the Koran that it showed, and the understanding of the life of Muhammad that it exemplified. There were some negative reactions, some who said that having the woman speak was blasphemous and had polluted the mosque, but those voices were, by comparison, few.

60. The Prince of the Faithful is the official title of the reigning king. The Community of Faith here refers to the members of the Moroccan nation.

61. Since the Iranian revolution, the king has been ever more adept at mobilizing popular Islam. He appears considerably less often in military garb, a favorite performative dress of his in the 1960s and 70s, usually worn along with dark sunglasses. The king now visually underplays his base in the strong arm of power even though he has actually increased military power during this same period (1979 to present). The king nowadays appears somewhat less often in French suits than before and wears the sacred and unifying white robes more frequently.

62. For example, see Combs-Schilling, *Death and the Female Saint* (forthcoming), on the women of Seksawa, who with the institution of the 1957 Family Code lost many of their rights to press for divorce and their automatic right to half of all the goods acquired since marriage. For centuries, until this postcolonial legal innovation, the women of Seksawa were seen as contributing equally to the economic standing of the conjugal household and hence as having a right to half the goods. The people of Seksawa have been Muslim for a thousand years. They consider themselves pure of faith. When the Family Code was passed, the men of Seksawa tried to protect their women's rights by passing ordinances in local councils that would have continued to guarantee women these rights. But the legal representatives of the nation ruled these ordinances illegal on the basis that the family code was universal and had to apply to all. In the code, men rather than women are guaranteed rights to press for divorce (in the law women have the right to divorce only in a few exceptional circumstances, such as the case of impotency) and divorced women have a right to only 100 days of support from their husbands.

63. In point of fact, Morocco's tradition over the last seven centuries has been enormously diverse and flexible. Hence those who claim a unified, singular, and unvarying Islamic tradition are a product

of the present, not the past, a new phenomenon on the scene as Mervat Hatem argues when analyzing Islamic fundamentalism in Egypt. See her "Thinking the Unthinkable: The Egyptian Islamist Discourse as a Stepchild of Modernity and the Nation State (1970–1990)" (paper presented at the Institute for Research on Women and Gender, Columbia University, 6 February 1995).

64. The billion dollar estimated cost for the mosque comes from the *New York Times International,* 5 October 1993, in the article entitled "Casablanca Journal, World's Tallest Minaret." *Le Monde* of 30 August 1993 estimates the cost at approximately $750 to $800 million. No official calculation of the cost of the mosque has ever been released.

65. Kably, "Legitimacy" (Chapter 2 in this book), 25.

· NINE ·

Themes of Authority in the Life Histories of Young Moroccans

Gary S. Gregg

INTRODUCTION

Discussion of Arab-Muslim political culture has a long and checkered history, its low point marked by Rafael Patai's still popular *The Arab Mind,* which goes so far as to blame Arab states' military weakness on infant care practices that leave their leaders more enamored of rhetoric than of action. Unfortunately, critiques by psychologists such as Ali Banuazizi[1] and Halim Barakat[2] have failed to check this sort of thinking. David Pryce-Jones, for example, opens his widely read *The Closed Circle* with a discussion of what social scientists have learned about the Middle East's shame and honor code and concludes that

> What otherwise seems capricious and self-destructive in Arab society is explained by the anxiety to be honored and respected at all costs, and by whatever means. . . . Consistent within itself, shame-honor ranking is unsuited to a technical context because it prevents reason being an agreed value.[3]

Certainly, if "shame-honor ranking" were "unsuited to a technical context," then Japan, long crowned by social scientists as the world's premier shame-honor culture, would be mired in technological stagnation.

In spite of the shadow cast by such works, the last decade has seen a resurgence of interest in political culture among academics.[4] This stems from a convergence of factors, including a growing use of cultural analysis in historiography and the increasing global importance of religious, ethnic, and nationalist ideologies. In the case of the Middle East, a deepening pessimism about the prospects for progressive change, coupled with the need to understand the roots and potential of Islamic fundamentalism, also appear to be driving this trend.[5] Ahmed Dabashi's *Authority in Islam,* Fuad Khuri's *Tents and Pyramids,* and Kanan Makiya's *Cruelty and Silence* develop provocative analyses of political culture, as does Roy Mottehedeh's *The Mantle of the Prophet,* with its effective use of biography and dramaturgic concepts to provide an account of the Iranian revolution. Political scientists generally have viewed Moroccan politics through the lenses of history and political economy rather than that of culture.[6] But John Entelis's *Culture and Counterculture in Moroccan Politics* and Elaine Combs-Schilling's *Sacred Performances* focus explicitly on political culture, and the theme of this book suggests a broadening interest in this framework.

In this chapter, I do not develop an interpretation of Moroccan political culture but offer, more modestly, some psychological observations I hope may contribute to such an undertaking. As a psychologist studying the identities and developmental paths marked out within the matrix of Moroccan culture, I view political culture through the perspective of individual lives and, in particular, of a dozen very ordinary young adults I interviewed in depth. These individuals describe often acute conflict over alternative models of authority, autonomy, and loyalty, which many seek to resolve by synthesizing identities that construct their lives as callings in the Weberian sense.[7] I believe the character of the conflict they experience and the synthesis they seek can help us understand how young Moroccans may draw on their mixture of heritages to reimagine political relations. Their shifting among alternatives suggests that great volatility underlies their often provisional accommodations to the partly modernizing, partly underdeveloped conditions in which they live.

BACKGROUND: LIFE HISTORIES AND IDENTITY

In 1987 and 1988 I tape-recorded life history interviews in Moroccan Arabic with nine men and three women in the Ouarzazate area, a growing provincial capital and tourist center south of the Atlas Mountains. In their twenties at the time, most of the interviewees had grown up in villages, but all had at least some high school education. I followed a study-of-lives methodology, eliciting the narratives during six to twenty-five hours of loosely structured interviews, which included a series of projective tests. This replicated research I had done with working- and middle-class Americans in the Detroit area. My objective in both cases was to study how culture shapes two processes emphasized in the work of Erik Erikson: the developmental tasks faced during young adulthood and the organization of identity, which Erikson describes as a system of values and beliefs about one's world, anchored by commitment to a vocation.[8] In *Self-Representation*,[9] which was based on the American interviews, I argued that individuals select a subset of culturally provided integrative symbols, mythemes, and narrative schemas, and tailor them to identities that more or less suit their personalities and life situations. Culture does not so much assign identities as require individuals to work within a particular language of identity if they are to make their lives intelligible to themselves and to their communities. I also proposed a model of the representational grammar that thought uses to fashion identity. This centers on the multiplicity of self-representations and on the pivotal role played by key symbols[10] whose structurally ambiguous, reversible meanings enable them to articulate contradictory identities and integrate them in a dialogic or contrapuntal structure.[11] The interviews I conducted in Ouarzazate are forcing me to modify and broaden this model, but they basically support it. Moroccan integrative symbols, mythemes, and narrative schemas differ profoundly from American ones, but the grammar-like processes by which individuals fashion them into identities appear to be similar.

Here I examine representations of authority in the life narratives. Because I could not guarantee the security of tapes, I cautioned my interviewees not to comment on the monarchy, the war in the Sahara, or the Muslim brothers. The life histories thus lack manifest political attitudes but are rich in discussions of familial, cultural, and religious authority. These discussions present a kind of latent politics, showing the models of authority that can be drawn on to represent or construct political relations. Just as I found these young Moroccans, like the Americans I had studied, engaged in an inner dialogue among multiple identities, so I found them embracing multiple models of authority.[12]

The life narrative approach thus affords a different view of political culture than historians or political scientists typically take. Rather than beginning from a description of the political system and tracing its features to their cultural roots, as Entelis has sought to do, or tracing its legitimating symbols into individual psyches, as Combs-Schilling has sought to do, the life narrative method looks from the bottom up, from the perspective of single personalities. This cannot account for, let alone predict, the course of political events, but it has the advantage of bringing to light a broad and complex field of authority relations. Analyses that begin with a political system and trace its cultural or psychological roots run the danger of highlighting only those prototypes of authority and resistance called into play by that particular political system. Other important cultural and psychological models may be missed, producing a narrow and perhaps distorted image of political culture.

In fact, I think most discussions of Moroccan political culture underestimate the potential for either democratic or authoritarian reimaginings of the body politic. In the following sections I present excerpts from some of the life narratives to illustrate the shifting and conflict among multiple models that, I believe, make for both flexibility and volatility.

AMBIVALENCE

The Americans I interviewed tended to construct their identities in terms of symbols, mythemes, and stories that refer to social class and race, about which they show considerable ambivalence, often shifting between empathic identification and emphatic rejection of stereotypically represented others. In the Moroccan life histories, by contrast, gender and religion appear as two of the most prominent dimensions of identity, both marked by a similar sort of ambivalence. The Americans made surprisingly little use of national identifications or civilized versus primitive oppositions, typically preferring to embrace and condemn contrasting lifestyles (for example, between ethnic groups, working people, and welfare recipients; materialistic businesspeople and spiritual New Agers, etc.). For the Moroccans, however, contrasts between French and Moroccan, Christian and Muslim, European and Arab, and modern and traditional ways of life frequently emerged as central themes. Certainly the fact that their interviewer was Christian, European, and modern heightened the salience of these oppositions, but after decades of ubiquitous European intrusion they saturate popular culture in Morocco. Most of the young people I interviewed strongly articulated what I would call secular and even Eurocentric views on cultural matters but with equal conviction voiced religious views that often echoed Islamist themes. Such contradictions, appearing as ambivalence and inner debate, encompass issues of both authority and personal autonomy.

Khadija, for example, struggled against her mother and, with her father's support, became a secretary and lived an independent life after dropping out of high school. But when she found herself isolated, confused, and under attack by her mother's relatives, she consented to an arranged marriage, only to rebel in its first days and get divorced six months later. She had returned to work as a secretary in the Ministry of Health when I interviewed her:

> It's like I separate myself into two parts, I become like two personalities, like there are two Khadijas. . . . Sometimes I give my imagination free reign, and I don't even live in Morocco any longer: I'm in Europe, living with Europeans, speaking French— no more Arabic. I'll forget I'm Moroccan or that I'm a Muslim. . . . I imagine myself at a swimming pool naked, *par exemple*, smoking a cigarette and drinking a beer. *Au même temps*, I think about Allah, about Islam, because at that time Islam affects me, understand? And I regret it: why did I insult Allah? It's as if I mocked Allah.
>
> At that time, the stronger Khadija is the one who's a Muslim, and she reproaches the weaker one who made that error. . . . When this happens to me, I regret it at the same time: I'll say "I shouldn't think that," I'll say "I'm Khadija, I'm Moroccan." I'll come back to Islam, to the Koran and what it says. I struggle, quarrel with myself (*kenser'a*). . . . This struggle makes life difficult for me.

For Majid, conflicts over autonomy and authority have focused on his relationship with his father. Known in his village as a well-bred child and nicknamed Nizam (orderly, disciplined), he did well in school and went off to attend high school in Ouarzazate. There he lost his way, he says, because he "couldn't find someone who could help him make his way in life" and drifted toward delinquency. When his father became gravely ill, Majid impulsively enlisted in the army, became a radio technician, and developed a strong loyalty to his commanding officer, who acted as his patron and protector. When his father recovered, however, he began a series of confrontations with junior officers that escalated until, facing prison for a second time, he offered to let himself be shot on the spot and talked his commander into giving him a discharge. He came home and got a post teaching elementary school in a High Atlas village, where living alone, he began reviewing his life:

> One night I was sitting on a sack of hay thinking over my life, and I found it not good. I was thinking about how I came into the

world: a human being was born, he came out of my own mother's womb, and he was clean. He didn't know anything about smoking or drinking or lying or stealing. Why have I now dirtied my head and filled it with all these things? Why didn't I stay like I was born, clean? I decided: that's enough.

I asked myself what to do, and I decided to become clean like the first time I came out of my mother's womb: I must start praying and devote myself to religion. . . . I must model myself on somebody who has good manners and all the rest and who can help me make my way in life and give me some advice. . . . I asked Allah to put me on the right path and take care of my affairs and keep me away from the bad path. And things have worked out well.

Majid's conversion reunited him with his father, but he soon had to choose between moving to Casablanca to marry the woman he loved, a sophisticated second cousin with a good job, or staying in his father's house in the village and accepting an arranged marriage to a stranger. He chose the latter, and now four children later feels he made a mistake that has trapped him in a narrow, insignificant life. When I left, he was seeking ways to move to Casablanca and work with one of the large mosques to spread Islamic education.

Hussein was twenty-five when I interviewed him and had been sitting at home unemployed since failing his university examinations two years before. Pressed by his father to get a job but rebuffed by the local *bureaux,* Hussein said he felt increasingly useless, angry, and depressed as he watched months turn into years of sitting *la khadma la redma* (with neither work nor rest). Long a nominal Muslim who believed that if he followed the dictates of reason his life would automatically conform to the ethical spirit of the Koran, he had recently begun listening to cassette sermons of Shaykh Kishk, the Egyptian Islamist.

Toward the end of nearly twenty hours of interviews, I asked Hussein about the poetry he likes, and two verses came to mind. "Only yesterday I heard some verses of poetry from Shaykh Kishk," he said, and gravely quoted a couple of lines that translate roughly as: "People flock to men who have gold/And say they are good men/But from the poor they just flee." This attitude characterizes our modern era, Hussein explained, in which "nobody will approach you or be your true friend" if you aren't wealthy. This echoes the anger he repeatedly aimed at the bourgeois, Frenchified elite for their contemptuous treatment of ordinary Moroccans, an elite whose guard dogs chase beggars from the gates of their villas. "And," he said without breaking stride, "there are some verses about gazelles, the pretty girls." His gravity gave way to delight as he recited: "When I kissed her and she kissed me/She said: You kissed my cheek/Don't be lazy about my neck." Then he recited another: "When I kissed her, she said/Don't go too far, it's Ramadan./But you're like the moon [I said]/And kissing you is worthier than fasting." These verses, coming to mind together, convey an ambivalence over the Islamist moral program and indeed over conventional religious morality that runs through Hussein's interviews bur rarely takes shape as a self-conscious inner debate as it does for Khadija. Rather, at points he enthusiastically endorses orthodox views of his religious, familial, and social duties, and at other points he voices the skeptical, sensual, or blasphemous sentiments of the classical Arab poets Abu al-'Ala and Abu Nuwas, of popular singers, and of others he sometimes mistakenly identifies as poets of the *jahiliya* (pre-Islamic) era.

Even more prominent in the interviews are Hussein's shifts between modernist and traditionalist views of the underdeveloped world he is caught up in. Officially, Hussein takes a thoroughly modernist stance: he depicts the traditional rural world as a static, closed one of deprivation and disempowering patriarchal authority, and presents himself as moving into a modern urban world of culture and sophistication. His childhood memories center on repeated beatings from his "despotic," "'Antar-like" father[13] and "lion-like" first-grade teacher. He says he feels crippled by the residue of "fear" these left in him, and while he recognizes "the father's right" to rule his sons' affairs, he insists it is a father's responsibility to "understand" rather than tyrannize his sons. But he also admires his father's strength, courage, honesty, and generosity—the familiar cluster of traits comprising manly honor. Developmentally, he explains, an adolescent wants autonomy:

> When a son reaches thirteen or fifteen he wants to take care of himself (*ykallif bi-rasu*). He doesn't want that paternal authority (*saytara abuwa*). . . . He wants a little freedom for himself. He begins to feel that he has entered the age of manhood, and he wants to cut off that relationship [in which] he is like a child.

At another point he says:

> A son always tries to resemble his father. . . . That's because he sees his father has authority (*saytara*) and has power (*quwa*), and therefore the child always tries to resemble the father—and without conscious awareness. . . . So the child takes on the personality of his father.
>
> But when someone comes to visit them, by car—and the father doesn't have a car—he comes in a fancy car, and his father is in traditional clothes but the visitor has come in modern clothes, in a suit, and he's elegant (*aniq*), the child no longer emulates his father, but that other guy. . . . He's attracted by the elegance (*anaqa*), maybe, of that man, and then maybe he'll begin to think of that man in order to develop a personality like his.

Two elegant urbane men have recently figured as models for Hussein. One is a wealthy neighbor whose client he was seeking to become in his quest for a job, a modern man with so much "understanding" for his son that he bought him a book picturing a naked woman on its cover, a request Hussein says his father would reject with scorn. The other was a law professor whose impassioned style crystallized Hussein's desire to become a defense attorney and spend his life fighting to restore the rights of the wrongly accused—before he flunked out of the university, that is.

This ambivalence over paternal authority appears in the story he composed to a Thematic Apperception Test (TAT) picture depicting an older and younger man (which I had redrawn to portray the older man in more traditional garb).[14] He began composing a modernist story. The father and son live in different epochs, he says: the son's epoch is modern and clean; the father's is old and dirty. The father has rejected the son's plans for himself, and the son in turn is rejecting his father's advice, saying, "You lived in your era, and this is our era." Then he shifts:

> But a time will come when he'll arrive at a predicament he can't get out of, and then he'll begin to think about his father's advice, then he'll understand his father's important role. Times change, but the ideas stay the same. If you don't follow them, there will come a time when you're brought up short in front of yourself (*twaqqaf qudamik*), and you come to regret it: why didn't you do what he advised?
>
> Whatever the son's ideas were, they mustn't be different from the ideas of the father. They must always be tied together (*murtabit baynathum*). If one cuts the chain of ideas or the chain of traditions or customs, you can't live, even if you live in the middle of a big city.

This story in fact reflects Hussein's own experience: when he went to the university he rebelled against his father's advice to stay home and take a low-level extension job with the Ministry of Agriculture, but he now has to admit that he erred.

Such reversals of values intertwine with his modernist outlook throughout the interviews, sketching a traditionalist view that associates the modern urban world with sickness, pollution, chaos, delinquency, and abandonment before cold, corrupt functionaries and unpredictably malicious *makhzan* authorities. In contrast to this involution-and-decline view of modernity, Hussein describes the tribal world of his grandfathers as one of physical strength, longevity, natural beauty, and security; as a world in which pastoralist fathers "hit their sons with the tent post," empowering them by bringing them a bride and giving them a meaningful role in the family. Hussein hardly wishes he could turn back the historical clock, but this romanticized picture of the tribal past lives on in his imagination, and his life narrative traces a movement that circles continually: now in flight from the disempowering patriarchal authority of the *qabila* (tribal) world toward the empowering enlightenment and self-cultivation of *hadara* (urbanity); now in flight from the disempowering bureaucratic and state authorities of the *hadara* world toward the empowerment and security of *qabila*.

Gender relations appear to be marked by similar ambivalence. For Majid and Khadija, this has crystallized in their inner struggles over the value of egalitarian relationships versus arranged marriages. Saïd, a French teacher and the most "modern" person I interviewed, debated for months over whether to marry his college-educated lover (a businesswoman in Casablanca) or the traditional daughter of a local landowner. Finally, he arranged his own marriage to the latter. Hussein says he wants an egalitarian relationship with a wife. He angrily indicts "our fathers" for mistreating their wives and idealizes the egalitarianism of the French wedding ceremony, with its emphasis on standing side by side, holding hands, and exchanging vows. But when he imagines replacing his father as his household's head, he shudders at the prospect of "policing" its women, railing that women have be policed because they possess instincts of contrariness (*ghara'iz mukhalifa*)—the *fitna* (chaos, disorder, rebellion) Fatima Mernissi has written about.[15]

Rachida, a devoutly religious elementary school teacher, describes how she fought at every step of her career against the men of her household. She repeatedly asserts women's equality in impassioned terms, insisting that a woman "has to be able to take care of her affairs in life herself. Herself! It's not the man who should be taking care of her business." Then she succumbs to a fear of *fitna* and says men should have authority over women because "there would be conflict, chaos (*al-fawda*), and things like that":

> If there isn't that hierarchy (*irtifa'a*), if the man and woman are equal, each one responsible for himself, there won't be agreement. . . . If one sees a modest woman (*mar'a hashumiya*), you'll probably find that her husband compels her to be a modest woman. . . . There must be a man there to control them (*sirhum*). If he doesn't, squabbling will develop (*ghadi ynud sad'*). Understand?

Presented with so little context, these passages may exaggerate the intensity of ambivalence, but they illustrate the chronic conflicts that many young adults experience. Their ambivalent efforts to fashion models of authority and loyalty show the truth of Halim Barakat's argument that we misunderstand the dynamism and volatility of Middle Eastern societies if we simply see change-minded secular modernists meeting resistance from religious-minded traditionalists and try to gauge the social bases and strengths of each side. As Barakat insists, the desire for change is nearly universal, with individuals struggling within themselves over conflicting values.[16]

AUTHORITARIANISM

A brief survey of the current political scene in Morocco, in which popular support appears split between a monarch and an Islamist opposition, naturally raises questions about authority and authoritarianism: must not this be a deeply authoritarian culture? A number of scholars appear to be pessimistically concluding that there is something fundamentally undemocratic about Middle Eastern cultures or psyches.[17] Some, such as Barakat and Sharabi,[18] point to the tenacity of patriarchal or neopatriarchal authority, which we see Hussein invoking in order to reverse the initial wish-for-independence theme of his TAT story. Others, such as Fuad Khuri,[19] point to the deeply embedded interpersonal game of becoming "first among equals." While Entelis and Combs-Schilling stop short of describing Moroccan culture as undemocratic, their conclusions imply as much.

I want to suggest that the studies of authoritarianism inspired by the Frankfurt School, and especially those by Fromm and Adorno et al.,[20] still provide a useful conceptual framework, especially if their more detailed psychodynamic interpretations are left aside as perhaps peculiar to the European context. They viewed authoritarianism not as a set of manifest political opinions but as a latent psychological structure rooted in ambivalence over obedience and rebellion that is resolved by loyalty to a leader figure and displacement of the originally rebellious hostility onto vulnerable out-groups. And they situated authoritarianism not in traditional social relations but in modernizing conditions in which the security afforded by traditional attachments has broken down and the new ideal of individual autonomy cannot be achieved. That is, they theorized that authoritarian forms of psychological integration are most likely to come to the forefront in conditions of underdevelopment that resemble those in which many young Moroccans now live.

In the more traditional agropastoral communities around Ouarzazate, authority and loyalty continue to be structured around three models: (1) patriarchal authority in families and households, (2) a Big Man patron-client system that welds together lineage and clan-like factions,[21] and (3) a set of egalitarian beliefs and practices used to create horizontal bonds at all levels. Patriarchs and patrons typically show tyrannical and benevolent faces alternately. They are expected to intimidate and inspire fear in their clients as well as in their enemies but also to moderate exploitative authority and empower clients who find themselves in tyranny's shadow. The horizontal models structure much more protodemocratic relationships and the spirit of the old "five-fifths" system[22] remains alive and well. Many rights and duties continue to be allocated by balance-of-power arrangements crafted by gerrymandering naturally unequal groups into roughly equal *ikhsan* or *'azm*[23] that share or rotate whatever is at issue. Irrigation and pasture rights, the formation of multi-family producer cooperatives, and the finance and management of village projects continue to be organized by these principles in many areas. Women also continue to apportion household work and leisure by a system of turns (*nawbat*) that recognizes their equal needs and responsibilities. And in this region at least, the role of the saint or *faqih* as neutral peacemaker and healer of relationships remains a highly salient and attractive model of authority and emerges as critical to the identities of at least two of those I interviewed.

This adds up to a complex field of cross-cutting prototypes of authority and loyalty, one that cannot be termed authoritarian—at least as this concept was formulated to describe movements seeking to build homogeneous in-groups around compliance to single sources of authority, typically by cleansing themselves of impurities. But it is also not a republican world as some colonial ethnographers liked to imagine.[24] The traditional North African world contains a wide range of both protoauthoritarian and protodemocratic models, and the critical questions concern how political elites draw on these in order to build a nation and how ordinary individuals draw on them to imagine a national community. Here is the crucible in which either authoritarianism or democratic tolerance might be forged from traditional prototypes that are neither.

Fromm and Adorno thus sought to investigate the creation of authoritarianism and argued that in times of social crisis, underlying or latent psychological orientations would prove more important than overt political attitudes. Their empirical studies were methodologically crude and incomplete by contemporary standards[25] but still led them to an important finding: a small proportion of those they surveyed appeared to be true characterological democrats, an equally small proportion true authoritarians, and the majority ambivalent and therefore susceptible, they predicted, to fascist propaganda. None of the Moroccans I interviewed were searching for a charismatic leader to follow into blind obedience and hatred of out-groups, and in fact the most classically authoritarian personalities I've interviewed were Americans.[26] But the life histories do show pronounced ambivalence over forms of authority and personal autonomy in all spheres. And they contain numerous instances, clear to a Western-trained psychologist, of claims to personal autonomy compromised by retreats to models of neopatriarchal authority[27] that modernist aspirations have pushed into a kind of latent status: Majid's, Khadija's, and Saïd's marriages; Hussein's return to the "chain of traditions" linking father and son; Rachida's return to the need of husbands to compel their wives' modesty. These are not authoritarian per se but show the pervasive tension between more egalitarian, autonomous representations of relationships and more potentially authoritarian models.[28] In the next section I consider the broad role of paternal and patronal figures in these Moroccans' efforts to "become modern" and then conclude with some observations about their efforts to synthesize identities that divinely sanction modernist aspirations.

FATHERS AND PATRONS

Most discussions of authoritarianism focus especially on its paternal forms, and recent Moroccan autobiographical literature depicts a land of tyrannical, if not authoritarian, fathers: the Lord of Chraïbi's *Simple Past*; the Haj Mohammed of Ghallab's *Le Passé enterré*; Hajj 'Abd al-Rahman's father Mansure in Eickelman's *Knowledge and Power in Morocco*; the fathers of Mohammed Mrabet and Larbi Layachi in the accounts they told to Paul Bowles, *Look and Move On* and *A Life Full of Holes*. Chraïbi, for example, begins with a schoolboy's walk home to dinner: "The Lord is waiting for me. His law is indisputable. My life is ruled by it." Twenty pages of beatings, insults, and stomach knotted in fear later, he reflects: "This man is essentially strong, combining the two factors that make for a strong man: time and forgetfulness. That is the way I had always perceived him. From that came the respect and admiration that I had never ceased to feel for him, the whole of my long hatred of him."[29] Such portraits appear to justify Sharabi and Mukhtar's attack on the "feudal bourgeois" family and Bouhdiba's critique of the "castrating" world of fathers for helping transmit antidemocratic values through generations. Without rejecting this view, it is important to recognize the ways in which it oversimplifies.

One morning early in our field work among the Imeghrane confederation,[30] I set out to conduct a census of a small Dadès Valley village. At the first house on my list, I ran into a tall young man in his twenties making charcoal in a freshly harvested field. I introduced myself, we chatted, and I began to ask him who lived in his household. After a few minutes his father arrived, berated his son for stupidly letting too much air get into the coals and sent him off to the house on a made-up errand. I assumed the real problem had been that his son talked to me on his own initiative, so that afternoon when I found another twenty-something son home alone and happy to tell me about his household, I kept putting him off until his father returned. When he finally arrived, the father sat with his son and me, more like a friend than a patriarch, I thought, and after finishing his tea said, "Oh, go talk to my son. He'll tell you whatever you want to know." As I developed friends in the village and told this story to them, I learned that the second pair were generally admired for their mutual respect, and the first father viewed as something of a crackpot whose belittling displays of authority had undermined his son's ability to take on adult responsibilities. As I came to know more and more families, I saw a much greater variety of authority relations than the literature had led me to expect.

The life histories show a similar range of paternal styles and debates over their merits. One young man described a bullying, brutal father; a few said they had stern, formal, principled fathers; and a pair depicted pampering, indulgent fathers. One had been virtually abandoned at birth and raised by a kind foster family; the father of another died when he was young; and another's father was a remote and ineffective heavy drinker. The numbers don't matter because this can hardly serve as a representative sample, but it illustrates the variety to be found behind the stereotype of authoritarian patriarchy. Perhaps most important, those who described more authoritarian fathers also had memories of them as warm, nurturing, generous, or funny, as well as recollections of protective, mentoring relationships with other adult men. And those who described more companionable or absent fathers had memories of abuse by tyrannical relatives or teachers. Fathers appear in most of the life histories as complex characters with admired and criticized qualities (much as they do in interviews with Americans), with their actions judged as they approximate more purely despotic versus saintly or prophetic prototypes. In fact, it is the contrast between tyrannical exploitative authority and protective, beneficent authority that runs so saliently through the life histories. This may form a deep current in North African culture, underlying the ubiquity of hagiographic contests between the power of saints' *baraka* versus sultans' swords and between the appeal of religious rhetoric versus political rhetoric that depicts the conflict between prophet and pharaoh.

Hussein again provides an example. As he stews in unemployment, unable to find a patron who can open doors to *les bureaux*, Shaykh Kishk's sermons have begun to provide him with images of prophets as ideal models of empowering authorities. Indeed, his knowledge of the Koran is nearly limited to stories of the prophets, which he enthusiastically retold, and he also takes special interest in accounts of ordinary believers visited by prophets who either heal them or empower them to defeat despots. He repeatedly emphasizes the moments in which divine figures appear so powerful as to terrify but then prove themselves benevolent, enabling the initially frightened hero to face and vanquish pharaohs and strong men of various sorts. Most important, he insists, the Prophet was no tyrant but guided the Muslim community with compassion. "Allah forgives you, and He wants others to forgive you. You have to become generously forgiving (*musamih karim*), to not be a person who is tough (*'asabi*) or selfish (*anani*)." He recounts a story in which the Prophet asked a new convert who didn't want to pray or fast to simply live among Muslims, allowing the man's own sense of propriety to guide him toward an eventual integration with the community: "And so it was that he began to pray and fast without the stick (*al-'asa*) or force."

Above all, the young Moroccans I interviewed appear to be searching for patron or mentor figures. For some, grandfathers, uncles, cousins, and older brothers have played this role; for others, a neighbor or family friend. Nearly all recall a charismatic or compassionate teacher who, at least for a brief period, inspired and brought out the best in them. But few have relationships of this sort now. I write *patron or mentor* because I believe that in the modern context of near-universal education and bureaucratic careers, the traditional patron role has evolved to an important degree toward the sort of mentor relation Daniel Levinson and his colleagues found so critical for American men's development. A mentor may play a number of roles critical to a young adult's honing of a life dream, entrance into an occupation, and consolidation of a life structure:

> He may act as a teacher to enhance the young man's skills.... As a sponsor, he may use his influence to facilitate the young man's entry and advancement. He may be a host and guide, welcoming the initiate into a new occupational and social world and acquainting him with its values, customs, resources and cast of characters. Through his own virtues, achievements and way of living, the mentor may be an exemplar that the protégé can admire and seek to emulate. He may provide counsel and moral support in time of stress.[31]

As young people look to the state and its officials to provide them with opportunities and guarantee a modicum of security, it appears that this ill-defined figure—benevolent but exacting, a lightning rod for ambivalence—increasingly animates political imaginations and debates about authority and loyalty. The mentor figures sought in the life narratives appear to transform traditional kinship-based models of patriarchs and patrons into relationships that are more characteristically found in institutions of civil society and that suggest more democratic conceptions of political relations. But they also easily metamorphose into charismatic leader figures, such as Shaykh Kishk.

SYNTHESIS

The life histories show not only inner strife, however, but potentially important points of synthesis and resolution. They suggest, I believe, that there may be a widely shared resolution that signals a major cultural transformation under way, in a sense, beneath the surface of the political system. Listen to how

Hussein, no radical of either left or right, described the identity he consolidated in his second year at the university:

> I wanted to become a lawyer to stand up for the poor, weak people (*nas da'ifa*)! It wasn't for money; I really wanted to help people. Like if a family was accused or under suspicion, even if they had no money, I would work with them. If a rich person came to see me, I would charge him more and keep the extra to help the others.
>
> My main goal is to give their rights back to them. And to have an innocent relationship between myself and Allah. When you do good with people, you do good with Allah. I don't care whether people recognize what I do but that Allah recognizes the good I do: that's my main objective.

This formulation does exactly what Erik Erikson says an identity should do: it configures the core tensions comprising his personality to form a role in society that recruits his personal energies to broader social commitments, thereby giving shared moral and political meanings to what otherwise would be merely personal conflicts. It also builds a bridge: it links what is in many ways a very traditional personality structure, built around the deeply internalized honor-modesty schema, to a modern career and cause. By combining courage, defense of innocent victims, challenge of corrupt authority, worldly sophistication, and personal elegance, Hussein constructs an ideal modernist image of honorable manhood.

In addition, this is one of the few but important points at which he conjoins his modernist and religious views, and it matters a great deal to him that his life's work maintains an "innocent relationship with Allah." It essentially formulates his profession as a calling, in the Weberian sense. I see this in many life histories, including Rachida's, Majid's, and Saïd's, if perhaps not in Khadija's: the construction of achievement and career aspirations legitimated as a religious calling. This is not the modernity of Goethe's Wilhelm Meister and Faust, the first statements of the distinctly psychological view of individual development as an organic unfolding of inner potentials. These narratives contain very little of the explicit rhetoric of self-cultivation so characteristic of American life narratives, and they are not modern in that particular twentieth-century, Western, middle-class sense that many are now terming postmodern. Rather, they more closely resemble the early Protestant notion that one's earthly life should be lived as a single good work witnessed by God and rewarded in the afterlife.

Robert Bellah has shown how the dissemination of the samurai Bushido code and emergence of new religious movements throughout the Tokugawa period facilitated Japan's capitalist transformation, as did the Protestant ethic in Europe: a broad diffusion of the samurai class's Bushido ethic and consequent synthesis of Shinto nationalism promoted a melding of modernist social ambitions and religious values, symbolized by the mission and power of a state headed by a divine emperor who would foster development at home and expel the barbarians from abroad. And John Waterbury has shown how the Berbers of the Moroccan Sous region, the same *tashilhit*-speaking group as those in the Ouarzazate region, developed a Protestant ethic–like variant of Islam as they became famously successful self-sacrificing entrepreneurs and merchants.

I believe this to be the underlying psychocultural movement political scientists need to consider: the transformation of the traditional patriarchal, patronal, honor-modesty schema into a modernist achievement-career schema, via the linkage of the latter to religion as a calling. The young Moroccans I interviewed are not seeking leaders to obey but mentor figures. They are not seeking an "escape from freedom" but a social and ideological framework of security, justice, and meaning within which to achieve honorable careers. For most, however, this means not the secular liberalism of Hume or Bentham but a modernist-religious synthesis that more closely resembles that of Calvin. Ernest Gellner has described this sort of "Weberian ethic" in his discussion of "Algerian puritanism,"[32] and Ellis Goldberg has drawn attention to resemblances between Islamic activists and Protestant reformers.[33] These parallels could yield yet another reductionistic account of Middle Eastern political culture, but they have important implications that make them worth investigating. Above all, the cultural synthesis of modernism and religion has a personal side, which appears in the form of a modernist achievement orientation, and a political side, which appears as spontaneous support for a number of key Islamist themes.

Models for imagining the body politic in more democratic, tolerant terms are powerfully present in the representations and inner debates of those I interviewed. It is a short step, I would suggest, from a religiously grounded demand that the state provide a framework of opportunity and fairness to a democratic demand for equal opportunity, justice, and participation in the decisions of the state. But it is an equally short step from constructing life as a religious calling to believing that modernization requires implementing the religious order on earth and cleansing society of the irreligious. On the question of which step young Moroccans are more likely to take, my small set of interviews provides no prediction.

Here social psychological models of authoritarianism may prove useful. There are several, ranging from the classic works by Fromm, Adorno et al, and Joel Kovel's psychohistory of American racism,[34] to the nonpsychodynamic approaches of Herbert Kelman and V. Lee Hamilton[35] and Henri Tajfel.[36] The theoretical challenge lies in linking the latter models, which provide good accounts of the cognitive and group processes that generate and amplify ethnocentric stereotyping, with the psychodynamic models that account for the emotional power of distinct symbolic or ideological configurations that structure and trigger this sort of thinking. Mottahedeh may have pointed the way by employing dramaturgic metaphors to describe how the assimilation of Iranian political events to the martyrdom schema of the Ashura passion play "moved great numbers of Iranians across the emotional barrier between the audience and the actors."[37] Group and cognitive processes, rather than national character, most likely explain the postrevolutionary rigidification of self-conceptions he describes: "Among every category of

Iranian there seem to be large numbers who see the love of ambiguity that gave Iranian culture a flexible exterior and a private interior as something no longer tenable, a freedom that history no longer permits."[38]

Caution must be exercised, however, especially in view of how easily social psychological theories can yield reductionistic analyses. If psychological approaches have relevance, it can only be in the context of historical and political-economic analyses, as part of an examination of how institutions of civil society shape local loyalties and of how political systems shape cultures and psyches. Traditional culture is not weighing anything down or holding anything back or rearing an ugly authoritarian head. It is providing a broad range of representations from which political forces may select, reject, and refashion models for building the future. Psychological theories may help understand how underdevelopment fosters authoritarian forms of personality integration but not for describing the weight of tradition.

Demographic conditions, combined with the spread of literacy, media, and raised aspirations appear to be creating the sort of mass of individuals that many scholars have identified as a critical precondition of authoritarianism. Perhaps most important, the declining ability of fathers to economically control and empower their children may lead to increasingly brutal but futile assertions of power at home[39] and to more authoritarian searches for empowering figures in the political arena. To the extent that the economic and political framework frustrates the raised, modernist aspirations of a growing number of educated young adults, provides them with little security, and confronts them with bureaucratic corruption and Kafkaesque threat, the authoritarian models will most likely strengthen at the expense of the democratic.

NOTES

1. Ali Banuazizi, "Iranian 'National Character': A Critique of Some Western Perspectives," in L. Brown and N. Itzkowitz, eds., *Psy-*

chological Dimensions of Near Eastern Studies (Princeton, NJ, 1977).
2. Halim Barakat, "Beyond the Always and the Never: Critique of Social Psychological Interpretations of Arab Society and Culture," in H. Sharabi, ed., *Theory, Politics and the Arab World* (New York, 1990), 132–59.
3. D. Pryce-Jones, *The Closed Circle* (New York, 1991), 50–1.
4. See, for example, L. Pye, *Asian Power and Politics: The Cultural Dimensions of Authority* (Cambridge, Mass.: Harvard University Press, 1985); S. Huntington, "The Clash of Civilizations?" *Foreign Affairs* 72, no. 3 (1993): 22–50; L. Hunt, *The Family Romance of the French Revolution* (Berkeley: University of California, 1992); B. Anderson, *Imagined Communities* (New York, 1991).
5. See Y. M. Choueiri, *Islamic Fundamentalism* (Boston, 1990); F. Mernissi, *Islam and Democracy: Fear of the Modern World*, trans. Mary Jo Lakeland (Reading, Mass., 1992); F. Burgat and W. Dowell, *The Islamic Movement in North Africa* (Austin: University of Texas Press, 1993); Hisham Sharabi, *Neopatriarchy* (New York: Oxford University Press, 1988); and Bassam Tibi, *Islam and the Cultural Accommodation of Social Change* (Boulder, Colo., 1985).
6. See, for example, A. Laroui, *The History of the Maghrib: An Interpretive Essay*, trans. Ralph Manheim (Princeton: Princeton University Press, 1977); J. Waterbury, *The Commander of the Faithful: The Moroccan Political Elite—A Study in Segmented Politics* (New York: Columbia University Press, 1970); R. Leveau, *Le Fellah marocain, défenseur du trône*, 2nd ed. (Paris, 1985).
7. See Weber's original formulation, Max Weber, *The Protestant Ethic and the Spirit of Capitalism* (New York, 1958), and R. N. Bellah's application of it to Japan, *Tokugawa Religion: The Values of Pre-Industrial Japan* (Boston, 1957).
8. See especially Erikson's *Childhood and Society* (New York, 1950) and *Youth, Identity and Crisis* (New York, 1968).
9. Gary Gregg, *Self-Representation: Life Narrative Studies in Identity and Ideology* (New York, 1991).
10. S. Ortner, "On Key Symbols," *American Anthropologist* 75 (1973): 1338–46.
11. For an analysis of self based on Bakhtin's notion of dialogue, see H. Hermans and H. Kempen, *The Dialogical Self* (San Diego,

1993). I have sought to describe the dialogical structure of identity by developing an analogy to tonal music, which I believe provides a more general model; see Gregg, *Self-Representation;* idem, "Multiple Identities and the Integration of Personality," *Journal of Personality* 63, no. 6 (September, 1995).

12. This complexity should come as no surprise, especially in light of works such as R. Mottahedeh's *Loyalty and Leadership in Early Islamic Societies* (Princeton: Princeton University Press, 1980) and of course, Ibn Khaldun's Bedouin versus urban typology.
13. 'Antar is a mythic warrior figure of tremendous strength and ferocity.
14. The TAT test consists of a series of drawings that the interviewee is asked to make up stories about and presumably projects important emotional tensions, relational paradigms, and developmental conflicts into the characters and plots. For principles of administration and interpretation, see Henry Murray, *Thematic Apperception Test* (Cambridge, Mass.: Harvard University Press, 1943), for the original test material, and D. Rapaport, M. Gill, and R. Schafer, *Diagnostic Psychological Testing* (New York, 1968).
15. Fatima Mernissi, *Beyond the Veil* (Bloomington: Indiana University Press, 1987).
16. Barakat, "Beyond the Always and the Never."
17. See especially Huntington, "Clash of Civilizations?"
18. Halim Barakat, *The Arab World: Society, Culture, and State* (Berkeley: University of California Press, 1993); Sharabi, *Neopatriarchy;* Hisham Sharabi and Mukhtar Ani, "Impact of Class and Culture on Social Behavior: The Feudal-Bourgeois Family in Arab Society," in Brown and Itzkowitz, eds., *Psychological Dimensions*.
19. Fuad Khuri, *Tents and Pyramids: Games and Ideology in Arab Culture from Backgammon to Autocratic Rule* (London, 1990).
20. Erich Fromm, *Escape from Freedom* (New York, 1941) and *The Working Class in Weimar Germany* (Cambridge, Mass.: Harvard University Press, 1980); T. W. Adorno et al., *The Authoritarian Personality* (New York, 1950).
21. Marshall Sahlins, "Poor Man, Rich Man, Big-Man, Chief: Political Types in Melanesia and Polynesia," *Comparative Studies in Society and History* 5 (1963): 285–303.
22. David Hart, "Segmentary Systems and the Role of 'Five Fifths' in

Tribal Morocco," in A. S. Ahmed and D. M. Hart, eds., *Islam in Tribal Societies* (London, 1984), 66–105.
23. *Ikhs* is the Tashelhit Berber word and *'azm* the Arabic word for "bone," which traditionally was used for the lineage and clan levels of organization. Among the Imeghrane, at least, there is a much broader application, which suggests they more abstractly mean "a social group, which along with similar social groups, makes up a social whole," just as bones make up the skeleton of a body.
24. Robert Montagne, *Les Berbères et le Makhzan dans le sud du Maroc* (Paris, 1930).
25. For critiques and reevaluations of these works, see R. Christie and M. Jahoda, eds., *Studies in the Scope and Method of "The Authoritarian Personality"* (Glencoe, Ill., 1954), and Daniel Burston, *The Legacy of Erich Fromm* (Cambridge, Mass.: Harvard University Press, 1991).
26. See chapter 6 of my *Self-Representation* for an example.
27. Sharabi, *Neopatriarchy*.
28. These interpretations clearly reflect a Eurocentric view that regards autonomy, independence, and separation from one's family as developmentally progressive and prolonged attachment and dependence as regressive. I do not endorse this view but believe that the struggle to modernize—that is, to break out of the kinship-based subsistence economy and into the bureaucratized salaried sector—creates it in the experience of the Moroccans I interviewed.
29. D. Chraïbi, *The Simple Past* (Washington, 1990), 1, 21.
30. G. Gregg and A. Geist, *The Socio-economic Organization of the Ait Imeghrane* (Ouarzazate: Office Régional de Mise en Valeur Agricole de Ouarzazate, 1988).
31. Daniel Levinson, C. Darrow, E. Klein, M. Levinson, and B. McKee, *The Seasons of a Man's Life* (New York, 1978), 98.
32. Ernest Gellner, "The Unknown Apollo of Biskra: The Social Base of Algerian Puritanism," *Muslim Society* (Cambridge: Cambridge University Press, 1981), especially 170–1.
33. Ellis Goldberg, "Smashing Idols and the State: Protestant Ethic and Egyptian Sunni Radicalism," in J. Cole, ed., *Comparing Muslim Societies* (Ann Arbor: University of Michigan Press, 1992).
34. Joel Kovel, *White Racism: A Psychohistory* (New York: Columbia University Press, 1970).

35. Herbert C. Kelman and V. Lee Hamilton, *Crimes of Obedience* (New Haven: Yale University Press, 1989).
36. Henri Tajfel, *Human Groups and Social Categories* (Cambridge: Cambridge University Press, 1981).
37. R. Mottahedeh, *The Mantle of the Prophet: Religion and Politics in Islam* (New York, 1985), 374.
38. Ibid., 379.
39. This theme lies at the heart of Chraïbi's *The Simple Past*. As father and son realize that the son has been lost to a Western notion of liberty, the Lord's actions become increasingly brutal and futile.

Part Four

PROSPECTS

· TEN ·

The Cultural Legacy of Power in Morocco

Rahma Bourqia

Political theory tells us that state power and control are established over society through various channels and means. Legal institutions, the degree of military coercion, ideology, the charisma of the leader, and a specific traditional culture differentiate one state from another. The Weberian approach has theoretically refined the nature of state control by advancing notions of legitimacy and the monopolization of violence. Legitimacy not only makes control acceptable; it also allows the state to avoid, postpone, elude, or set aside violence. Moreover, once the process of legitimating the state is established and its mechanisms are fully functioning, violence is paradoxically justified, and the system of control becomes a legitimate intervention into society. Thus cultural legitimacy becomes the basis on which the power of the state is constructed. By isolating the cultural sphere in order to examine this process of legitimation, this study looks at the cultural *fil conducteur* that has caused the Moroccan state to redefine itself over time, despite periodic political upheavals and the challenges of modernity that have led to a blending of traditional and more contemporary forms of power.

What kinds of imagery are found in the discourse of state power at the level of popular culture? The vernacular language conveys images of power that are part of the collective representations shared by the Moroccan people. These images are expressed in idioms and sayings loaded with meaning about state power and its dimensions in society. A Moroccan saying goes "Three things cannot be overcome: fire, flood, and the *makhzan*." When a person finds himself faced by an indomitable opponent, he will say, "Only God and the *makhzan* can defeat you." Other sayings such as "The *makhzan* takes care of itself" (*makhzan qad b-shaghalu*) or "We cannot match up to the *makhzan*" (*washntqadu m'a l-makhzan*) express the same idea. These sayings and others like them reveal a representation of power in the Moroccan *imaginaire* that endows the state with absolute authority and raises its status in the collective consciousness.

The notion of the *makhzan* and the meaning it conveys are still part of the Moroccan lexicon of power. While the word *dawla* (state)[1] is often used by the media and has become common in the vernacular language, it has not completely replaced the older *makhzan*, which is still used by people in their everyday language. Both words are used when talking about state control and the bureaucracy or when describing the services the state provides to its citizens, such as education, health care, and other forms of economic and social development. *Makhzan* and *dawla* are not only two separate terms; they are also two superimposed images in the collective consciousness. *Makhzan* is inherited from the past, while *dawla* is produced by the era of modernity. The key questions are how these two images have converged in the collective consciousness and how they are both maintained. To answer these questions, we need to examine the context in which the images of the *makhzan* and the state have been formed.

The accumulated cultural legacy of the Moroccan state is inscribed in the historical process that legitimated power, as well as in the mechanisms used by the state to appropriate important religious, cultural, and modern symbols. The process of legitimation draws its strength from the popular representations of power and from the symbols that arise from different elements of society. In the light of recent historical developments, these forms are identified as twofold: first, the scriptural and popular forms of religion that have engaged with the Moroccan state at various phases of its existence and, second, Islamism, modernization, and development, which are the emergent forces of the present era. The legitimacy of state power has rested on the management of these competing forces and on the appropriation of their significant symbols.

THE POWER OF RELIGIOUS SYMBOLS

Historical and historiographic accounts have shown that in precolonial Morocco, the sultan constituted the pole of the *makhzan* system. This meant that the dynasty and the form of government, although separate in practice, were tightly linked in a representation of power elaborated by historical discourse. Sharifism, the religious attribute of the state, was an acquired source of legitimacy beginning with the Idrisid dynasty in the ninth century. In order to maintain its legitimacy and to manage it as an inheritance, the 'Alawi dynasty supported an elaborate form of reproduction through the ritual of allegiance (*bay'a*). The *bay'a* as event and as written text carries symbols that reproduce a legitimate form power. Texts of allegiance draw a parallel between the *bay'a* to the sultan and the allegiance of benediction (*bay'a ridwan*) granted by God to the Prophet. The text of the *bay'a* reminds us of this founding event and of its sacred origin—that is, the advent of Islam, when Muhammad was sent by God as a messenger, thus forging a link between the accession of the sultan to the throne and the archetypal events of the *bay'a ridwan*. Furthermore, in the forefront of those who present the *bay'a* are those who untie and tie (*ahl al-hall wa-al-'aqd*)—that is, the elite of society, its religious scholars, merchants, notables, and aristocratic families (*al-ashraf*). The presence of the latter group in the ritual implicitly creates a kind of hierarchy within the *ashraf* itself, with the sultan appearing not only as a *sharif* different from the others but of a higher rank as well.²

The ritual of allegiance is also associated with a place. That place is Fez and the shrine of Mawlay Idris, which evokes the moment when the dynasty was founded. The allegiance of the people of Fez was considered to be the most important, initiating the process of gaining other allegiances. Fez is therefore not merely a city; it is also a symbolic place where legitimate power begins. According to Ibn Zaydan, historian of the 'Alawi dynasty who wrote in the early part of the twentieth century, the texts of allegiance used to be displayed on the walls of the sanctuary of Mawlay Idris, so that "people would benefit from their *baraka*."³ The *baraka* of Mawlay Idris was reinforced by the *baraka* of the texts. By bringing together sharifism and *baraka*, the historical discourse reiterates a configuration of power that integrates religious and saintly elements. The historical discourse also stresses the fact that the sultan is the commander of the faithful and is thus the first imam. In his person, the synthesis between *khilafa* (succession to the Prophet) and *imama* (spiritual guidance) is realized, a fact that has been a subject of debate between Shi'i and Sunni Islam for centuries. The presence of religious symbols at critical turning points in history and their reproduction give place and meaning to the legitimacy of power and continually restructures legitimacy in the Islamic field.

Moreover, in this representation of power we also find symbols relating to the sacred field itself that are articulated around the notion of *baraka*. In the collective mind, is not *baraka* a symbol of power in its most sacred form? *Baraka* can be defined as a beneficial force derived from a divine origin yielding abundance and prosperity in the physical order.⁴ The ultimate sources of *baraka* are the sayings of God in the Koran and those of his Messenger, the Prophet Muhammad. By a sort of transmission, God has empowered all the descendants of the Prophet and all those who are close to God (that is, saints) with *baraka*. These sacred individuals are able to communicate their spiritual potential to others during their lifetime and afterward. In the popular culture, *baraka* can be imbedded in words, things, or persons. It is also found in phrases that invoke the name of God, such as *bismillah* (in the name of God), and that solemnly inaugurate every act of a Muslim. In the past, customary law made use of *baraka* as a spiritual force in arbitrating disputes between individuals. Judicial oath-taking (*hluf* in Arabic and *tagallit* in Berber) occurs in the sanctuary of the saint.[5] The oath "in the name of this *baraka*" taken in a sacred place or over a loaf of bread—such as "I have not said or done such a thing"—is used as proof of innocence and shows the importance of *baraka* in enforcing customary law and in regulating social life.[6] Although *baraka* is diffused in words, things, and places, it is transmitted through a process of polar attraction whereby all forms of it converge around the sacred object. Some individuals are endowed with more *baraka* than others. Their sanctity is known through their deeds (*karamat*), and popular culture has preserved stories and myths about these exceptional performances.

This polarizing of sanctity in the sacred sphere is transferred to the political one where it functions as an additional value to the political power. Sultans would seek the *baraka* of saints, and ultimately they themselves would become sources of this *baraka*.[7] In listing the accomplishments of Mawlay Isma'il, Ibn Zaydan emphasizes the generosity of the sultan and the prosperity people enjoyed during his reign because of his *baraka*.[8] The historian al-Nasiri also states that when 'Abd al-Rahman Ibn Hisham became sultan and the people offered their allegiance to him (which the author refers to as *bay'a mubaraka*), the country enjoyed peace and prosperity; the rains came and prices fell, proving his blessedness to the people.[9] The *baraka* of the sultan brings rain, a highly significant belief in a semiarid culture. Writing about sultan Mawlay Hasan I, the same author says: "When he came to the throne, people were happy because of his auspicious person."[10] Thus, the person of the sultan is endowed with benediction, investing him in the collective mind with the attribute of *baraka* in addition to his sharifian origins.

This *baraka* raised the image of Mohammed V in the imagination of Moroccans to the extent that he "appeared on the moon," a myth that stays in the memory of those who experienced the end of colonialism. Mohammed V, father of the nation and hero-savior of his country from French rule, became the symbol of nationalism. In popular as well as in official discourse, his image was elevated to the status of sainthood. The monarchy draws the image of its continuity from the sultan's glorious deeds and from the saintliness derived from these acts in the popular mind, reinforced by the discourse of the media. Moreover, this saintliness is concretized in space: the *darih*, the sacred burial place, is a symbol of the heroism of a sultan. At the same time, the *darih* is an Islamic monument visited by diplomatic delegations and the general public. The image arising from these symbols is a trilogy of sanctity: great leader, miracle worker, and wise one.[11]

The sultan is endowed with *baraka*, which he transmits to his heir, who then becomes the one who inherits his secret (*warithahu sirrihi*). It should be noted that the notion of *sirr* (secret) or, as Dermenghem puts it, "la fine pointe de l'âme des mystiques du XVII siècle," or the spiritual center of being, belongs to the Sufi lexicon.[12] Here *sirr* is considered as the locus of the union with God. By introducing the notion of *sirr* to qualify the inheritance of benediction, this image stresses the bond between the sultan and his son that carries saintliness forward from one generation to the next. Thus, the presence of the king in a given place and contact with him are sources of blessing. His appearance is auspicious. Historically, this process has functioned through the integration of religious and sacred symbols. How has this heritage adapted to changes in the nature of the state, and what are the implications of these changes for the representation of power in the contemporary period?

DEVELOPMENT AND ITS RITUALS

Management of the legacy of power has to be understood within the context of change that has occurred in Moroccan society since independence in 1956 and its impact on the processes of legitimation. An investigation into these processes implies adoption of what Georges Balandier has called a dynamic approach. This approach takes into account the heterogeneous nature of a society made up of contradictory elements belonging to "different ages."[13] These various elements are incorporated into existing traditions and reformulated so that the articulation between the old and the new is not one of coexistence or contradiction, as Balandier puts it, but rather is an integration into new strategies. In the process of legitimation, these elements of "different ages" constitute symbolic references from which the state draws the symbols required by historical contingency.

Since independence, the Moroccan state has taken on the project of developing society in the fields of education, health, agriculture, and other areas. In supervising development projects and modernizing various economic sectors, the state has created an image of itself as the ultimate provider of goods and services in society. In the popular mind, the *makhzan* is capable of meeting most of the needs of its citizens. The state educates children by creating schools, offers health care, distributes land, builds roads and dams, extends electricity to outlying villages, and finds jobs for youth. Thus, a new process of legitimation through development takes place. This process involves rituals repeated in time and space that sanctify activities relating to development.

In their study of traditional societies, anthropologists usually focus on social, political, and religious rituals in their established form. However, societies have also elaborated political rituals in the "modern" sphere relating to modernity and development that sustain the process of legitimation. In a speech made after independence, King Mohammed V declared that "we have finished the minor jihad and are ready to start the major one," meaning that Moroccans had left behind the colonial period and were entering the era of nation-building. In using the word *jihad*, the speech evoked a notion belonging to the Islamic semantic field that was loaded with meaning. Jihad is an effort oriented toward conquering physical and spiritual space.[14] The symbol of jihad was deployed to insert the idea of struggle and sacrifice into the development effort.

State development and modernization of society are not achieved without rituals. The ritual of laying the cornerstone (*wada'a al-hajar al-asasi*) that initiates every state project and the opening ceremony (*tadshin*) that marks the start of operations publicly and solemnly stress the accomplishments of state power. These rituals are usually performed by ministers of state in an atmosphere of pomp and ceremony. The procession, the gathered crowds, the dance troupes, and the ceremony itself create an atmosphere that celebrates the achievements of the state. The gestures of the official state representative such as the laying of a cornerstone or the cutting of a ribbon are surrogates for the acts of a holy man filled with *baraka*. Each of these rituals is meant to impress, to demonstrate the prestige of the state, to exhibit its power as an initiator of development, and to crystallize the image associating the state with splendor and modernity. The timing of the opening ceremony often coincides with a period of national celebration, which vivifies collective memory and reminds those present that they share a common history. These festivities also endow rituals with symbolic efficacy and perpetuate a certain representation of power.

MONOPOLIZATION OF THE LANGUAGE

The state derives its symbols of legitimacy from different referential fields: religion, saintliness, and modernity. The deployment and use of these symbols is part of the process of monopolizing them. The word *makhzan*, derived from the Arabic verb *khazana* (to store up goods, money, supplies, or arms), expresses the idea of hoarding or storing up goods in a container.[15] It also suggests that the process of legitimation occurs by constantly renewing the contents of the container and by accumulating symbolic capital. The process of legitimation works through the appropriation of the language and symbols of development that imply an adoption of modernization as a historical necessity. The lexicon of modernization includes concepts such as development, democracy, human rights, and equal rights for women. Furthermore, the socialist vocabulary, which served as a defender of the dispossessed, is no longer the sole property of the political parties of the opposition. Problems of youth unemployment and issues of housing and education are also part of the official discourse of the state. The opposition parties no longer have the privilege of being distinguished by their language or by being the sole producers of a discourse of marginality and discontent. During the electoral campaign in 1993, the uniformity of jargon across the political spectrum undermined differences in program and orientation between the left and the right. This led to an inflation of democratic terminology ending in its own devaluation, creating a crisis of meaning. As a result, there is no consensus among political parties and between the parties and the state about the meaning of such key terms as *democracy* and *human rights.*

Moreover, the field of political discourse is regulated by the principle of inclusion and exclusion, which is one of the mechanisms of power. Among these various discourses, the discourse of the state is most capable of appropriating and monopolizing symbols of modernity and secularization because it is the most authoritative. In undertaking this process, the state runs the risk of assuming "secularization as a historical necessity."[16] This risk is overcome by means of a strategic dose of the language of modernity—neither embracing it excessively nor renouncing the right to adopt it selectively. From the state's point of view, too much reference to modernity might imply, on the one hand, a willingness to renounce the heritage of legitimacy, causing an outcry among those who defend that heritage; on the other hand, too small a dose would open the way for a militant defense of modernization.

RESHAPING THE RELIGIOUS FIELD

Because the religious field is contested space, the state refuses to yield its claim to it. The notion of "the field" as defined by Pierre

Bourdieu is "a space . . . in which a struggle is taking place to impose a definition of the game and the cards needed to win it."[17] Various Islamist groups have entered this field in an attempt to compete with the state. As Bruno Etienne puts it: "Although Islamist discourse is devalued, it has forced the modern political system to make readjustments."[18] Furthermore, the state is attempting to dominate this field by extending its reach, driving other competitors to the margins.

In order to thwart Islamist movements and to dominate Islamic discourse, some political regimes have attempted to introduce a "reislamization from above" through their systems of education. In Morocco this linkage has always existed: it was present in the traditional education system and became integrated into the modern state system after independence. Today, religious education is taught in primary and secondary schools as well as at the religious universities, and departments of Islamic studies have been created within the state-run universities.

The state takes it on itself to be the primary custodian of religion. According to the Moroccan constitution, the king is the commander of the faithful whose mission is to ensure that Islam is being respectfully observed. The management and monitoring of religious affairs are in the hands of a special ministry that supervises the mosques and nominates the imams. The state also safeguards respect for religious principles during the sacred month of Ramadan by prohibiting the sale of alcohol to Muslims and by punishing those who publicly eat or drink during the daytime. Throughout Ramadan, the king presides over religious talks in which outstanding religious scholars participate. He also is the patron of an Islamic-style architecture that expresses religious intentions in space. The recent building of the Hasan II mosque in Casablanca is a symbol of the splendor of the monarchy as well as an expression of its faith. The process of constructing this vast monument—funded to a large extent through public contributions—not only enabled the administrative apparatus to test its efficiency and the extent of its authority but also led to an important popular mobilization that activated the power of religious symbols in the public mind. That the state can readily assume the role of guardian of the faith is sustained by the fact that in Morocco, Islam is well-established as a referent of self-identity. There is no identity crisis in Morocco, as is the case in Algeria, where colonialism carried out a project of forcibly assimilating Algerians to the French identity. Although Moroccans find themselves within concentric circles of identities (Moroccan, Arab, Berber, African, North African, Muslim), the Islamic element has always been the core one.

The literature written on the various expressions of Islam has elaborated a typology of Islam: Islam as refuge, Islam as protest, Islam as culture. It is worth interrogating each type in its relation to the state. The process of political integration works together with the process of religious integration through the ulama. Although the discourse of the men of learning is esoteric and does not often reach the people at large, religious scholars have always been open to answering questions raised within the Muslim community. The development of the literature of *nawazil* (legal precedence) in Morocco and in the Maghrib is a concrete sign of the role played by the *fuquha'* in responding to social problems and in attempting to integrate new subjects into Islamic discourse. Using jurisprudential mechanisms, the ulama have come to accept certain innovations (*bid'a*) that are necessary (*darura*) in Muslim society. By developing these mechanisms, the practice of *fiqh* ensured the flexibility of Islam in integrating and legitimizing the changes occurring within the Muslim community.

Men of learning have always kept a certain distance between themselves and political power. For example, during the nineteenth century, intervention of the ulama in political affairs was confined to legitimizing the power of the *makhzan,* which solicited legal opinions concerning important questions raised in the community through the procedure of consultation (*istishara*). At present, the ulama are organized in an official institution, the High Council of the Ulama. Although their role as an ideological body is somewhat diminished, they still carry on their tasks at the educational level and are responsible for the training of youth in religious institutions. However, their status as custodians of the Islamic faith and as exclusive holders of Islamic knowledge has been overshadowed by the rise of new competitors; namely, the Islamists who contest their passivity in applying Islamic principles in the sociopolitical arena. Indeed, the Islamist movement seems to be gaining ground and invading the religious field, as shown by such indicators as the increase in the number of informal groups and associations with Islamist orientations, the widespread dissemination of Islamic literature among students, and the appearance of newspapers and underground cassettes. Its activities—thus far concentrated in the cities and in the universities—are a sign of a certain malaise of youth confronting problems of unemployment as well as a crisis of ideology. However, this movement is challenged in turn by the state as custodian of the religious field. Moreover, it is undermined by the weakness of its own internal organization and by the specificity of Islamism in the Moroccan cultural context.

The morphology of Islamism in Morocco is characterized by what we might call Islamist pluralism, where we find that different groups do not necessarily share the same objectives or hold the same political ambitions. Islamist groups reproduce a segmented social structure where vertical differences are often more important than horizontal similarities. This segmented character prevents Islamism from being expressed through a unified and activist movement sustained by a coherent social and political program. In most Islamic societies, according to Etienne, "the transition from the village to the city, from kinship to anonymity, cannot take place without problems"—that is, it cannot be achieved without disturbing the structure of society.[19] This rupture has supposedly created a frustrated urban population that is the best client of Islamism.

Such an assumption is questionable in the Moroccan context. Although the displacement of immigrants from rural to urban settings has created dissatisfaction, we might ask to what extent there is continuity among these people, bearing in mind they have carried with them some enduring cultural patterns. At the level of the social organization, we notice that the people living on the peripheries of the large cities continue to have organized links with their rural villages of origin.[20] Traditional patterns of social organization are noticeable even within political parties, where linkages among people belonging to the same party often evoke kinship relations and traditional alliances. This relative continuity of traditional forms of social and political organization inhibits the mass enrollment of youth in Islamist groups.

Moreover, Islamism in Morocco fits within what Mohammed Tozy calls *"neo-turuqism."*[21] Islamism, expressed through the development of formal groupings called associations (*jam'iyat*), is different from Sufism yet is influenced by it. Sufism constitutes its organizational and spiritual background. Abdessalam Yassine, a Moroccan Islamist leader, points out the difference between them, saying that Islamism is oriented toward political and social action while Sufism is not. Nevertheless, there is a link between them: "Once I met someone who said to me, 'There is a sufi master in Morocco. You should go and see him.' . . . I was associated with him for six years. . . . In 1974, I decided to do something to—how shall I put it?—to leave that ambiance of the *tariqa* and to take action. A sufi logic? It is true there are sufis—I think the majority—who have set a limit for themselves by saying that we do not wish to have a dialogue with those in rule."[22] The majority of Moroccan Islamists do not want to start a dialogue with those in power, and they continue to preach a return to the sources of true Islam. Their Islamism at this time does not openly call for a new political order, as is the case in Algeria.[23]

Through the medium of newspapers and the written word, the Islamist movements have produced public leaders known outside Islamist circles. However, no emblematic figure has emerged thus far. Through their writings and oratory, Islamist leaders stand out as articulate preachers rather than as political heroes. The process of hero-making does not occur readily in a culture where popular Islam does not leave much room for the creation of new heroes. In this Islam, sanctity was diffused among various places and individuals, offering a plurality of hagiographic myths. The impact of the *quth,* or the pole of sanctity,[24] was always confined to a limited geographical space and did not lend itself to the appearance of national religious figures. Furthermore, the process of hero-making takes place in the context of popular mobilization. So far, this has not happened in Morocco, where the state has taken the lead in projects requiring mass organization. Islamism has been constricted on all sides: by a popular Islam that historically has captured the collective consciousness, by the orthodoxy of the ulama as authorized custodians of religion, and by a state that monopolizes religious symbols and controls the religious sphere.

In sum, isolating the cultural sphere of state power and stressing the process of its monopolization and reproduction of traditional and modern symbols is not simply a matter of reducing its power to the content of those symbols. Rather, as we have tried to show, the complexity of the Moroccan state system, with its various layers of direct and indirect control over a society that constantly seeks ways to elude authority, requires a more refined explanation.[25] Throughout history the state has been continually forced to redefine itself by reinventing the cultural means of survival needed to maintain the centrality of its system of power. In this regard, the Moroccan political system seems not to fit readily into existing frameworks of analysis developed in Western political theory but requires instead its own distinctive paradigms in order to be fully understood.

NOTES

1. It should be noted that the translation of the term *dawla* as "state" (French *état*) does not fully embrace the meaning of the term in Arabic, which also involves the idea of dynasty.
2. See A. Laroui, *Les origines sociales et culturelles du nationalisme marocain* (Paris, 1977), and R. Bourqia, "L' Etat et la gestion du symbolique au Maroc précolonial," in R. Bourqia and N. Hopkins, *Le Maghreb: approches des mécanismes d'articulation* (Rabat, 1991), 137–51.

3. 'Abd al-Rahman Ibn Zaydan, *Al-'izz wa-al-sawla fi ma'alim nuzum al-dawla*, 2 vols. (Rabat, 1962), 1:27.
4. *Encyclopedia of Islam* (new edition), s.v. "Baraka."
5. "Le recours au serment consacre donc . . . l'autojurisdiction des plaideurs, ou plutôt il consacre donc . . . entre eux . . . le principe d'une véritable rivalité mystique, transposition sur le plan supraterrestre du litige concret qui le divisait tout d'abord. Au moins l'un d'eux va jurer; on verra bien qu'il pousse l'impudence morale jusqu'à défier les forces occultes qui constituent la *baraka*, influence privilégiée du marabout, l'adversaire est tranquille, il a maintenant satisfaction, désormais c'est entre le marabout et l'auteur éventuel d'un faux serment, le marabout reconnaîtra les siens." G. Marcy, *Le droit coutumier Zemmour* (Paris, 1949), 71.
6. In Moroccan culture, bread, grain, and food in general are considered to be endowed with *baraka*, explaining the reason it is central in oath-taking.
7. The sultans used to visit the saint Mawlay Idris near Fez.
8. 'Abd al-Rahman Ibn Zaydan, *Durar al-fakhira bi ma'athir muluk al-'Alawiyin bi Fas al-zahira* (Rabat, 1937), 37.
9. Abu al-'Abbas Ahmad Ibn Khalid al-Nasiri, *Al-istiqsa' li-akhbar duwal al-Maghrib al-'aqsa*, 9 vols. (Casablanca, 1954–6), 9:4.
10. Ibid., 128.
11. B. Etienne, "Recherche héros positif désespérement," *Pouvoirs: Revue française d'études constitutionnelles et politiques* 62 (1992): 74.
12. E. Dermenghem, *Le Culte des saints dans l'islam maghrébin* (Paris, 1954), 35.
13. G. Balandier, *Sens et puissance* (Paris, 1971), 219.
14. *Encyclopedia of Islam* (new edition), s.v. "Djihad."
15. R. Dozy, *Supplément aux dictionnaires arabes* (Beirut, 1968).
16. E. Zakariya, *Laïcité ou islamisme: les arabes à l'heure du choix* (Paris, 1971), 13.
17. P. Bourdieu, *Choses dites* (Paris, 1987), 117.
18. B. Etienne, *L'islamisme radical* (Paris, 1987), 124.
19. Ibid., 135.
20. R. Bourqia, "Espace physique, espace mythique: Réflexion sur la représentation de l'espace tribal chez les Zemmour," in Abdellatif Bencherifa et Herbert Popp, eds., *Le Maroc. Espace et société: Actes du colloque maroco-allemand* (Passau, 1989), 247–61.

21. Quoted by Etienne, *L'Islamisme radical,* 165. *Neo-turuqism* means the renewal of traditional religious lodges in the form of modern organizations such as associations.
22. See F. Burgat, *L'Islamisme au Maghreb* (Paris, 1988), 22–3.
23. According to a study carried out in 1994 among students of Mohammed V University on attitudes and values, strong pro-Islamist opinions were not expressed. The results were as follows: 54.9 percent of students pray regularly, 44.7 percent are in favor of the *hijab;* 15.4 percent are for polygamy; 25.7 percent consider that the Prophet or a religious personality is a model for youth. However, 59.8 percent of the students would like to migrate to a Western country if the occasion presented itself, and 90.2 percent think that Morocco's relation with the West should be one of cooperation rather than imitation or rupture. This survey revealed also that only 5 percent among the students read Islamic newspapers. See R. Bourqia, R. El Harras, and M. Bensaid, "La jeunesse estudiantine: valeurs et stratégies" (Rabat, 1995).
24. A term used to refer to a sufi leader.
25. The issue of direct control is not discussed here but could be considered from a political science perspective though an analysis of the evolution of political institutions.

· ELEVEN ·

The Elections of 1993 and Democratization in Morocco

Henry Munson, Jr.

To what extent has democratization occurred in Morocco? I attempt to shed some light on this question by discussing the legislative elections of 25 June 1993, which I observed as a member of an international delegation of monitors invited by the Moroccan government.[1] I describe these elections as I observed them in a popular quarter of Casablanca and in the coastal city of Bouznika. I then analyze the significance of these elections in the context of the political evolution of Morocco in the late twentieth century. While conceding the possibly dangerous consequences of suddenly holding completely free elections in a previously autocratic regime—one thinks inevitably of Algeria—I stress that when elections come to be seen as playing a strictly cosmetic role, they cannot perform their intended political functions. Instead of channeling popular discontent, they simply aggravate it.

THE DIRECT LEGISLATIVE ELECTIONS OF JUNE 1993

The direct elections of June 1993 involved the two-thirds of the parliament elected directly by the voters. The indirect elections of September 1993 involved the one-third of parliament elected by local communal and municipal councils and the chambers of agriculture, artisanry, labor, and commerce and industry. Later partial elections held in April 1994 involved the election of fourteen members of parliament to replace thirteen representatives whose elections in June 1993 were annulled by the Supreme Court because of electoral fraud and one representative who had died.

The relative success of the opposition parties in the direct elections of June 1993 led some observers to believe that they represented a significant step away from the controlled elections of the past.[2] The alliance of the principal opposition parties—the "social democratic" Union Socialiste des Forces Populaires (USFP) and the centrist and Islamic reformist Istiqlal—won ninety-one out of 222 seats (41 percent), forty-eight for the USFP and forty-three for the Istiqlal. The two less significant Marxist parties, the Parti du Progrès et du Socialisme (PPS) and the Organisation de l'Action Démocrate et Populaire (OADP), won six and two seats, respectively.[3] While the various progovernment parties won most of the seats as usual, the opposition was nonetheless considerably more successful in June 1993 than it had been in recent decades. This led some Moroccans, especially people with strong commitments to one of the opposition parties, to hope that a new era of real democratization had begun. That hope, however, gave way to bitter disillusionment on 17 September 1993, when the indirect elections were marred by widespread fraud, and the USFP won only four of the 111 seats at stake and the Istiqlal won nine.[4] Even with the addition of the four seats won on 17 September by a union linked to the USFP, the USFP-Istiqlal alliance that won 41 percent of the 222 seats at stake in June won only 15 percent of the 111 seats at stake in September. The results of the September 1993 indirect elections led to widespread protests, including the resignation of the head of the USFP, Abderrahmane Youssoufi, who went into exile in France.[5] The direct elections in June were unquestionably relatively free when compared with the indirect elections of

September. But even in June, the government intervened in some districts to ensure the victory of particular candidates. This was the case, for example, in al-Hayy al-Hassani, a popular quarter of Casablanca, and the city of Bouznika.

AL-HAYY AL-HASSANI

The two main candidates in the district of al-Hayy al-Hassani in Casablanca were Mohamed Karam of the USFP (and the USFP-Istiqlal alliance) and Maati Bouabid of the government-controlled Union Constitutionnelle (UC) (*al-hizb al-dasturi*). Karam, who was in his late forties in 1993, is a lawyer and a prominent member of Morocco's principal human rights organization, the Organisation Marocaine des Droits de l'Homme (OMDH). He is also a member of the Central Committee of the USFP. Maati Bouabid, who appears to be in his late sixties, is also a lawyer. He too was once a prominent spokesman of the Moroccan Left.[6] But, like many other Moroccans, Bouabid eventually discarded the leftist views of his youth. In 1979, he became prime minister and in 1983 the head of the Union Constitutionnelle, one of a series of parties the government has created to ensure its control of parliament.[7] Educated Moroccans often refer to the Union Constitutionnelle as one of Morocco's *cocotte-minute* or pressure-cooker parties conjured up on short notice by the government. It was in fact created within a matter of weeks in April 1983, when Bouabid was prime minister.[8] Virtually all of its members are civil servants and their dependents. The head of the UC office I visited in al-Hayy al-Hassani, along with several other election observers, was a young woman who conceded that she was being paid her regular salary as a government employee during the electoral campaign.

According to the Moroccan Ministry of the Interior, there were 88,638 registered voters in the electoral district of al-Hayy al-Hassani in 1993. (Each electoral district is supposed to have about 90,000 voters, though some rural districts actually have fewer than 30,000.)[9] The district is inhabited by most of Morocco's urban social strata, from the very poor in squatter settlements to the very rich in villas, although most of the inhabitants are closer to the poorer end of the spectrum. There were 190 polling places (*bureaux de vote* or *makatib al-taswit*) in al-Hayy al-Hassani, concentrated in seventeen schools.

Each polling place I saw was in fact a classroom. The president of the voting station and from two to four assistants were generally seated behind a long table. On this table were displayed the various ballots, each party having its own color, as well as the envelopes in which ballots were supposed to be sealed, and the wooden ballot box in which the envelopes were supposed to be placed. On another side of the classroom was a flimsy folding voting booth with a curtain on one side. After presenting his or her voter's identification card, the voter took one ballot of each color and an envelope. Once in the booth, with the curtain closed, the voter was supposed to place the ballot in the envelope, lick it shut, and then leave the voting booth and place the envelope in the ballot box on the long table. As for the ballots they did not select, voters were supposed to discard them into a wastepaper basket. A number of Moroccans told me that when people were paid to vote for a certain candidate, they had to show the ballots for the other candidates as proof that they had voted for the right person. Some people who earned money this way actually placed empty envelopes in ballot boxes, thus deceiving those who paid them and protesting the nature of the elections at the same time.

Moroccan law stipulates that candidates have the right to have a poll watcher in every polling place in the district in which they are running. On 25 June 1993, the party poll watchers generally sat at school desks, as I did, after showing the people in charge my letter of authorization from the Ministry of the Interior. The USFP and Istiqlal poll watchers tended to be educated activists thoroughly familiar with the electoral laws. The poll watchers of the government parties (notably the UC) were often shabbily dressed and seemed to be relatively uneducated and confused by the election process. None of the UC poll watchers I met appeared to have any real commitment to the party. In fact, one UC poll watcher could not remember his party's name when I asked him. Another UC poll watcher acknowledged that he was observing the election simply because someone in the UC had promised him a job if he did so. This same individual acknowledged matter-of-factly that the government would declare Bouabid of the UC the winner in al-Hayy al-Hassani no matter how many votes he received.

In addition to Karam of the USFP-Istiqlal alliance and Bouabid of the UC, there were other candidates in al-Hayy al-Hassani representing the generally progovernment parties of the Rassemblement National des Indépendants (RNI) and the Mouvement National Populaire (MNP) as well as the two Marxist parties—the Organisation de l'Action Démocratique Populaire (OADP) and the Parti du Progrès et du Socialisme (PPS). Everyone in al-Hayy al-Hassani, including government officials speaking off the record, said that the only serious candidates were Karam and Bouabid. The actual results I recorded suggest that the only real choice for most voters was between voting for Karam and placing an empty envelope in a ballot box.

I was present in polling place 103 at the al-Hana' School when the votes were counted. I arrived there at 7:50 in the evening, ten minutes before the polls closed. I had visited this polling place, along with seven others in al-Hayy al-Hassani, earlier in the day and had seen nothing wrong. The count took place in the presence of poll watchers from the progovernment MNP and UC as well as one from the USFP. (Some parties did not take advantage of their right to have poll watchers in every polling place.) The three observers and I kept tallies of our own.

The final results for polling place 103 were as follows: 120 votes for Karam (USFP-Istiqlal alliance), eighty-seven null votes (almost all empty envelopes), thirty-eight votes for Bouabid (UC), and insignificant totals for the remaining candidates. Null votes constituted 30 percent of the 294 votes cast, and the rate of participation was 65 percent, or 294 out of 449 voters. (According to the Moroccan government, the rate of participation at the national level was 63 percent.)[10] Similar results were recorded by an official of the American consulate-general in Casablanca who observed the vote count in polling place 4 at the Ibn Hamdis Bennis School in al-Hayy al-Hassani. He recorded the following figures: 129 votes for Karam, 100 null votes, and forty-eight votes for Bouabid, with the other candidates winning fewer than twenty votes each.

On the morning of 27 June 1993, Mohamed Karam gave me photocopies of the official vote tallies (*procès-verbaux* or *mahadir*) for eighteen of the 190 polling places in al-Hayy al-Hassani. Each of these documents was signed by the head of the polling place and his assistants. According to Moroccan law, Karam's poll watchers were entitled to receive 190 copies of the official vote tallies, one for each polling place in al-Hayy al-Hassani. But as in many other electoral districts (notably Ben Ahmed, Bouznika, Moulay Rachid, and Tiflet, to cite only the best-known cases), local authorities simply refused to give most party poll watchers the copies of the official vote tallies to which they were entitled.

The results in all the eighteen official vote tallies from al-Hayy al-Hassani for which I have copies show Karam winning, followed by null votes (except in three cases where null votes were not recorded), with Bouabid trailing far behind. One of the official vote tallies came from polling place 103, where I was present during the count. The figures in it are identical to those I recorded.

At 9:35 on the evening of the election, after the count had been completed, a crowd of USFP and other party poll watchers came to the door of the classroom I was in and asked me to help them because the presidents of their polling places were not giving them the copies of the official vote tallies to which they were entitled. They said things like "Le caméra ouvert, ça passe très bien" (On camera, it all goes very well) and "Tout ça c'est une comédie pour les médias étrangers" (All this is a comedy for the foreign media). I heard Moroccans make such statements every day during the twenty days I was in Morocco from 9 to 29 June 1993.

The observers claimed they had not received a single official vote tally for the entire school. They said they were in effect prisoners because the school was surrounded by police. They even suggested that I go out the front door because the police would not stop an American, while one of them would jump over the wall surrounding the school. We would then meet and call someone (I was not sure whom). I stressed that I wanted to stay in my polling place to see if the poll watchers there received their official tallies.

Then suddenly, like magic, the head of the school-cum-electoral center, a short man whose glasses kept sliding down his sweaty nose, emerged out of the darkness and assured me that everything was fine and that I should not listen to the USFP observers. He assured me that all the poll watchers would get their copies of the official vote tallies. And indeed they eventually did. Afterward, many of the poll watchers came up to me and thanked me because they believed that it was thanks to my presence that they had received the official tallies to which they were legally entitled. I cannot prove that. But it is true that the school I was in was the only voting center in al-Hayy al-Hassani where all the party poll watchers received copies of the official vote tallies. It seems unlikely that this was simply a coincidence.

On 3 July 1993, the USFP newspaper *Al-Ittihad al-Ishtiraki* published the results of the election in al-Hayy al-Hassani as recorded by USFP poll watchers in all 190 polling places in this district. These figures correspond to those in the official vote tallies of which I have copies as well as those I recorded myself and those recorded by an official of the American Consulate in Casablanca, except for a few typographical errors and minor errors concerning candidates other than the USFP-Istiqlal candidate Karam and the Union Constitutionnelle candidate Bouabid. It seems therefore that the results published in *Al-Ittihad al-Ishtiraki* were quite accurate with respect to the votes received by Karam and Bouabid. They showed Karam winning 18,528 votes as opposed to 7,241 votes for Bouabid. The official results announced by the government gave 29,799 votes to Bouabid and 11,160 to Karam.[11] The residents of al-Hayy al-Hassani with whom I discussed the official results said they were ludicrous (although no one dared question them in front of government officials).

I left al-Hana' School on the night of the election at about midnight. I then went to visit Taieb Cherkaoui, the head of the local electoral commission for the prefecture of 'Ayn Shuq-al-Hayy al-Hassani, with whom I had spoken several times. In his office, I told him about all I had seen and heard at al-Hana' school, and he said he knew nothing about it and that no complaints had been made to the electoral commission. He insisted that the official vote tallies were in fact being given to the party poll watchers. As we spoke, two officials of the United States consulate in Casablanca walked in. I was, to say the least, surprised to see my two fellow Americans in the middle of the night in a popular quarter of Casablanca.[12] It turns out that they had been visiting Karam's headquarters and he had told them his poll watchers were not getting their copies of the official vote tallies. So they asked Taieb Cherkaoui about this. Cherkaoui became rather upset by this line of questioning and finally opened the door to his office and had the members of the local Electoral Commission brought in, one of whom I had met before at the local office of the RNI (Rassemblement National des Indépendants). I began telling the members of the Commission what I had seen and heard at al-Hana' School and asked them to give me whatever information they had on electoral fraud. One man then whispered to me in literary Arabic, "Laysa huna" (not here). He and his colleagues were obviously afraid to speak in front of Cherkaoui and the other local authorities. By now it was about one in the morning. I left al-Hayy al-Hassani and returned to my hotel.

According to Karam and his poll watchers, policemen removed the ballot boxes from six polling places in al-Hayy al-Hassani before the votes in them had been recorded in an official vote tally. According to the Moroccan newspaper *Libération,* the ballot boxes in polling places 76 and 77 were taken away in a car with the license plates 221-11/2.[13] When Karam's poll watchers tried to prevent the removal of the ballot boxes, they were beaten. Morocco's government-controlled television channel announced Bouabid's victory at 1:45 a.m., whereas votes were still being counted at the central vote counting center of al-Ulfa until 2 a.m. Some of Karam's supporters took to the streets to protest what they referred to as the government's blatant falsification of the election results. Karam and his wife managed to calm them down before the protests evolved into a full-fledged riot.

According to Moroccan law, appeals of election results are supposed to be submitted within six days of an election, and they are supposed to be judged within forty days of their submission. It was over nine months after the 25 June 1993 elections when the Constitutional Chamber of the Supreme Court finally rejected the appeal of the al-Hayy al-Hassani results in April 1994, *after* new elections had already been publicly scheduled for 26 April 1994 to replace the thirteen representatives whose elections in June 1994 the Supreme Court had already declared invalid as well as one representative who had died. It should be noted that there were 210 appeals of the June 1993 results, involving 132 of the 222 seats at stake.[14] Only thirteen were accepted by the Supreme Court.

BOUZNIKA

Bouznika is a small city of some 30,000 inhabitants about forty kilometers southwest of Rabat and fifty kilometers northeast of Casablanca. The two main candidates for parliament here during the elections of 25 June 1993 were Abdelkamel Reghaye and Ahmed Zaïdi. Reghaye, a former finance minister dismissed after price increases for basic foods sparked the Casablanca riots of 1981 and a millionaire once indicted for embezzlement, was the candidate of the Rassemblement National des Indépendants (RNI) (*al-tajammu' al-watani li-al-ahrar*). Like the UC (Union Constitutionnelle), this is one of the parties the Moroccan government has created over the years to ensure its control of parliament. One wing of the RNI claims to want to transform it into a legitimate centrist-conservative party independent of the government. Reghaye is apparently among the RNI leaders who want to maintain the party's traditional ties to the government.[15] Reghaye's principle opponent in Bouznika was Ahmed Zaïdi of the USFP. Zaïdi is a well-known television journalist. In addition to being president of the Moroccan Press Club, he is president of the local council of one of the two administrative districts into which Bouznika is divided.

At 3:40 a.m. on 26 June, the day after the election, a picture of Reghaye appeared on Morocco's government-controlled television. The Moroccan Ministry of the Interior thereby declared him the winner. This sparked the widespread protests that have become known as "the events of Bouznika." The government's declaration that Reghaye won the election outraged Zaïdi's supporters because the fifty official vote tallies they had obtained, out of the 120 to which they were legally entitled, all showed Zaïdi winning by a landslide. Indeed, the official vote tallies obtained by poll watchers, as well as their unofficial vote counts, indicated that Reghaye actually came out ninth in a field of ten candidates, and the tenth one had done nothing to publicize his candidacy. Awareness of these early results led Zaïdi's supporters to begin celebrating his victory the night of the election. Then the government declared Reghaye the winner, and the elation of Zaïdi's supporters turned to outrage.[16]

Early in the morning of 26 June, hundreds of people in Bouznika joined a march to protest the official election results, walking in the direction of the Royal Palace at Skhirat. Some of the protesters waved the Moroccan flag. Others carried pictures of King Hasan II and his father Mohammed V, who died in 1961. Some chanted slogans like "O God, this is an abomination" (*allahumma inna hada munkar*).[17] A large number of policemen, brought in by truck and car, attacked the protesters near the bridge over the Oued Cherrat. Dozens were wounded and arrested. The marchers then divided into three groups. The first stayed on the road toward the Royal Palace, the second ran into the forest near Oued Cherrat, and the third went to the nearby beach on the shores of Atlantic. All three groups were pursued by police. The protesters on the beach, many of whom were women, were dispersed by policemen on foot and by a helicopter. Many marchers ran into the waves and dunked their heads in the salt water to protect their eyes from the blinding sand stirred up by the helicopter's rotating propeller blades.[18]

Eventually, the government allowed the protesters to select a delegation of ten people to meet with several officials who promised that the election in Bouznika would be investigated, though this did not end the protests. By noon on Saturday, 26 June, the day after the election, most of the marchers who had not been arrested were back in Bouznika. It was apparently on this day that the people of Bouznika began a general strike to protest the election results. Stores and cafés shut down, and there was little or no traffic on Bouznika's streets. The police and the auxiliary forces (*al-quwat al-musa'ida*) continued arresting people, allegedly beating many of them.

On the morning of Sunday, 27 June, two days after the election, yet another protest march proceeded toward the Royal Palace in Skhirat. The police surrounded it and prevented the marchers from leaving the city. The police also attacked a large crowd numbering in the thousands, according to some sources, gathered around the house of Zaïdi's father al-Hajj 'Umar al-Zaïdi. Among those injured was an old woman who had to be taken to a hospital. Protests also continued Sunday morning. Police began encircling Bouznika's popular quarters so as to regain control of the city.

On Sunday, 27 June, I drove to Bouznika from Casablanca with my fellow election observers, Raqiya Humeidan and Roland Amoussouga. They, along with Denis Sullivan, were members of the observer team in Casablanca, of which I was in charge. On the road from Casablanca, which is the old road to Rabat now largely supplanted by the new multilane highway, we saw some trucks full of soldiers headed north in the direction of Bouznika.

Having seen these trucks, and having heard a great deal about the suppression of a veritable insurrection in Bouznika, I was amazed by the absolute stillness we encountered when we entered the city. The road from Casablanca to Rabat is also Bouznika's main avenue, and it was virtually deserted. Stores and cafés were closed, and there were few cars and almost no pedestrians. I did not know about the general strike at the time, and I was beginning to think that perhaps my contacts in Casablanca and the opposition newspapers had exaggerated the extent of the protests and the government's response to them.

We drove all the way through Bouznika seeing only one policeman directing traffic on the way. Then I noticed a public fountain on the northern outskirts of the city in the direction of Skhirat and Rabat. An old man in threadbare clothes had filled several plastic bottles at the fountain and was now walking toward us by the side of the road. I asked our driver to stop. I lowered the window and told the old man, in Moroccan Arabic, that we had heard that Bouznika was full of policemen suppressing protests about the election. But we had seen nothing on the main street. The old man then pointed at a field in the distance, where we saw policemen in gray uniforms charging a large crowd. He said the police were arresting people in all the popular quarters. Then he said, bitterly, "This is freedom in Morocco" (*hadi hiya al-hurriya fi'l-Maghrib*).

This old man was not the sort of Moroccan one expects to find lamenting the lack of freedom in Morocco. He was not a professor or a journalist or a lawyer. His teeth were rotten at the edges. His Western suit was old and rumpled, as if bought at a flea market and often slept in. And he had just filled some dirty plastic bottles at a public water fountain. I have known many men like this old man in the villages and popular quarters of Morocco, and most of them had always looked on elections as a game in which they had no part except to vote as they were told to vote by local government officials. Yet this man was clearly outraged by what was happening in his city.

After thanking the old man for his help, we drove back into Bouznika and turned into a dusty side street. The contrast with the silence of the deserted main road could not have been greater. We saw policemen in gray uniforms and antiriot gear on almost every corner. They all wore helmets with transparent plastic visors and carried transparent plastic shields. One had the impression of being in an occupied city.

We drove down the dusty street toward the open space at its end where dozens of policemen were rounding up and beating people with billy clubs. I pulled out a camera and took several pictures. Raqiya Humeidan then told me, "Look, Henry, the people are happy you are taking pictures." I looked out and saw children and young adults flashing the V for victory signal as well as raising their thumbs in the air. They were clearly delighted that foreigners were there to tell the world what was happening in Bouznika while the government newspapers declared that Moroccans had voted "in freedom, serenity, discipline, and joy."[19] Some of the young people on the sidewalks also shouted "Long live the King" (*'ash al-malik*) despite their manifest disapproval of what the king's policemen were doing in their city. After taking some pictures, I asked the driver to turn around and head back to the road to Rabat. We all felt immensely relieved to be back on the main highway.

On 30 June 1993, at 5 p.m., Ahmed Zaïdi was called into the office of the director of the government-controlled television station where he worked as a broadcast journalist. The director, Mohamed Issari, told him, "We need your office and your service car. As for the rest, we shall decide later." He was allowed to return to work after a month's suspension.[20]

On 16 August 1993, the Constitutional Chamber of the Supreme Court nullified the election results at Bouznika. In late December 1993, Ahmed Zaïdi's lawyer Khalid Soufiani sent a letter to Morocco's Minister of State for the Interior and Information, Driss Basri (generally referred to simply as the Minister of the Interior), reminding him that Moroccan law stipulates that when an election is annulled, a new one has to be held within six months. Thus, a new election had to held in Bouznika no later than 16 February 1994.[21] A spokesman for the Ministry of the Interior responded by saying that the Constitutional Chamber of the Supreme Court had not notified the ministry of any nullifications, and it could not organize new elections without such notification.[22] When asked by opposition members of parliament why new elections were not being scheduled, the president of parliament also claimed that he had never been officially informed of the Supreme Court's nullification of any of the June elections.[23] When a member of parliament asked the Moroccan Minister of Justice, Mohamed Idrissi al-'Alami Mchichi, in late December 1993 if he was aware of the Supreme Court's nullifications of some of the election results of June, he answered that "the decisions of the Constitutional Chamber are not published in the Official Bulletin, and only those concerned with such decisions can request access to them."[24]

As has already been noted, the government did eventually schedule "partial elections" on 26 April 1994 for the thirteen districts where the June results had been declared invalid by the Supreme Court, plus one district where the parliamentary representative had died. This time, Zaïdi won, and Reghaye was not even a candidate.[25]

THE JAMAÏ AFFAIR

On 16 November 1993, the Moroccan newspaper *L'Opinion*, published by the Istiqlal party, printed an article in which its editor-in-chief, Khalid Jamaï, summed up the history of Moroccan elections since the early 1960s as follows:

> The scenario always seems to be the same. Each time the opposition warns that the new elections are likely to be marred by fraud. But that does not stop it from taking its chances. Then its apprehensions prove to have been justified. The opposition then condemns, threatens, caves in, and ends up accepting and in effect legitimating what it had denounced, what it had condemned. . . . Then there are new elections. Once again there are warnings. Once again the democratic process is subverted. And a new disillusionment prevails, but it runs deeper than before. The years

pass, the leaders of this opposition grow old, but they begin to understand that by their repeated concessions, they simply legitimate political practices that have ended up creating an illusory democracy. Meanwhile, the spectator (the citizen, in this case) gradually leaves the theater as the show ends by becoming absurd and he ceases to feel involved.

Then comes the moment when this opposition realizes that it has simply been running after a mirage.

Morocco's Minister of State for the Interior and Information, Driss Basri, who has been running Morocco's elections since the late 1970s, summoned Jamaï and the publisher of *L'Opinion*, Mohamed Idrissi Kaïtouni, to the Ministry of the Interior. As soon as Jamaï entered his office, Basri shouted, "Who are you?" (*shkun nta?*). He warned the journalist that "stronger and better men than you have gone to prison."[26] Jamaï reacted by describing the incident in an open letter to Basri published in the Istiqlal's newspapers *L'Opinion* on 22 November 1993 and *Al-'Alam* on 24 November 1993. In his letter, Jamaï said that Basri's summons and threat reminded him of how his father had been summoned to the office of the Pasha of Fez seventy years earlier because of his involvement in the nationalist movement opposed to French rule. This letter transformed Jamaï into something of a national hero, at least in the eyes of many educated and politically conscious Moroccans. The coverage of Jamaï's clash with Basri in both the Moroccan and European press undoubtedly prevented Basri from dealing with Jamaï as he would have liked. Be that as it may, the fact that a Moroccan journalist was able to publish such a scathing critique of Morocco's electoral system demonstrates that Moroccan newspapers have far more freedom than do their counterparts in much of the rest of the Arab world.

THE RISKS INHERENT IN RISK-FREE ELECTIONS

The basic logic underlying Morocco's electoral system is similar to the one that prevails in Tunisia, Egypt, and Jordan.[27] Parliamentary elections are designed to make sure that the opposition wins enough seats to remain part of the system but never enough to really change or challenge it. Such an ostensibly risk-free system is meant to serve as a kind of safety valve. The opposition gets to let off steam without ever posing a threat. The opposition parties have no real power, but their parliamentary representatives can make fiery speeches that are printed in their party's newspaper and read by the party faithful. Occasionally, leaders of the opposition parties are even given ministerial positions that have no real impact on basic government policy but that are nonetheless a source of status and influence. This kind of system is designed to enhance a regime's legitimacy both internationally and domestically, without running the risks associated with elections that determine who governs whom. But such ostensibly risk-free elections do in fact involve risks, notably the risk that people will cease to take them seriously. This risk is very real in the Moroccan case.

Virtually all Moroccans are aware of the cosmetic role played by Morocco's parliament and the elections to it.[28] This awareness was one reason for the widespread indifference to the June 1993 elections that was noted by many members of the observer delegation.[29] This indifference was reflected in statements from almost all Moroccans I heard except for government officials and party activists. People of all social strata, from professors to unemployed laborers, referred to the elections as a spectacle staged largely for the benefit of the Western media. As one taxi driver put it, "Les élections sont du cinéma." In the popular quarters of Moulay Rachid and al-Hayy al-Hassani in Casablanca, young people repeatedly told me that they saw no reason not to sell their votes to the government parties since their votes and the elections did not mean anything anyway. In one popular quarter of Casablanca where I accompanied a candidate campaigning door-to-door, even a group of women married to policemen told me the elections were meaningless. (Their husbands were not at home.)

Resentment of the illusory character of Morocco's parliamentary elections is widespread, especially among educated Moroccans in the cities. One index of this is the high rate of null votes cast on 25 June. As already noted with respect to al-Hayy al-Hassani, voters were supposed to place one of a number of ballots in an envelope. Many voters simply placed empty sealed envelopes in ballot boxes to protest the nature of the electoral process. Less frequently, voters would put all the ballots in a sealed envelope. One member of the observer team even found that people put scraps of paper and pieces of cigarette carton in ballot envelopes. A small percentage of such votes may have been due to ignorance. But the fact that the highest rates of null votes occurred in big cities, where literacy is far greater than in the countryside, makes it clear that the null votes were to a large extent a protest vote.[30] Indeed, some Moroccans actually told members of the IFES observer delegation that they had placed empty envelopes in ballot boxes to protest the nature of the election.

According to the Moroccan government's official figures, 13 percent of all votes cast on 25 June were null votes.[31] But in fourteen out of fifteen polling places in Casablanca for which I have data on such votes, they constituted 25 to 36 percent of the total. In Casablanca as a whole, over 20 percent of all votes were null. This was also true in all of Morocco's major cities (Fez, Marrakesh, Oujda, Rabat, and Tangier). In central Tangier, 50 percent of all votes cast were null. That is, one out of every two voters in central Tangier placed an empty envelope (or an envelope with more than one ballot in it) in a ballot box. In Casablanca, some members of the observer team came across districts where null votes actually outnumbered the votes of winning candidates. In rural areas, on the other hand, where voters tend to be less politically sophisticated as well as less educated, null votes were generally less than 10 percent of the total. This pattern of high null rates in urban areas as opposed to low ones in the countryside has persisted since the early 1960s, and, according to the Moroccan government's figures, the rate of null votes in 1993 was four times as great as in 1963.[32]

This would appear to reflect the increasing dissatisfaction with the nature of Moroccan elections that one often hears expressed by educated Moroccans. (The percentage of literate Moroccans increased from 13 percent in 1960 to 45 percent in 1991.)[33] It is of course possible, however, that the null votes also reflected other forms of discontent unrelated to the elections per se.

Having looked at the null vote in the 1993 direct elections, one should also consider the rate of participation—63 percent according to the official figures.[34] The comparable rates for the 1963, 1977, and 1984 direct legislative elections, again according to the official figures, were 73, 82, and 67 percent.[35] These figures should not be taken at face value. It is well known that local administrative officials force people to vote by threatening to withhold essential documents from them if they do not.[36] If it were not out of fear of the local *muqaddim* and shaykh, and the possibility of selling one's vote for a little pocket money, rates of participation in Morocco's parliamentary elections might well dip below 30 percent. I have heard Moroccan scholars suggest even lower figures.

CONCLUSION

One of the main functions of a controlled electoral system like Morocco's is supposed to be to provide an outlet for popular discontent that might otherwise lead people to support movements seeking to overthrow the current political order. But when such a system comes to be seen as utterly unrelated to the real distribution of power, it may well serve to aggravate rather than contain popular discontent. One can of course argue that recent events in Algeria and elsewhere illustrate the dangers of overly rapid democratization and that in a country like Morocco maintaining law and order and generating economic growth are more important than allowing people to choose how they are to be governed. This is not an implausible argument. Many Moroccans are keenly aware of, and worried by, what has been happening in Algeria since January 1992. Many even acknowledge quite frankly that they prefer rigged elections to free elections that could lead to an Algerian-style chaos. But the fact remains that the Moroccan electoral system's lack of credibility undermines its political efficacy as a means of channeling popular discontent.

The Moroccan government needs to enhance the credibility of the opposition political parties as well as that of the electoral system itself in order to dilute the appeal of the militant Islamic fundamentalists, who are very influential among Morocco's students and unemployed educated youth.[37] Cautious but real democratization would not entail as much risk in Morocco as it would in some Arab countries because the monarchy is still widely seen as a crucial source of stability.[38] Even if fraud were eliminated, parliamentary elections would continue to produce a majority of representatives inclined to endorse whatever the government wanted endorsed, especially in rural areas and among the urban poor.[39] Real progress toward democratization would of course mean that elections would have to be linked to real power. The parliament would have to become more than a debating club, and the composition of governments would have to reflect electoral results. But the monarchy would retain enough power to ensure the regime's stability and continuity.

In Morocco, as opposed to many other countries in the Arab world, some of the legal mechanisms needed to make this happen are already in place. While some revision of the Constitution of 1992 would be needed, the crucial task would be to make people obey already existent laws. This is in turn related to the complex issue of civil society and its relationship to democracy, which I cannot explore here.[40] For present purposes, the crucial point is that risk-free elections can in fact be riskier than they seem.

NOTES

1. The International Foundation for Electoral Systems (IFES), which organized the "monitoring and observation delegation," and the

United States Agency for International Development, which funded it, are not responsible for the views expressed in this chapter. Some of the data presented here appear in the final report of the IFES mission: T. C. Bayer, *Morocco Direct Legislative Elections, June 25, 1993: Report of the IFES Monitoring and Observation Delegations* (Washington, D.C.: International Foundation for Electoral Systems, 1993). Some passages of this chapter were first published in Arabic as part of a summary of a report I wrote for IFES, which appeared in the 5 September 1993 issue of the Moroccan newspaper *Al-Ittihad al-Ishtiraki* under the title "Intikhabat 25 yunyu ja'at aqall sufuran fi al-tazwir min al-intikhabat al-sabiqa lakinaha ma'a dhalik lam takun naziha" (p. 2). Some passages of this chapter also appeared (in French) in my response to François Soudan's criticism of my report in *Jeune Afrique*, no. 1716 (25 November–1 December 1993). This response was published in the 18 January 1994 issue of the Moroccan newspaper *Libération* under the title "H. Munson, observateur, persiste et signe" (p. 1). I submitted this response to *Libération* after *Jeune Afrique* declined to publish it. I would like to thank Bahman Bakhtiari, Jean-François Clément, Dale Eickelman, George Joffé, Mohamed Karam, Susan Gilson Miller, Augustus Richard Norton, and I. William Zartman for their comments on earlier versions of this chapter. I would also like to thank all those who commented on the abbreviated oral versions presented at the Johns Hopkins University's School of Advanced International Studies on 17 December 1993 and at Harvard University's Center for Middle Eastern Studies on 8 April 1994. These people are of course in no way responsible for the views I have expressed. In transliterating Moroccan names of both people and places, I have generally used the spellings used by Moroccans themselves.

2. See M. Bennani-Chraïbi, "Sujets en quête de citoyenneté: le Maroc au miroir des législatives de juin 1993," *Maghreb-Machrek*, 148 (April–June 1995): 17–27; D. F. Eickelman, "Re-Imagining Religion and Politics: Moroccan Elections in the 1990s," in J. Ruedy, ed., *Islam and Secularism in North Africa* (New York, 1994), 269–70; R. Leveau, "Les hésitations du pouvoir marocain," in *Le Maghreb face à la contestation islamiste,* Manière de voir 24 (Paris: Le Monde diplomatique, 1994), 56–9; M. Benhassen Tlemçani, "La Leçon des élections législatives au Maroc," *Cahiers*

de l'Orient, 31, 3 (1993): 129–36. For overviews of Morocco's electoral history, see A. al-Dagharni, *Al-intikhabat wa al-ahzab al-siyasiya al-maghribiya* (Rabat, 1990); the essays by de Mas, Santucci, and Sehimi in B. Lopez García, G. Martin Muñoz, and M. H. de Larramendi, eds., *Elecciones, participacion y transiciones politicas en el Norte de Africa* (Madrid, 1991); and the articles by Zartman, el-Mossadeq, and Tessler in I. W. Zartman, ed., *The Political Economy of Morocco* (New York, 1987).

3. *Libération*, 21 September 1993. (All references to *Libération* refer to the Moroccan newspaper with this name, unless the French one is specifically indicated.)
4. Ibid., 19–20 September 1993.
5. The pervasive falsification of the September indirect elections was well documented in the Moroccan opposition newspapers published during the following week. See, for example, the 19–20 September issue of *Libération*. The role of the indirect legislative elections in ensuring the government's control of parliament is discussed in M. Sehimi, "Maroc: partis politiques et stratégies électorales," in Lopez García et al., *Elecciones*, 224.
6. M. Monjib, *La Monarchie marocaine et la lutte pour le pouvoir* (Paris, 1992), 311, 345–66 n. 155.
7. al-Daghirni, *Al-intikhabat*, 229.
8. M. Sehimi, "Maroc," in Lopez García et al., *Elecciones*, 226–7.
9. Bayer, *Morocco*, 27.
10. Bennani-Chraïbi, "Sujets en quête de citoyenneté," 18.
11. The first of these figures was published on p. 4 of the 26 June 1993 issue of the government-controlled paper *Maroc Soir*. It and the second figure were also given to me over the phone on 13 August 1993 by Tom Bayer of IFES. He read them from a brochure printed by the Ministry of the Interior.
12. François Soudan has asserted that these two officials accompanied me as I visited polling places in Casablanca. That is not the case. See François Soudan, "Le grand malaise," *Jeune Afrique* no. 1716 (25 November–1 December 1993): 17. The fact that Soudan refers to me as "Henry Morton" in this article, along with a number of other errors, suggests that he never read the report he criticizes.
13. *Libération*, 27–28 June 1993.
14. Bayer, *Morocco*, p. 88.
15. *Maroc hebdo*, 14–20 May 1993. I have actually heard various

interpretations of the split within the RNI. Some on the left say it was entirely manipulated by the Ministry of the Interior. Some say it is just a power struggle between individuals looking out for their own interests. One prominent member of the RNI told me he could not discuss the real reasons for the split.
16. *Al-Ittihad al-Ishtiraki,* 28 and 29 June 1993.
17. Ibid., 27 June 1993.
18. Ibid., 28 June 1993.
19. *Le Matin du Sahara et du Maghreb,* 26 June 1993.
20. *Maroc hebdo,* 2–8 July 1993, and personal communications from a lawyer involved in the appeal of the Bouznika results.
21. *Libération,* 29 December 1993.
22. Ibid., 31 December 1993.
23. Ibid., 5 and 7 January 1994.
24. Ibid., 25 December 1993.
25. *al-Nashra,* 30 May–5 June 1994.
26. *al-'Alam,* 24 November 1993.
27. See, *inter alia,* A. M. Amawi, "The 1993 Elections in Jordan," *Arab Studies Quarterly* 16 (Summer 1994): 15–27; Eva Bellin, "Civil Society in Formation: Tunisia," in Augustus Richard Norton, ed., *Civil Society in the Middle East,* 2 vols. (Leiden, 1995), 1:120–47; Roger Owen, "Socio-economic Change and Political Mobilization: The Case of Egypt," in G. Salamé, ed., *Democracy without Democrats: The Renewal of Politics in the Muslim World* (London, 1994), 183–99. The general issue of elections in autocratic regimes is discussed in G. Hermet, R. Rose, and A. Rouquié, eds., *Elections without Choice* (London, 1978).
28. M. Bennani-Chraïbi, *Soumis et rebelles: les jeunes au Maroc* (Paris, 1994), 185–6.
29. Bayer, *Morocco,* 4, 35, 92, 104, 106; Bennani-Chraïbi, "Sujets en quête de citoyenneté."
30. M. Sehimi, *Juin 1977: Etude des élections législatives au Maroc* (Casablanca, 1979), 62–6; al-Dagharni, *Al-intikhabat,* 150.
31. All data on null votes in this paragraph are from Appendix G of the IFES report on the June 1993 elections unless other sources are given.
32. O. Marais, "L'Election de la chambre des représentants," *Annuaire de l'Afrique du Nord 1963* (Paris, 1965): 98; J.-C. Santucci, "Les Elections législatives marocaines de juin 1977," in *Développe-*

ments politiques au Maghreb (Paris, 1979), 224; Sehimi, *Juin 1977,* 62–6; A. Claisse, "Elections communales et législatives au Maroc (10 juin 1983–14 septembre et 2 octobre 1984)," *Annuaire de l'Afrique du Nord 1983* (Paris, 1985): 658; P. de Mas, "Pouvoir et migration au Maroc: Dynamiques électorales divergentes dans le Rif et le Sous," in Lopez García et al., eds., *Elecciones,* 93; al-Daghirni, *Al-intikhabat,* 150.
33. *Libération,* 16–17 January 1994.
34. *Maroc Soir,* 26–27 June 1993.
35. Marais, "L'Election," 98; Santucci, "Les Elections," 224; Claisse, "Les Elections," 657.
36. Bayer, *Morocco,* 21, 54, 60; Bennani-Chraïbi, "Sujets en quête de citoyenneté," 25–6.
37. H. Munson, Jr., *Religion and Power in Morocco* (New Haven: Yale University Press, 1993), 149–79.
38. Ibid., 142–4, 178–9.
39. Bennani-Chraïbi, "Sujets en quête de citoyenneté," 25–6.
40. See Norton, *Civil Society in the Middle East.*

· TWELVE ·

Interpreting Political Reform in Morocco

Susan E. Waltz

For thirty years, Moroccan political dissidents, expatriates in Europe, and international human rights groups charged Morocco with serious violations of human rights, and for an equally long period of time, the powers that be ignored or denied such allegations. On more than one occasion it was claimed that Morocco held no political prisoners and that the military prison at Tazmamert was a figment of the imagination. Before television audiences in December 1989, King Hasan II declared, "If I knew that even 1 percent of what Amnesty International says is true, I wouldn't be able to get a wink of sleep."[1]

Dramatic developments after 1990 suggested the opening of a new era. In 1991, one by one, the prison doors began to swing open. "Disappeared" Saharans reappeared, near-dead inmates at Tazmamert returned to life, and by early 1992 more than 400 of the world's longest-held political prisoners were set free. At the same time, institutional reforms were implemented by the monarchy. In 1990, the king created a royal council on human rights, the Conseil Consultatif des Droits de l'Homme (CCDH), and in 1992 he personally oversaw the drafting of a new constitution that alludes to international standards of human rights. He also approved new laws to restrict the practice of *garde-à-vue* detention, and late in 1993, he created a new Ministry of Human

Rights. Finally, in July 1994, the king announced his intent to "turn the page," and a comprehensive amnesty emptied Moroccan prisons of all but about fifty political prisoners.[2]

Arrests and reports of torture abated after the 1994 amnesty, but during the first phase of the reforms a series of arrests and unfair trials raised questions about the government's intentions. Even as dramatic events were unfolding in 1991, more than 120 people were imprisoned for political offenses.[3] Noubir Amaoui, Secretary-General of the Confédération Démocratique du Travail, served more than half of a two-year sentence imposed in April 1992 for criticizing Moroccan authorities in an interview with the Spanish press. Moreover, the government's unwillingness to explain the fate of several hundred Saharans it held in secret detention for nearly two decades and to account for more than thirty deaths at Tazmamert continue to cast a shadow over the process of reform.[4]

The messages have been mixed and are difficult to interpret. What significance do measures of clemency and the creation of new institutions hold? Are they harbingers of new political dynamics or merely symbolic gestures to appease internal opposition forces and Western critics, without limiting arbitrary power? Conventional approaches to Moroccan politics do not take us far enough toward answering these difficult questions. The monarch is the centerpiece of Morocco's political system, and in studying Moroccan politics it is common to begin with the powers of state that accrue to the monarchy. That approach directs attention to formal structures such as the constitution, parties, and parliament and to political culture that revolves around respect for the monarch as *amir al-mu'minin*. While such approaches help identify players and interrelationships, they tend to obscure other dynamics.

An alternative approach is to look at political activity on the periphery of the political game that authorities judge intolerable and consequently attempt to repress. As recent scholarship suggests, questions about who suffers repression and why may provide rich insight into political dynamics.[5] The consideration of repression permits inference about acceptable political behavior and the treatment of opponents, and more important, it points to the boundaries of the political game. By their nature, reforms that involve curbing such practices as torture, disappearances, and political imprisonment involve aspects of the political system that have not worked well. In any political system repression is costly and points up the limits of political accommodation. It is the idea of boundary, and political taboo, that is challenged by the current reforms. It is arguably the experience of those who play at the margins that best illustrates the need for such reforms, and it is at the margins that the effective bounds of political activity are most clearly established. Questions that bring this issue into focus may clarify the extent to which reforms alter the parameters of political life and thereby help establish their significance.

THE PARAMETERS OF ACCEPTABLE POLITICAL BEHAVIOR

The Moroccan political system tolerates considerable ideological diversity, and political parties enjoy a fairly large, if clearly bounded, political space in which to joust. Thirteen parties, for example, representing diverse interests and ideological leanings, competed for parliamentary seats in 1993 elections. The press, likewise, represents a broad political spectrum. The king towers above these contests: routine politics in Morocco has for decades turned on political competition and the construction of political alliances, with royal patronage as the central reward. Accordingly, one legitimate approach to Moroccan politics focuses on the ideological positions of winners and losers of favor and patronage.[6] Even if the most significant activity of political parties amounts to a contest for royal favor and power continues to concentrate in the throne, for many within the Moroccan polity the political system has worked reasonably well, and much can be learned from studying the mainstream of political activity.

The political left has commonly been identified as Morocco's principal opposition, though in recent years Islamists have also been labeled as opponents of the regime. In both cases, it is tempting to associate political marginality with ideological position. In fact, the experiences of both the left and the Islamists suggest that a finer analysis is required. Their histories reveal differential treatment of groups having a similar ideological position, suggesting that being part of the opposition is not only a function of ideological position but also a function of their group's relation to the monarchy, the size of the party or the group, and its position toward major national issues, such as the question of the Sahara.

THE POLITICAL LEFT

The political left has been the most frequent target of repression in Morocco, though only the particulars of its relationship with the monarchy explain the apparently arbitrary and inconsistent quality of the reprisals sometimes directed its way. Paradoxically, the moderate socialist left has for many years suffered intermittent but harsh reprisals from the political authorities, whereas relatively outspoken criticism of social policies by more radical parties has been viewed with greater tolerance. To illustrate this paradox and isolate its governing principle, the left may be divided into three components: the socialist left, represented by the Socialist Union of Popular Forces (USFP) and its forbear, the National Union of Popular Forces (UNFP); radical parties, represented by the Party of Social Progress (PPS) and the Organization of Democratic and Popular Action (OADP); and inchoate radical groups such as Il'al-Amam.

The relationship between the monarchy and the UNFP (and after 1974, the USFP) has long been a rocky one.[7] In the winter of 1959–60, UNFP leader Abdallah Ibrahim briefly served as prime minister; four years later, after a grossly unfair trial, twenty-one newly elected UNFP members of parliament were imprisoned on charges of plotting against the king. In 1965, one of the UNFP's most outspoken and popular leaders, Medhi Ben Barka, was abducted and presumably assassinated while in France, and by 1972 Fqih Basri, another charter member of the UNFP, had been sentenced to death no fewer than four times.[8] From 1963 to 1976, at least a dozen political trials involving the UNFP or affiliated student groups took place,[9] and one of those came even in the midst of royal overtures to the party. In 1971, Hasan II reportedly summoned UNFP leader Abderrahim Bouabid to the palace at Fez, but Bouabid declined: the king's prosecutor in Marrakesh was asking for forty-eight death sentences and Bouabid was needed to defend his UNFP colleagues.[10] After air force officers attempted a coup d'état in 1972, hundreds more UNFP members and supporters were arrested on charges of a plot against the king. Their 1973 trial at Kenitra marked the UNFP's nadir: the seventy-two defendants acquitted by the court—including thirteen Rabat barristers—were kept in custody for more than three years.[11]

The USFP emerged out of a split within the UNFP in 1974 and soon eclipsed the parent party, but for both factions tensions with the palace remained high. Relations ameliorated somewhat in the late 1970s, when USFP leaders willingly served as emissaries to promote Morocco's cause in the Western Sahara, but they deteriorated once again in 1981. Following riots in Casablanca, hundreds of USFP members with no apparent connection to the unrest were arrested,[12] and the party's leadership were charged with capital crimes for too-adamant support of Morocco's claim to the Western Sahara!ced[13] Those charges were eventually dropped, but rank-and-file members of the USFP's radical wing shuffled in and out of prison throughout the 1980s.

By contrast to the UNFP/USFP, political parties of the more radical left have operated in relative freedom. In fact, the further leftist PPS and the OADP enjoy such favor that they have been dubbed the "king's leftists."[14] Though many of their founding members spent long years as political prisoners and the groups themselves were once forced to operate clandestinely, both of these smaller groups were ultimately allowed to form parties and claim a seat or two in parliament. The PPS, a permutation of the dismantled Moroccan Communist Party, was sanctioned in 1974. A decade later, the OADP was allowed to form as an outgrowth of the once outlawed 23 March Movement,[15] the political crimes of its Secretary-General Mohammed Bensaïd—twice condemned to death in absentia—apparently forgotten.[16]

If the PPS and the OADP were permitted full participation in the political system, the experience of certain less organized—but ideologically indistinguishable (and related)—groups has not been so fortunate. Remnants and outgrowths of the Progressive Front, organized during the student unrest at the beginning of the 1970s, continued to suffer harsh repression into the 1990s. Two groups, the 23 March Movement and Il'al-Amam, formed the backbone of the Front, and their Marxist-Leninist rhetoric implicitly called the absolute authority of the monarchy into question. The liberationist position many adopted toward the Western Sahara isolated them further. Beginning in 1972, successive waves of arrests, followed by being held incommunicado, secret detention, and a mass trial, resulted finally in lengthy prison sentences for 173 individuals.[17] Although many Frontistes spent long years in prison, as noted above, the March 23 movement was eventually allowed to reformulate itself into the OADP. Il'al-Amam, on the other hand, was identified as the extremist group par excellence. In 1984 and 1985, some seventy-two individuals were imprisoned for efforts to revive the moribund political association, and many radical leftists unaffiliated with the OADP or PPS remained in prison until the 1994 amnesty.[18]

Experiences across the range of leftist groups in Morocco point to the centrality of the relationship to the royal power and the relatively minor role played by ideological position. Rather than ideology, it is a combination of size, influence, and political opportunism that explains the differential treatment of the three sets of leftist groups over the past several decades. As the largest and most popular leftist party, the UNFP/USFP also offered the most credible threat to the palace's control of politics. Mohammed V could not easily curb Prime Minister Ibrahim's independence in 1959, and it was the party's popularity at the polls in 1963 that won them the ire of his son and successor, Hasan II. The potential threat posed by the USFP also helps explain the position of favor enjoyed for more than twenty years by the PPS. Forerunners of the PPS had been banned through the 1960s, and their leader, Ali Yata, spent many years in prison. It was only when the USFP emerged in 1974 that the new—and potentially rival—PPS was allowed to form.

Strategic positioning on the Saharan question also accounts for some of the differential treatment of leftist groups. Hasan II advanced the Saharan cause as an issue of territorial integrity and for nearly two decades has lent the monarchy's rich pageantry to its service. The *frontistes* were harshly punished in part because they dared to raise questions of self-determination for the disputed territory, and conversely, militants from the March 23 movement were rewarded with permission to form a legitimate party soon after they published a clear position in support of Morocco's claim. In the late 1970s the USFP also received royal favors for its enthusiastic support of the Saharan cause: national fervor in the service of unity—and the monarchy—for a time softened the palace's view of the party. This issue, however, could be treacherous, even for a party with sizable influence. As noted above, Bouabid and his colleagues learned in 1981 that there was considerable danger in advocating a position more royalist than the king's.

As the varied experiences of the leftist political organizations make clear, political opposition in Morocco is not simply a matter of ideology. Ideology may predispose a group toward an oppositional stance or status, but the pattern of a precipitous fall from grace and an equally arbitrary rehabilitation establishes the concern with power politics as the principal political dynamic in Morocco and points back to the palace as the real source of power in the kingdom. This dynamic is seen easily in the history of the left, but it is likewise apparent in the experience of Islamists more recently identified as the political opposition.

ISLAMIST GROUPS

Political nuances that explain the palace's differential responses over time and across the range of leftist groups also explain the equivocal treatment of Islamist groups in a land where the king is commander of the faithful and defender of the faith. Although the king has explicitly denounced fundamentalism (*intégrisme*), and though Islamists arrested in 1983 and 1984 were given particularly harsh sentences, in 1991 some leniency was extended toward them, and rumors circulated that an Islamist party might be allowed to come to the political table.

In general, Islam has not offered the same new possibilities for political expression in Morocco as elsewhere in the Maghrib, and neither al-Shabiba al-Islamiya (Islamic Youth) led by Abdelkrim Muti nor al-'Adl wa'l-Ihsan (Justice and Charity) of Abdessalam Yassine have grown to the proportions known by the FIS in Algeria or al-Nahda in Tunisia. All the same, events in Iran that resulted in the 1979 overthrow of the Shah were worrisome in Rabat. During the summer of 1983 and after the political unrest of January 1994, Moroccan authorities arrested several dozen Islamists. Most of them were secondary school students affiliated with Muti. They were accused of having brandished portraits of Ayatollah Khomeini and importing tracts of "Iranian inspiration,"[19] but two European attorneys observing the trial raised doubts about the evidence, noting that the tracts in question featured photographs of Hasan II rather than the Iranian leader.[20] Despite the questionable evidence the court found all seventy-one defendants guilty of plotting against the monarchy. Sentences were exceptionally harsh, and for the first time in more than a decade the court called for the death penalty. Two successive trials in 1985, involving followers of Muti and a former associate Abdelaziz Enaamami, involved similar charges and similarly harsh sentences.[21]

From 1985 through the onset of the Gulf conflict in 1990, only the troublesome figure of Yassine pressed Islamic politics. Yassine had been in and out of prison following the publication of an impertinent open letter to the king in 1974, but from 1985 until 1988 he was allowed to operate more or less freely. Waves of arrest then began in 1989, after many of Yassine's numerous visitors refused to cooperate with police surveillance. His group, Justice and Charity, was declared illegal, and Yassine himself was placed under house arrest. Although protests were launched by Moroccan human rights groups and lawyers associated with such groups provided defense, Yassine's closest associates—the complete executive bureau—were soon thereafter imprisoned and remained so for two years.

The Justice and Charity movement was supposedly decapitated and formally dismantled, but in the meantime, the Gulf War and anti-Western sentiments fueled Islamism in Morocco. In early 1991, 10,000 Islamists took to the streets of Rabat, brandishing copies of the Koran and waving pro-Iraqi slogans, in a display of their potential force. In this shifting political climate, Yassine appeared both as a possible valuable client and as potential threat, and the government made no effort to disguise its new interest. Two semiofficial delegations were sent to meet with him, their mission to find grounds for an understanding.[22] A declaration of fealty to the monarch, it was speculated, could open the door for the creation of a formal Islamist party. So long as Islamists were willing to play by the rules that left the monarchy unquestioned, they too might be admitted to the game of politics.[23] Since 1991 the government has backed away from negotiations with the Islamists, but its position remains equivocal, enough to accommodate both tolerance or repression as best suits the purposes of the political system.

REPRESSION AND NEGOTIATION

From the experiences of both Islamists and the left, much can be learned about the parameters of political dynamics as they occur in Morocco. Both repression and negotiation clarify the rules that have governed the relationship between state and society. Repression has not been sparked by criticism of socioeconomic policy (as it was in many other countries of the region and as it was in the United States in the 1920s) or by ideological concerns (again, by contrast to other countries in the region and to the United States in the 1950s), nor has it impeded the practice of religions other than Islam. The exercise of power makes clear the fundamental axiom that the king is sacrosanct and his authority supreme, while calling attention to many lesser rules that buoy that principle. It is forbidden by law, for example, to publish an article offensive to the king and the royal family, and it is not politically or socially acceptable to inquire into royal finances. Criticism and public debate have been permitted, even encouraged, so long as they have neither implicitly nor explicitly contested the monarchy, Islam, Morocco's territorial integrity (including the Western Sahara), or the king himself.

The king plays a direct and central role in Moroccan politics, but he also frequently serves as arbiter of the political contest. The punishment for not abiding by prescribed rules has been exclusion or, in the extreme, outright expulsion. Egregious offenses to the central precept have received harsher responses, but regular players who temporarily contest the game, or who contest it in a relatively minor way, have been subject to milder and more temporary punishment. It has not been uncommon for high-ranking officials to be dismissed, ostracized, and even imprisoned and then subsequently courted and reintegrated to government function. The quality of arbitrariness frequently attached to both reprisals and measures of clemency have served to reinforce an object lesson about the king's raw power. Disjointed reprisals and unexpected amnesties throw players off balance even as they underscore the discretionary—and thus enhanced—powers of the monarch.

CHANGING THE RULES OR RULING THE CHANGE?

The political consensus around God, king, and country left the king's own power virtually unchallenged for more than two decades. By the late 1980s, however, forces inside and outside

Morocco began to exert pressures for reform. In 1988, a new human rights group, the Organisation Marocaine des Droits de l'Homme (OMDH), was constituted from among Morocco's elite. By contrast to two existing but then inactive groups, the Ligue Marocaine des Droits de l'Homme (LMDH) and the Association Marocaine des Droits de l'Homme (AMDH), many of the original OMDH members were not affiliated with political parties.[24] The OMDH was able to evade early efforts to control it, and its patent success in articulating political concerns and attracting media attention without eliciting reprisals unleashed new political energy. The AMDH and LMDH took on new life, and human rights fired the imagination of the USFP, which moved to tighten its relation with the new organization.

Although the OMDH no longer stands as distant from political parties as it once did, the very appearance of a significant, independent force on the political scene was a marked change in the political game. As I have argued elsewhere, it is doubtful that OMDH members would have escaped repression except for the support they received from Morocco's allies in France and the United States. In addition to expressing concern that the OMDH be allowed to operate freely, in accordance with Moroccan law, Western governments at the insistence of their own citizens pressed Morocco directly about its human rights record.[25]

These convergent pressures formed a very important backdrop for measures of clemency and reform enacted by the king. Not only did numerous individuals who had transgressed the sanctioned parameters make a dramatic reappearance after years of being banished from public memory as well as political life, but liberalizing innovations were formally introduced to the game of politics in the form of the Conseil Consultatif des Droits de l'Homme (CCDH), a new constitution, legislative elections, and most recently, a Ministry of Human Rights. As argued at the outset of this chapter, however, the trappings of a formal political system may reveal little about the primary dynamic in political relationships. Moroccan politics, and not simply the Moroccan state, have been governed by the king. To what extent has this basic rule been modified? That question can be addressed across the four institutional reforms that the monarchy has announced at home and abroad. Of particular interest is finding evidence that the king has ceded any significant measure of power or that the arbitrary nature of governance has been curtailed.

THE CONSULTATIVE COUNCIL ON HUMAN RIGHTS

By spring 1990, the OMDH had established itself as a political actor, Morocco's human rights record was under scrutiny in France, and an embarrassing and widely publicized incident with an Amnesty International delegation fueled discussion among political elites. Human rights (*al-huquq al-insan*) had worked its way onto Morocco's national agenda, and somewhat tardily the monarchy sought control of it. On 8 May, the king announced the creation of a royal council, the CCDH, and within a few weeks government ministers, academics, representatives of political parties and civic groups, including human rights groups, and a number of prominent citizens, had been named to the new and nominally independent thirty-six member body.[26] The CCDH was created to "put an end to hearsay about human rights,"[27] and as such it served strategic purposes. To what extent, however, has it affected the rules of political play in Morocco?

From the outset, critics argued that the CCDH could be only a propaganda tool, legitimating government policy and practice, and on these grounds the AMDH even refused to participate. As part of its initial charge the CCDH was instructed not to transgress the dictum of God, king, and country.[28] Even so, the CCDH in 1990 appeared to take its responsibilities seriously, and in a limited way it criticized official policies and practices, proposing reforms or advising restraint. Its first memorandum to the king, for example, cautiously suggested a political amnesty, and it also proposed legal reforms to establish clear limits on the allowable period of *garde-à-vue* and preventive detention.[29]

The early initiatives seem largely to have come at the urging of the CCDH's most politically credible members, those who already had an established record of interest in human rights and who were from the start the most active members.[30] Progressively, though, the role of these members was curtailed, and the CCDH came more squarely under government control. An inquiry into the 1990 riots in Fez quietly died, and in 1991 a small group of CCDH members who issued a maverick protest about judicial process were quickly reined in.[31] In 1992 the CCDH secretariat refused to consider dossiers submitted by domestic rights groups, echoing instead the oft-repeated official denials that Morocco held any political prisoners.[32]

Its own waning commitment notwithstanding, however, the CCDH had an appreciable impact on politics in Morocco. Largely because human rights groups (reinforced by diplomatic pressures of Western allies) pushed for the reforms, several measures cautiously advanced by the CCDH in its first months have ultimately been enacted. Thus, after stalling for a year—during which time both parliament and human rights groups pressed for reforms[33]—the king in 1991 enacted the suggested reform of laws concerning preventive detention. Three years later, the CCDH was invited to prepare lists of prisoners to benefit from the general amnesty it had first proposed in 1990.

For actors interested in reform, the CCDH offered a unique opportunity to compare rhetoric and reality. Morocco's domestic human rights groups have regularly tested the credibility of new political commitments by creating a competitive atmosphere and pressuring even those CCDH members with the greatest interest in defending the status quo. On more than one occasion the OMDH protested apparent manipulation by the government and threatened to withdraw its representative. The CCDH's significance relative to human rights practice—and to the rules of political play—lies not in its power to carry out reforms but in its inability to resist pressures for change. Despite rather than because of palace initiative, the CCDH has called into question the rules of political fair play, and the monarchy's control over the body it created has not been effortless.

THE HUMAN RIGHTS MINISTRY

With the appointment of a new cabinet following elections in 1993, Hasan II also announced the creation of a new Ministry of Human Rights. Among human rights activists and regime critics, the initial appointment of Omar Azziman to head it immediately gave the new ministry a credibility for which the CCDH still struggled. As a well-respected law professor and early supporter of the OMDH, Azziman lent the new ministry his own reputation for integrity and sincerity in matters concerning human rights.

On several occasions in 1994, Azziman pleased public audiences with frank speech. Lingering issues concerning political disappearances and indemnities for those treated unjustly were not resolved, however, and by consequence questions were raised about the actual powers accorded to the new ministry. The creation of the Human Rights Ministry, like the CCDH, appeared to be primarily a symbolic gesture, inasmuch as the new minister's role lacked definition and remained dwarfed by the powerful Ministry of the Interior; nevertheless, it offered further indication that concern about rights and accountability had registered in the palace.

The replacement of Azziman with the controversial figure of Mohammed Ziane in February 1995, however, raised new doubts about the intent to press forward on human rights issues. Long a controversial figure in Moroccan politics, in 1989 Ziane had served as defense attorney for Yassine and the Justice and Charity Islamist movement and since 1990 had participated in the CCDH. He had long been an opponent of the left in parliament, however, and antipathy deepened in 1992 when he formally registered his support of the government case against labor leader Noubir Amaoui. Several Moroccan human rights groups registered their displeasure with his appointment by refusing to work with his office.[34]

THE 1992 CONSTITUTION

In 1959 Mohammed V ceded to demands from the nationalist Istiqlal party for a constitution, without yielding any real powers. The first constitution, in fact, was used to reinforce the monarchy by legalizing the principle of primogeniture, which had not been fully established by historical practice. Morocco's first three constitutions (1959, 1970, and 1972) did not so much limit the monarch's powers as elaborate them. Constitutional provisions have legitimized the monarch's prerogatives to promulgate law, dissolve parliament, and amend—or suspend—the constitution. The courts have reinforced these considerable powers by systematically refusing judicial recourse against acts promulgated by the king;[35] no instance has power to reprove a king who steps beyond constitutional provisions, as was the case in 1983, when Hasan II personally assumed the legislative function at the end of the parliamentary term.[36]

Morocco is a constitutional monarchy, but the monarch has effectively accrued power beyond constitutional law, and no constitution has challenged that situation. The 1992 constitution, drafted at the king's initiative and under his close supervision, nevertheless did create some political openings. The notion of human rights had been endorsed by the monarchy more than a decade earlier with the ratification of several international human rights treaties, but it was finally anchored in the local political and legal context by placing it prominently in a preambular passage. More significant from a practical perspective, the new constitution made provision for the prime minister rather than the king to appoint the ministerial cabinet. That provision was ignored, however, in the immediate aftermath of the 1993 elections. In November 1993, Hasan II reappointed Karim Lamrani to a fourth term as prime minister, and subsequent efforts—ultimately unsuccessful—to draw opposition figures into the ministerial cabinet were negotiated by the king, not Lamrani. Opposition parties were openly critical of the king's apparent disregard of the new rules (to the extent that USFP chief Abderrahmane Youssoufi exiled himself to France), and the replacement of Lamrani by Abdellatif Filali in 1994 was seen by many as the king's intent to abide at least by the spirit of the new constitution. Although Filali is father of the king's son-in-law and long served as Morocco's foreign minister, he is known for the independence of his judgment and his politics. Filali's independence notwithstanding, critics may justifiably remain skeptical about the royal intentions to put the palace at the service of the constitution: early in 1995 the palace attempted to entice Istiqlal leader M'Hamed Boucetta to become the prime minister but refused to allow the replacement of longtime Interior Minister Basri.[37] Despite such machinations, it is important to recognize that in contrast to previous regimes, Filali's office did directly negotiate many ministerial posts in 1994 and again in 1995.[38] King Hasan's withdrawal from direct control of the political process, symbolized by even partial respect for the new constitutional provisions, may over time create new political space.

PARLIAMENT AND THE 1993 LEGISLATIVE ELECTIONS

By provision of the 1992 constitution, two-thirds of the 333 seats in parliament were to be elected directly, while the remaining 111 seats were to be elected through professional and trade associations. The Kutla (Democratic Bloc), a coalition of the Istiqlal, USFP, and smaller parties frequently identified as opposition, narrowly won a plurality in the first set of partial elections, but their relatively poor showing in the indirect contest deprived them of a parliamentary majority.

Opinions vary about the fairness of the 1993 elections and some documented charges of fraudulent tallies in certain Kutla-favored districts raise serious questions about the government's willingness to permit the opposition to come to power.[39] If the elections did not give Kutla parties control of the government, however, they did appear to strengthen the voice of opposition parties in a parliament that had begun to take itself seriously. Increasingly, ministerial reports have been subject to close scrutiny, and in June 1994 parliament made a very bold move, abrogating a royal *zahir* (decree) from 1935 authorizing repression of public demonstrations that had continued to serve as the legal basis for political imprisonment. Significantly, the parliamentary measure was initiated by two Kutla parties, the USFP and the Istiqlal.

CONCLUSION

Amnesties and measures of reform in the mid-1990s have been welcomed by parties and organizations representing the full spectrum of Moroccan political interests, but as the past experiences of the political opposition make clear, the true measure of reform lies in the extent to which the rule of law is enhanced. Because the king retains broad discretionary powers and continues to exert direct control over the *makhzan*, one might question the palace's determination to overhaul basic political structures and reorient political dynamics.

At the same time, the royal overtures have created a ripple effect that may ultimately expand political space in a significant way. In the past, broad powers extended by the monarch to the security forces have allowed arrests to go unregistered within the judicial system, confessions to be admitted as evidence despite clear indication of their extraction under torture, and certain prisoners to be held beyond the expiration of their imposed sentences. With the reform of preventive detention procedures and, more recently, the abrogation of the 1935 *zahir,* the effect on security agencies and the judicial system may have a significant impact on the way the opposition is treated and the extent to which it is tolerated.

Parliament's role in pressing these reforms merits emphasis.

Because laws are formally promulgated by the king and the Moroccan parliament has often seemed irrelevant to the political process, the new activism is important. It signals the interest of society in questions of social justice and human rights as a new element in the Moroccan political equation. The emergence of the OMDH in 1988 was the first clear sign of such a social awakening. The new human rights organization politely violated political taboos, and within six months human rights had caught the attention of Kutla parties. Both the AMDH and the LMDH found new life, and a Moroccan Charter of Human Rights was drafted in 1990. In the same year an international report on preventive detention brought hundreds to discussion sessions in Fez that lasted well into the night. In 1993, Moroccan women were circulating petitions for change in the Mudawwana (Morocco's code of personal status and family law), and when the shocking sex crimes of Casablanca police superintendent Mohammed Tabet were exposed, men and women alike framed the issue in terms of accountability and abuse of authority.[40] Simply cataloguing and publicizing the cases of political prisoners has been a major task for Moroccan human rights groups, and their purpose in these efforts has been to eliminate notions that abuses are isolated and to illustrate the existing limitations of law and legal practice.[41] In various ways, society expressed interest in mobilizing the protection theoretically afforded by law.

The net impact of recent reforms may lie in the openings they present to those who would advance the rule of law. While the reforms themselves change little in the monarch's exercise of power, the vehicles of reform—new institutions to promote human rights, constitutional reference to international human rights standards, and a reevaluated role for parliament and prime minister—give legitimacy to the discourse of legal rights and political fair play. Though power remains no less concentrated in royal hands, the reforms have already been instrumental in breaking age-old taboos, opening new channels of political expression, encouraging new voices, and sanctioning new language. The debate on establishing the state of right and law (*dawla al-haqq wa al-qanun*) is becoming the frame for the political discourse, thus opening the way for further change.

AUTHOR'S POSTSCRIPT, JULY 1998

By 1996, it was clear that reforms had not gone far enough. The 1994 Filali government was nearly the same as the old government, and political disaffection was rife. Moreover, Hasan II's sudden hospitalization in late 1995 reminded Moroccans of the monarch's mortality, and in early 1996, the World Bank delivered bad news about the economy's structure and long-term health. In March 1996, Hasan II announced another series of reforms, including the intent to establish a second parliamentary chamber and hold early legislative elections permitting *alternance*—that is, rotation of the prime ministry. The new Senate would be elected indirectly, but with its creation the controversial provision of the 1992 constitution that allowed one-third of the legislature's seats to be elected via professional and trade associations would disappear. The 1996 constitutional amendments were duly approved, and elections held in November 1997 returned a slim parliamentary majority in favor of a loose coalition of the Kutla and center parties. In due course, USFP leader Abderrahman Youssoufi was named prime minister.

New constitutional procedures were followed scrupulously in this round, and for the first time in modern history, a Moroccan prime minister drawn from the opposition selected his own cabinet—subject, of course, to the king's approval. Youssoufi now governs in uneasy alliance with Interior Minister Driss Basri, who retains considerable power even though his portfolio has been somewhat reduced. The prime minister must also attend to the pulse of the new Senate, dominated by Wifaq (pro-palace) parties and constitutionally imbued with powers to censure his government.

At the political fringe, Islamists remain under tight control (some of them in prison), and in 1997 several dozen leftists were arrested and tried for advocating a boycott of the elections.

Unemployed professionals have joined the ranks of the disaffected, and their protests, too, have tested the limits of political tolerance. Taboos around God, king, and the Western Sahara remain in place, but nevertheless, there is a political ambiance of cautious optimism and engagement unknown for many years. Morocco's political problems are far from having disappeared, but there appears to be new willingness to expand parliamentary powers and tolerate dissent. Those who have sought primarily to contain and restrain the arbitrary exercise of power find reason to hope that the reforms of this decade may yet deliver on their promise.

NOTES

1. J. de Barrin, "Royal Privilege and Human Rights," *Manchester Guardian*, 18 December 1990.
2. "King Hassan Gives Birthday, Youth Day Address," FBIS-NES-94-134, 13 July 1994.
3. Amnesty International, "Morocco, Continuing Human Rights Violations," MDE 29/06/92, October 1992.
4. See Amnesty International, "Tazmamert: Official Silence and Impunity," MDE 29/97/92, November 1992, and "Morocco: The Pattern of Political Imprisonment Must End," MDE 29/01/94, May 1994.
5. Two books by J. C. Scott, *Weapons of the Weak* (New Haven: Yale University Press, 1986) and *Dominance and the Art of Resistance* (New Haven: Yale University Press, 1990), contrast "hidden" and "official" transcripts of political discourse and point out the limits of political control, even where physical coercion is extensive. Likewise, J. Migdal, *Strong Societies and Weak States* (Princeton: Princeton University Press, 1988), presents engagement in "dirty politics" as evidence of the state's weakness rather than its strength.
6. See S. Ihraï, *Pouvoir et influence: Etat, partis, et politique étrangère au Maroc* (Rabat, 1986), 190–8; O. Bendourou, *Le Pouvoir exécutif au Maroc depuis l'indépendance* (Aix-en-Provence, 1986); and R. El-Mossadeq, "Political Parties and Power-Sharing," in I. W.

Zartman, ed., *Political Economy of Morocco* (New York, 1987), 59–83.
7. See J. Waterbury, *The Commander of the Faithful: The Moroccan Political Elite—A Study in Segmented Politics* (New York: Columbia University Press, 1970).
8. "Maroc: Les Révélations explosives du 'Fqih' Basri," *Jeune Afrique* no. 1383 (8 July 1987).
9. See Amnesty International, *Amnesty International Briefing on Morocco* (Nottingham, 1977). There were eight major trials in July–August 1976 alone.
10. G. Perrault, *Notre ami le roi* (Paris, 1990), 153.
11. Ibid., 198–205, and Amnesty International, *Briefing*, 4.
12. Lawyers' Committee for International Human Rights, "Morocco Briefing Memo" (New York, 1985), 11–18.
13. USFP leaders publicly protested the king's endorsement of a proposal that emerged at the 1981 OAU summit in Nairobi, calling for a referendum on the disputed territory. They argued that the Sahara's link to Morocco was not debatable. Over the past ten years the palace has approved a series of UN-negotiated terms but without apparent enthusiasm. See J. Damis, "The U.N. Settlement Plan for the Western Sahara: Problems and Prospects," *Middle East Policy* 1 (1992): 36–46.
14. "Les 'Gauchistes' de sa majesté," *Jeune Afrique,* no. 1306 (15 January 1986); "Un Parti pas comme les autres," *Jeune Afrique,* no. 1364 (26 February 1987).
15. The March 23 Movement derived its name from the 1965 riots in Casablanca that resulted in the declaration of a state of emergency and suspension of the constitution.
16. "Les 'Gauchistes' de sa majesté."
17. Amnesty International, "Briefing on Morocco," PUB 78/00/77, October 1977.
18. See Amnesty International, "Morocco: The Pattern of Political Imprisonment Must End," MDE 29/01/94, May 1994; and "Release of Detainees Viewed," FBIS NEW-94-141, 22 July 1994. Some activists within the Union Nationale des Etudiants Marocains (UNEM) incarcerated in a Fez prison apparently did not benefit from the amnesty (*La Lettre de l'ASDHOM,* no. 72, 16 November 1994.)

19. "Le Procès des intégristes de Casablanca: Treize des soixante et onze accusés sont condamnés à mort," *Le Monde*, 2 August 1984.
20. "Le Procès des intégristes de Casablanca: Deux observateurs français protestent contre la disproportion du réquisitoire'," *Le Monde*, 27 July 1984.
21. "Dix-neuf intégristes condamnés à perpétuité à Marrakech," *Jeune Afrique*, no. 1296 (6 November 1985). Enaamani led a group called "The Moudjahidin Movement" until his disappearance in September 1985. According to friends, he was "picked up" while living in France; followers of Muti claimed he was the victim of internal squabbles. Also see Henry Munson, Jr., "Morocco's Fundamentalists," *Government and Opposition* 26 (1991): 331–44.
22. "Maroc: Reprise du dialogue entre le palais royal et les islamistes," *Jeune Afrique*, no. 1601 (4–10 September 1991).
23. Hasan II's own views on Islamism were made clear in an interview with Jean Daniel, "Je ne laisserai pas l'intégrisme déformer l'islam," *Le Nouvel Observateur*, 28 March–3 April 1986.
24. The LMDH is affiliated with the Istiqlal party, and the AMDH originated within the USFP.
25. Susan Waltz, "Making Waves: The Political Impact of Human Rights Groups in North Africa," *Journal of Modern African Studies* 29 (1991): 481–504; idem, *Human Rights and Reform: Changing the Face of North African Politics* (Berkeley: University of California Press, 1995).
26. Among these were many individuals whose integrity was recognized and respected; however, questions were raised about the role of others, including Minister of the Interior Driss Basri and Ahmed Afazaz, who was the presiding judge in the 1977 political trial in Casablanca.
27. "Hassan Speech on Human Rights Council Creation," FBIS-NES-90-091, 10 May 1990.
28. "Discours historique de sa majesté le roi Hassan II à l'occasion de l'installation du Conseil consultatif des droits de l'homme, 8 May 1990," in *Conseil consultatif des droits de l'homme* (Rabat, 1992), 14.
29. See A. E. Mayer, "Moroccans: Citizens or Subjects? A People at the Crossroads," *New York University Journal of International Law and Politics* 26 (Fall 1993): 63–105.

30. The OMDH representative was part of the CCDH working group on pretrial detention, and it was this group that most ardently pressed for reforms to establish clear limits on the allowable period of *garde-à-vue* and preventive detention.
31. Their communiqué was then circulated by the Istiqlal paper *L'Opinion* ("Un Memorandum demande la 'suspension immédiate' des procès'," *Le Monde*, 2 January 1991, and "Human Rights Council Urges Suspension of Trials," FBIS-NES-91-001, 2 January 1991).
32. In July 1992 the OMDH criticized the CCDH for echoing the official position that Morocco no longer held political prisoners ("Maroc," *Le Monde*, 9 July 1992). Less than a month earlier the OMDH had released a list of 532 political prisoners as part of a dossier entitled "Pour qu'il soit mis fin à la détention politique," whose cover memorandum was circulated in the *Lettre de la fédération internationale des ligues des droits de l'homme*, no. 455/456, 14 August 1992. The question of political prisoners was not included in the CCDH's work plan for 1993 ("Council for Human Rights Outlines 1993 Program," FBIS-NES-93-035, 24 February 1993) and, as noted, it was not until Hasan II instructed the CCDH to present a list of candidates for amnesty in 1994 that the CCDH directed its attention to these cases ("CCDH Starts Work on Listing Prisoners for Release," FBIS-NEWS-94-135, 14 July 1994).
33. See two collections of press releases issued by the OMDH, *L'Organisation marocaine des droits de l'homme à travers ses communiqués et déclarations* (Casablanca, 1991 and 1993); Amnesty International, "Morocco: Update on Human Rights Violations," MDE 29/12/91, March 1991; and Amnesty International, "Morocco: Amnesty International's Concerns, February–June 1991," MDE 29/21/91 (July 1991).
34. See "Celui par qui le scandale arrive," *Jeune Afrique*, no. 1784 (16–22 March 1995); "Vers l'invalidation de Ziane?" *Jeune Afrique*, no. 1793 (18–24 May 1995); and "Droit de réponse à . . . Mohamed Ziane," *Jeune Afrique*, no. 1796 (8–14 June 1995).
35. A. Claisse, "Le Makhzen aujourd'hui," in J.-C. Santucci, ed., *Le Maroc actuel: Une modernisation au miroir de la tradition?* (Paris, 1992), 291.
36. Ibid.

37. "Maroc: L'Alternance à quitte ou double," *Jeune Afrique,* no. 1775 (12–18 January 1995).
38. See "King Hassan Appoints New Cabinet," FBIS-NES-94-110, 8 June 1994; "Maroc: Un coup pour rien," *Jeune Afrique,* no. 1783 (9–15 March 1995).
39. See untitled report submitted by Henry Munson, Jr. to the International Foundation for Electoral Systems (IFES), Washington, D.C., 22 July 1993, and a less critical story published by IFES, "Technical Observers see Progress in Morocco," *Elections Today,* 4 (Summer 1993): 5.
40. See "Sexe, pouvoir et vidéo," *Jeune Afrique,* no. 1681 (25–31 March 1993).
41. See "Présentation du dossier de presse relatif aux prisonniers politiques," in OMDH, *L'Organisation marocaine des droits de l'homme* (1991), 67–8.

Glossary

abid slaves.
adab literature or belles-lettres; good manners, refined behavior.
'alim scholar of Islamic legal studies.
aman guarantee of personal safety.
amin al-mustafad urban tax collector.
amir al-muminin lit., commander of the faithful; title of the Caliph.
'ar dishonor; imposition of an obligation.
'asabiya group feeling or solidarity (after Ibn Khaldun).
baraka blessing or abundance; God-given holiness; possessing an inherent spiritual power.
basha pasha or governor.
bay'a act of investiture of the sultan; pact between the sultan and the community.
bayt al-mal treasury house.
bid'a blameworthy innovation or deviation from orthodoxy.
dawla dynasty or state.
dhikr repetition of certain words in praise of God.
dhimmi/ahl al-dhimma protected person(s), either Jewish or Christian.
faqih (pl. *fuqaha'*) someone learned in Islamic law.
faqir (pl. *fuqara'*) poverty-stricken; a Sufi mendicant.
fatwa formal legal opinion given by a Muslim scholar such as a *qadi* or *mufti*.

fiqh Islamic jurispudence.

fitna rebellion against established authority.

hadara urban society; settled area as opposed to the *badawa*, or rural area.

hadith saying or report about the Prophet; collection of such sayings.

hadiya obligatory gift to the sultan.

haratin descendents of slaves brought from the Sahara.

harka military expedition sent by the sultan for punitive or fiscal purposes.

hayba fear, reverence, awe.

hijab head covering for the sake of modesty; veiling.

hijra migration; especially, a migration to rejoin the community of Islam.

hubus (pl. *ahbas*) pious endowment, known as *waqf* in the Islamic East.

hurm (pl. *hurumat*) religious sanctuary or refuge.

ikhwan members of a religious order.

imam prayer leader; spiritual leader of the Muslim community.

imama religious leadership of the *umma*.

jahiliya state of ignorance associated with pre-Islamic paganism.

jama'a tribal assembly.

jizya poll tax levied on non-Muslim populations (*ahl al-dhimma*).

karama (pl. *karamat*) miracle worked by a saint.

khalifa lit., caliph or successor to Muhammad; deputy or lieutenant.

kharaj tax on landed property.

khilafa caliphate.

khizana storehouse or treasury; library.

kuntrada contract; monopoly granted by the sultan.

madhhab one of the four schools of orthodox Islamic law.

madrasa (pl. *madaris*) religious college.

mahabba disciple's love for his master.

mahdi divinely guided one; messiah.

majdhub (pl. *majadhib*) one who is intoxicated by religious feeling.

makhzan lit., storehouse; in Morocco, state or administration.

makhazni government soldier or guard.

*maks (*pl. *mukus)* non-Koranic tax imposed in the market and at the gates of the city.

Maliki school of Islamic legal interpretation dominant in North Africa and ascribed to Malik b. Anas (d. 795).

mashwar courtyard adjacent to the palace used for ceremonial events.

millah (mellah) Jewish quarter of a Moroccan city.

mithqal specific weight; Moroccan coin worth ten dirhams.

mufti legal scholar authorized to issue fatwas.

mujahid one who fights for the Islamic faith.

mulk sovereign power.

muqaddim chief of an urban quarter; head of a brotherhood.

murabit inhabitant of a *ribat;* religious militant; saint.

murid novice or disciple of a Sufi master.

musalla prayer room or oratory; open-air mosque.

muʿtazila theological school stressing human responsibility and divine justice.

nadhir overseer of a *hubus.*

naqib head of a guild, association, or other social body.

qabila tribe.

qadi judge of Islamic law.

qaʿid tribal leader; army officer.

qasba casbah; citadel or fortress.

ribat outpost for waging the jihad.

rogui agitator, pretender to the throne.

rumat lit., sharpshooters; urban militia of Fez and other cities.

salafi religious reformer.

shafaʿa intercession of a saintly personage between the believer and God.

shariʾa lit., straight path; revealed law of Islam.

*sharif (*pl. *shurafaʾ* or *ashraf)* one who claims descent from the Prophet through his daughter Fatima and his son-in-law ʿAli.

shaykh al-yahud lit., chief of the Jews; head of the Jewish community.

talib lit., student; educated person, secretary.

tajir (pl. *tujjar*) *al-sultan* important merchant engaged in business with the sultan.

tariqa lit., way or path; fellowship of followers of a Sufi shaykh.

tashilhit dialect of Berber spoken in the southwest of Morocco.

tawhid unity; theological concept affirming the unity of God.

umma Muslim community.

'ushr (pl. *'ushur*) tithe; tax levied on agricultural products.

wali saint or holy man.

wird litany of a Sufi order passed from *shaykh* to *murid*.

zahir royal proclamation having the force of law.

zawiya (pl. *zawaya*) retreat or convent; religious order.

zwaq in popular belief, protection.

zwaq al-madfa protection afforded by a cannon.

A Selective Bibliography

Abitbol, Michel. *Témoins et acteurs: les Corcos et l'histoire contemporaine.* Jerusalem, 1977.

———. *Tujjar al-sultan: une élite économique judéo-marocaine au XIXe siècle.* Jerusalem, 1994.

Afif, Mohamed. "Les Harkas, hassaniennes d'après l'oeuvre d'Ibn Zaydan." *Hespéris-Tamuda* 19 (1980–81): 153–68.

Anderson, L. "The State in the Middle East and North Africa." *Comparative Politics* (October 1987): 1–18.

Aubin, Eugène, *Le Maroc d'aujourd'hui.* Paris, 1904.

Ayache, G. "Aspects de la crise financière au Maroc après l'expédition espagnole de 1860." *Revue Historique* 220 (1958): 3–41.

Beck, H. L. *L'Image d'Idris II, ses descendants de Fas et la politique sharifienne des sultans Marinides (659–869/1258–1465).* Leiden, 1989.

Bel, Alfred. *La Religion musulmane en Berbèrie.* Paris, 1938.

Bellin, Eva. "Civil Society in Formation: Tunisia." In Augustus Richard Norton, ed., *Civil Society in the Middle East.* 2 vols. Leiden, 1995.

Bendourou, Omar. *Le Pouvoir exécutif au Maroc depuis l'indépendence.* Aix-en-Provence, 1986.

Bengio J., and J.-L. Miège, "La Communauté juive de Tanger dans les années 1860, 'Les Actas'." *Maroc-Europe* 6 (1994): 151–65.

Bengio, J. "La Junta selecta: Le comité de la communauté juive de Tanger." *Maroc-Europe* 6 (1994): 167–214.

Bennani-Chraïbi, M. *Soumis et rebelles: les jeunes au Maroc.* Paris, 1994.

———. "Sujets en quête de citoyenneté: le Maroc au miroir des législatives de juin 1993," *Maghreb-Machrek* 148 (April–June 1995): 17–27.

Berque, Jacques. *Al-Yousi: problèmes de la culture marocaine au XVIIe siècle.* The Hague, 1958.

———. *L'Intérieur du Maghreb: XVe–XIXe siècle.* Paris, 1978.

———. *Structures sociales du Haut-Atlas.* Paris, 1955.

———. *Ulémas, fondateurs et insurgés du Maghreb.* Paris, 1982.

Bourqia, Rahma. "Don et théatralité: réflexion sur le rituel du don (*hadiyya*) offert au Sultan au xixe siècle." *Hespéris-Tamuda* 31 (1993): 61–75.

———. "Espace physique, espace mythique: Réflexion sur la représentation de l'espace chez les Zemmour." In A. Bencherifa and H. Popp, eds. *Le Maroc. Espace et société: Actes du colloque maroco-allemand.* Passau, 1989.

Brignon, Jean, et al. *Histoire du Maroc.* Casablanca, 1967.

Brown, K. L. *People of Salé: Tradition and Change in a Moroccan City, 1830–1930.* Manchester: Manchester University Press, 1976.

Brunschvig, Robert. *La Berbèrie orientale sous les Hafsides: Des origines à la fin du XVe siècle.* 2 vols. Paris, 1940–7.

———. "Sur la doctrine du Mahdi Ibn Tumart." *Etudes d'islamologie.* 2 vols. Paris, 1976.

Burgat, François. *L'Islamisme au Maghreb.* Paris, 1988.

Burgat, François, and William Dowell. *The Islamic Movement in North Africa.* Austin: University of Texas Press, 1993.

Burke, III, E. "The Image of the Moroccan State in French Ethnological Literature: New Light on the Origins of Lyautey's Berber Policy." In *Arabs and Berbers: Ethnicity and Nation-Building in North Africa*, edited by E. Gellner and C. Micaud. London, 1974.

———. "The Moroccan Ulama, 1860–1912: An Introduction." In *Scholars, Saints, and Sufis: Muslim Religious Institutions since 1500*, edited by N. R. Keddie. Berkeley: University of California Press, 1972.

———. *Prelude to Protectorate in Morocco, 1860–1912*. Chicago: University of Chicago Press, 1976.

Chelhod, J. *Les Structures du sacré chez les arabes*. Paris, 1964.

Cigar, N. "Socio-Economic Structures and the Development of an Urban Bourgeoisie in Pre-Colonial Morocco." *The Maghreb Review* 6, no. 3–4 (1981): 55–76.

Colin, G. S. *Chronique anonyme de la dynastie sa'dienne*. Rabat, 1934.

Combs-Schilling, M. E. *Sacred Performances: Islam, Sexuality, and Sacrifice*. New York: Columbia University Press, 1989.

Crapanzano, V. *The Hamadsha*. Chicago: University of Chicago Press, 1973.

al-Dagharni, Ahmad. *Al-Intikhabat wa-al-ahzab al-siyasiya al-Maghribiya*. Rabat, 1990.

Damis, J. "The U.N. Settlement Plan for the Western Sahara: Problems and Prospects." *Middle East Policy* 1 (1992): 36–46.

Dermenghem, Emile. *Le culte des saints dans l'islam maghrebin*. Paris, 1954.

Deshen, S. *The Mellah Society: Jewish Communal Life in Sherifian Morocco*. Chicago: University of Chicago Press, 1989.

Dozy, R. P. *Supplement aux dictionnaires arabes*. 3rd ed. Paris, 1967.

Drague, G. *Esquisse d'histoire religieuse du Maroc*. Paris, 1951.

al-Du'ayyif, Muhammad ibn Abd al-Salam. *Tarikh al-Du'ayyif: Tarikh al-dawla al-sa'ida*. Edited by A. al-'Amrani. Rabat, 1986.

Eickelman, Dale. *Knowledge and Power in Morocco*. Princeton: Princeton University Press, 1985.

———. *Moroccan Islam*. Austin: University of Texas Press, 1976.

———. "Re-Imagining Religion and Politics: Moroccan Elections in the 1990s." In *Islam and Secularism in North Africa*, edited by J. Reudy. New York, 1994.

El Mansour, Mohamed. *Morocco in the Reign of Mawlay Sulayman*. Wisbech, Cambridgeshire, 1990.

———. "Sharifian Sufism: The Religious and Social Practice of the Wazzani Zawiya." In *Tribe and State: Essays in Honour of David Montgomery Hart*, edited by E. G. Joffe and R. Pennell, 69–83. Wisbech, Cambridgeshire, 1991.

Ennaji, M. *Soldats, domestiques et concubines: l'esclavage au Maroc au XIXème siècle.* Paris, 1994.

Entelis, John. *Culture and Counterculture in Moroccan Politics.* Boulder, 1989.

Etienne, Bruno. *L'islamisme radical.* Paris, 1987.

Fattal, A. *Le Statut légal des non-musulmans en pays d'Islam.* Beirut, 1958.

Foucault, Charles de. *Reconnaissance du Maroc.* Paris, 1888.

García-Arenal, M. "The Revolution of Fas in 869/1465 and the Death of Sultan 'Abd al-Haqq al-Marini." *Bulletin of the School of Oriental and African Studies* 41, no. 1 (1978): 43–66.

———. "Mahdi, Murabit, Sharif: l'avènement de la dynastie sa'dienne." *Studia Islamica* 71 (1990): 77–114.

———. "Sainteté et pouvoir dynastique au Maroc: la résistance de Fès aux Sa'diennes. *Annales: E.S.C.* 4 (1990): 1019–42.

Geertz, C. "Centers, Kings, and Charisma: Reflections on the Symbolics of Power." In *Local Knowledge: Further Essays in Interpretive Anthropology.* New York, 1983: 121–46.

———. *Islam Observed.* New Haven: Yale University Press, 1968.

Gellner, Ernest. *Muslim Society.* Cambridge: Cambridge University Press, 1981.

———."Pouvoir politique et fonction religieuse dans l'Islam marocain." *Annales: E.S.C.* (1970): 699–713.

———. *Saints of the Atlas.* London, 1969.

Gellner, Ernest, and Charles Micaud, eds. *Arabs and Berbers.* Lexington, Mass.: Heath, 1974.

Gerber, J. *Jewish Society in Fez 1450–1700. Studies in Communal and Economic Life.* Leiden, 1980.

Goitein, S. D. *A Mediterranean Society: The Jewish Communities of the Arab World as Portrayed in the Documents of the Cairo Geniza.* 5 vols. Berkeley: University of California Press, 1967–88.

———. "Evidence on the Muslim Poll Tax from Non-Muslim Sources: A Geniza Study." *Journal of the Economic and Social History of the Orient* 6, no. 3 (1963): 278–95.

Gregg, G. *Self-Representation: Life Narrative Studies in Identity and Ideology.* New York, 1991.

Hammoudi, Abdellah. *Master and Disciple: The Cultural Foundations of Moroccan Authoritarianism.* Chicago: University of Chicago Press, 1997

———. "The Path to Sainthood: Structure and Danger." *Princeton Papers in Near Eastern Studies* 3 (1994).

———. "Sainteté, pouvoir, et société: Tamgrout au XVIIe et XVIIIe siècles." *Annales: ESC,* 34 (1980): 615–41.

———. "Segmentarity, Social Stratification, Political Power and Sainthood: Reflections on Gellner's Thesis." *Economy and Society* 9 (1980): 279–303.

———. *The Victim and Its Masks.* Chicago: University of Chicago Press, 1993.

Harris, W. B. "The Nomadic Berbers of Central Morocco." *The Geographic Journal* 6 (1897): 638–45.

Hart, David. "Segmentary Systems and the Role of 'Five Fifths' in Tribal Morocco." In *Islam in Tribal Societies,* edited by A. S. Ahmed and D. M. Hart. London, 1984.

Hirschberg, H. Z. *A History of the Jews in North Africa.* Vol. 2, *From the Ottoman Conquests to the Present Time.* Leiden, 1981.

Hopkins, J. F. *Medieval Muslim Government in Barbary until the Sixth Century of the Hijra.* London, 1958.

Hunwick, J. O. "Al-Mahili and the Jews of Tuwat: The Demise of a Community." *Studia Islamica* 61 (1985): 155–83.

Ibn Zaydan, Abd al-Rahman. *al-Durar al-fakhira bi-maathir al-muluk al-Alawiyin bi-Fas al-zahira.* Rabat, 1937.

———. *Ithaf alam al-nas bi-jamal akhbar hadirat Miknas.* 5 vols. Rabat, 1929.

———. *al-'Izz wa al-salwa fi ma'alim nuzum al-dawla.* 2 vols. Rabat, 1962.

Ifrani, Muhammed al-Segir. *Nozhet-Elhadi, histoire de la dynastie saadienne au Maroc,* translated by O. Houdas. Paris, 1889.

Kably, Mohamed. *Société, pouvoir et religion au Maroc à la fin du moyen âge.* Paris, 1986.

———. *Variations islamistes et identité du Maroc médiéval.* Paris, 1989.

Kenbib, M. *Juifs et musulmans au Maroc, 1859–1948*. Rabat: Mohammed V University, 1994.

———. *Les Protégés: Contribution à l'histoire contemporaine du Maroc*. Rabat: University Mohammed V, 1996.

Lahbabi, M. *Le Gouvernement marocain a l'aube du XXe siècle*. Rabat, 1958.

Laredo, A. I. *Les Noms des juifs du Maroc: Essai d'onomastique judeomarocaine*. Madrid, 1978.

Laroui, Abdallah. *Esquisses Historiques*. Casablanca, 1992.

———. *The History of the Maghrib*. Translated by Ralph Manheim. Princeton: Princeton University Press, 1977.

———. *L'Idéologie arabe contemporaine*. Paris, 1967.

———. *Islam et modernité*. Paris, 1986.

———. *Les Origines sociales et culturelles du nationalisme marocain (1830–1912)*. Paris, 1977.

Layachi, Larbi. *A Life Full of Holes*. New York, 1982.

Le Tourneau, R. *Fès avant le protectorat: étude économique et sociale d'une ville de l'occident musulman*. Casablanca, 1949.

———. "La Naissance du pouvoir sa'adien vue par l'historien al-Zayyani." In Institut français de Damas, *Mélanges Louis Massignon*, 3:65–80. 3 vols. Damascus, 1956–57.

———. "Sur la disparition de la doctrine almohade." *Studia Islamica* 32 (1970): 193–201.

Leveau, Rémy. *Le Fellah marocain: défenseur du trône*. 2nd ed. Paris, 1985.

Lévi-Provençal, E. *Documents inédits d'histoire almohade*. Paris, 1928.

Lewis, B. "L'Islam et les non-musulmans." *Annales: ESC* 35 (1980): 784–98.

———. *The Jews of Islam*. Princeton: Princeton University Press, 1984.

Lings, M. *A Moslem Saint of the Twelfth Century: Shaikh Ahmad al-'Alawi, His Spiritual Heritage and Legacy*. London, 1961.

Loewe, L., ed. *Diaries of Sir Moses and Lady Montefiore: A Facsimile of the 1890 Edition*. London, 1983.

Lopez García, Bernabe, Gema Martin Muñoz, and Miguel H. de Larramendi, eds. *Elecciones, participacion y transiciones politicas en el Norte de Africa*. Madrid, 1991.

Lourido-Díaz, R. *Marruecos en la segunda mitad del siglo xviii. Vida interna: politica, social y religiosa durante el Sultanato de Sidi Muhammad b. 'Abd Allah, 1757–1790.* Madrid, 1978.

———. *Marruecos y el mundo exterior en la segunda mitad del siglo xviii.* Madrid, 1989.

al-Manuni, Muhammad. *Mazahir yaqaza al-Maghrib al-hadith.* 2 vols. Rabat, 1973.

Marçais, Georges. *La Berbèrie musulmane et l'Orient au moyen âge.* Paris, 1946.

Marcy, Georges. *Le droit coutumier Zemmour.* Paris, 1949.

Mayer, A. E. "Moroccans: Citizens or Subjects? A People at the Crossroads." *New York University Journal of International Law and Politics* 26 (Fall 1993): 63–105.

Mercer, P. "Palace and Jihad in the Early 'Alawi State in Morocco." *Journal of African History* 18 (1977): 535–8.

Mernissi, Fatima. *Beyond the Veil.* Bloomington: Indiana University Press, 1987.

———. *Islam and Democracy: Fear of the Modern World.* Translated by Mary Jo Lakeland. Reading, Mass., 1992.

Miège, J.-L. *Le Maroc et l'Europe (1830–1894).* 4 vols. Paris: Presses Universitaires de France, 1961–2.

Michaux-Bellaire, E. "Les Impôts marocaines." *Archives Marocaines* 1 (1904): 56–96.

———. "La Maison d'Ouezzane." *Revue du Monde Musulman* V (1908): 50–51.

———. "L'Organisation des finances au Maroc." *Archives Marocaines* 11 (1907): 171–251.

Michaux-Bellaire, E., and G. Salmon. "El Qçar El-Kébir." *Archives Marocaines* 2 (1905): 1–228.

Miller, S. G., ed. and trans. *Disorienting Encounters: Travels of a Moroccan Scholar in France in 1845–1846: The Voyage of Muhammad as-Saffar.* Berkeley: University of California Press, 1992.

———. "Kippur on the Amazon: Jewish Emigration from Northern Morocco in the Late Nineteenth Century." In *Sephardi and Middle Eastern Jewries: History and Culture in the Modern Era,* edited by Harvey A. Goldberg. Bloomington: Indiana University Press, 1996.

Monjib, M. *La Monarchie marocaine et la lutte pour le pouvoir.* Paris, 1992.

Montagne, Robert. *Les Berbères et le Makhzan dans le sud du Maroc.* Paris, 1930.

Munson, Jr., Henry. *Islam and Revolution in the Middle East.* New Haven: Yale University Press, 1988.

———. "Morocco's Fundamentalists." *Government and Opposition* 26 (1991): 331–44.

———. *Religion and Power in Morocco.* New Haven: Yale University Press, 1993.

al-Nasiri, Ahmad Ibn Khalid. *Kitab al-istiqsa li-akhbar duwal al-maghrib al-aqsa.* 9 vols. Casablanca, 1956.

Nahon, M. I. "Les Israélites du Maroc." *Revue des études ethnographiques et sociologiques* (1909): 258–79.

Nordman, D. "Les Expéditions de Moulay Hassan." *Hespéris-Tamuda* 19 (1980–81): 123–52.

Paquignon, P. "Les Moulouds au Maroc." *Revue du Monde Musulman* 14 (1911): 525–36.

Park, T. K. "Inflation and Economic Policy in Nineteenth-Century Morocco: The Compromise Solution." *The Maghrib Review* 10, no. 2–3 (1985): 51–6.

Perrault, Gilles. *Notre ami le roi.* Paris, 1990.

Premare, A.-L. de. *Sidi Abd-er-Rahman el-Mejdub: mysticisme populaire, société et pouvoir au Maroc au 16ème siècle.* Paris, 1985.

al-Qadiri, Muhammad Ibn al-Tayyib. *Nashr al-mathani li-ahl al-qarn al-hadi 'ashr wa al-thani.* Edited by A. Tawfiq and M. Hijji. 4 vols. Rabat, 1977. Partial English translation by N. Cigar. *Muhammad al-Qadiri's Nashr al-mathani: The Chronicles.* Oxford: Oxford University Press, 1981.

Riley, James. *An Authentic Narrative of the Loss of the American Brig Commerce, Wrecked on the Western Coast of Africa, in the Month of August, 1815.* Hartford, 1847.

Rivet, D. *Lyautey et l'institution du Protectorat au Maroc, 1912–1925.* 3 vols. Paris, 1988.

Rollman, W. "The 'New Order' in a Pre-colonial Muslim Society: Military Reforms in Morocco 1844–1904." Ph.D. dissertation, University of Michigan, 1983.

Romanelli, S. A. *Travail in an Arab Land*. Edited and translated by N. and Y. Stillman. Tuscaloosa: University of Alabama Press, 1989.

Salamé, Ghassan, ed. *Democracy Without Democrats: The Renewal of Politics in the Muslim World*. London, 1994.

Salmi, A. "Le Genre des poèmes de nativité (Mauludiyya-s) dans le royaume de Grenade at au Maroc du XIIIe au XVIIe siècle." *Hespéris* 43, nos.–3–4 (1956): 335–35.

Salmon, Georges. "L'Administration marocain à Tanger." *Archives Marocaines* 1 (1904): 1–55.

———. "Le Droit d'asile des canons." *Archives Marocaines* 3 (1905). 144–53.

Santucci, J.-C., ed. *Le Maroc actuel: une modernisation au miroir de la tradition?* Paris, 1992.

Schroeter, Daniel. *Merchants of Essaouira: Urban Society and Imperialism in Southwestern Morocco, 1844–1886*. Cambridge: Cambridge University Press, 1988.

———. "Trade as a Mediator in Muslim-Jewish Relations: Southwestern Morocco in the Nineteenth Century." In *Jews among Arabs: Contacts and Boundaries,* edited by M. R. Cohen and A. L. Udovitch. Princeton, 1989.

Sebti, A. "Insécurité et figures de la protection au XIXe siècle: la *ztata* et son vocabulaire." In *La Société civile au Maroc*. Rabat, 1992.

Shatzmiller, M. "Les Premiers Mérinides et le milieu religieux de Fès: l'introduction des médersas." *Studia Islamica* 43 (1976): 109–18.

Shinar, P. "Traditional and Reformist Mawlid Celebration in the Maghrib." In *Studies in the Memory of Gaston Wiet,* edited by M. Rosen-Ayalon. Jerusalem: Hebrew University Press, 1977.

Smimou, Bahija. *Les reformes militaires au Maroc de 1844 à 1912*. Rabat: Fuculté des Lettres, 1995.

al-Susi, Muhammad al-Mukhtar. *al-Ma'sul*. 20 vols. Casablanca, 1960–63.

———. *al-Tiryaq al-mudawi fi akhbar al-shaykh sayyidi al-hajj Ali al-Susi al-Darqawi*. Titwan, 1960.

Tozy, M. "Champ et contre-champ politico-religieux au Maroc." Ph.D. diss. Aix-Marseille, 1984.

Vajda, G. "Un traité maghrébin 'Adversus judæos': Ahkam ahl al-dhimma du shaykh Muhammad b. 'Abd al-Karim al-Maghili." In *Etudes d'Orientalisme dédiées à la mémoire de Lévi-Provençal.* Paris, 1962: 805–13.

Waltz, Susan. *Human Rights and Reform: Changing the Face of North African Politics.* Berkeley: University of California Press, 1995.

———. "Making Waves: The Political Impact of Human Rights Groups in North Africa." *Journal of Modern African Studies* 29 (1991): 481–504.

al-Wansharisi, Ahmad Ibn Yahya. *Al-Mi'yar al-mu'rib wa-al-jami' al-mughrib 'an fatawa ifriqiya wa al-anadalus wa al-maghrib.* In *Archives Marocaines* 12, 13 (1908–1909).

Contributors

Rahma Bourqia, dean of the Faculty of Arts and Sciences of University Hassan II, Mohammedia, and also professor of sociology and anthropology at Mohammed V University in Rabat, is the author of *State, Power, and Society in Morocco* (in Arabic) (Beirut, 1991) and *Femmes et Fecondité* (Casablanca, 1996). She has coedited, with American colleagues, two conference proceedings sponsored by the American Institute of Maghrib Studies: *Le Maghreb: approches des mecanismes d'articulation* (Casablanca, 1991) and *Femmes, Culture et Société au Maghreb* (Casablanca, 1996).

M. Elaine Combs-Schilling is associate professor anthropology at Columbia University. Her publications include *Sacred Performances* (New York: Columbia University Press, 1989) and *Death and the Female Saint* (forthcoming).

Mohamed El Mansour is professor of modern Moroccan history at the Faculty of Arts and Sciences, Mohammed V University, Rabat, and formerly chair of the Department of History. He is author of *Morocco in the Reign of Mawlay Sulayman* (Cambridgeshire, UK: Menas Press, 1990).

Gary S. Gregg, associate professor of psychology at Kalamazoo College, conducted ethnographic and study-of-lives research in Morocco from 1983 to 1988. He is author of *Self-representation: Life Narrative Studies in Identity and Ideology* (New York, 1991) and has taught at Sarah Lawrence College and Harvard University.

Abdellah Hammoudi is professor of anthropology and director of the Institute for the Transregional Study of the Contemporary Middle East, North Africa, and Central Asia at Princeton University. He is the author of *The Victim and Its Masks: An Essay on Sacrifice and Masquerade in the Maghreb* (1993) and *Master and Disciple: The Cultural Foundations of Moroccan Authoritarianism* (1997), both published by the University of Chicago Press.

Mohamed Kably, rector of the University Sidi Mohammed Ben Abdellah, Fez, and professor of medieval history of the western Islamic world at Mohammed V University, Rabat, is the author of *Société, pouvoir et religion au Maroc à la fin du Moyen-Age* (Paris, 1986) and *Variations islamistes et identité du Maroc médiéval* (Rabat, 1989). He has been a visiting scholar at Bordeaux III University (1987) and at Harvard University (1994). In 1993, he was awarded the Grand Prix du Maroc.

Abdelfattah Kilito is a professor in the French Department of the Faculty of Arts and Sciences, Mohammed V University, Rabat. He was a visiting scholar at the Ecole des Hautes Etudes en Sciences Sociales (1989), the Collège de France (1990), and Harvard University (1996). His publications include *L'auteur et ses doubles: essai sur la culture arabe classique* (Paris, 1985), *L'oeil et l'aiguille: essai sur "Les mille et une nuits"* (Paris, 1992), and a novel, *La querelle des images* (Casablanca, 1995). He received the Grand Prix du Maroc in 1989.

Susan Gilson Miller is associate director of the Center for Middle Eastern Studies at Harvard University, where she directs the Moroccan Studies Program. She is a senior lecturer in the Department of Near Eastern Languages and Civilizations and author of *Disorienting Encounters: Travels of a Moroccan Scholar in France, 1845–46* (Berkeley: University of California Press, 1992), published in Arabic by the Faculty of Arts and Sciences, Rabat, in 1996.

Henry Munson, Jr. is professor of anthropology at the University of Maine. He is the author of *The House of Si Abd Allah: The Oral History of a Moroccan Family* (1984), *Islam and Revolution in the Middle East* (1988), and *Religion and Power in Morocco* (1993), all published by Yale University Press. In 1996–97, he was a fellow at the Woodrow Wilson International Center for Scholars, where he worked on his latest book, *Armies of God: "Fundamentalisms" of the Late Twentieth Century.*

Daniel J. Schroeter is associate professor of history at the University of California, Irvine, where he holds the Teller Family Chair in Jewish History. He has previously taught at the University of Florida, George Washington University, the University of Utah, and the University of Paris VIII. He is author of *Merchants of Essaouira: Urban Society and Imperialism in Southwestern Morocco, 1844–1886* (1988), recently translated to Arabic and published by the Faculty of Arts and Sciences, Rabat.

Susan E. Waltz is professor of international relations at Florida International University and author of *Human Rights and Reform: Changing the Face of North African Politics* (Berkeley: University of California Press, 1995) and "The Politics of Human Rights in the Maghrib," in J. Entelis, ed., *Islam, Democracy and the State in North Africa* (Bloomington: Indiana University Press, 1997).

Index

al-'Abbas (Mawlay), 110
'Abd al-'Aziz (Mawlay), 66, 67–69
'Abd al-Mu'min, 21
'Abd al-Rahman (Mawlay), 61–62, 86, 87, 88, 92, 229
'Abd al-Rahman ibn Hisham, 247
Abensur, Aaron, 118
Abu 'Inan, 20
Abu al-'Ala, 222
Abu Nuwas, 222
Acoca, Yamim, 89, 90
al-'Adl wa'l-Ikhsan (Justice and Charity), 289, 290, 295
adolescence, 143
Adorno, Theodor W., 226, 228, 235
'Alawi dynasty, 2, 74–75, 140, 178, 188, 245
Algeria, 203, 276–277; women in, 212–213n59; FIS in, 289
allegiance, ritual of, 245–246
Alliance Israélite Universelle (AIU), 124 n 27
Ahmad al-Mansur (Sultan), 36, 52–53, 180–181, 188
Almohad period, 23, 25
Almoravid state, 19–20; legitimacy of, 22; period, 23, 25
Amaoui, Noubir, 283

Amoussouga, Roland, 269
Anderson, Benedict, 176, 183, 204
Anglo-Moroccan treaty, 90
Ani, Mukhtar, 229
Arab Mind, The (Patai), 215
army, role of, 161–162
'ar rituals, 64–65
Association Marocaine des Droits de l'Homme (AMDH), 292, 299
Aubin, Eugène, 103
authoritarianism: *dar al-mulk* as, 132; modern, 159–163, 169–172; defined, 159–160
authority: relationship of youth to, 215–240; ambivalence about, 219–226; and authoritarianism, 226–229; models of, 227; paternal styles of, 230–231; patron figures and, 231–232
Authority in Islam (Dabashi), 216
Azziman, Omar, 295

al-Badia, palace of, 180–181
Balandier, Georges, 249
Banuazizi, Ali, 215
baraka, 6, 149–152, 246, 248, 257n6
Barakat, Halim, 215, 226

Basri, Driss, 271, 273, 297
Basri, Fqih, 286
Beaumier, Auguste, 92
Bellah, Robert, 234
Ben Barka, Medhi, 286
Benchimol, Haim, 118
Bendelac, Haim, 118
Bengio, Mordechai, 116
Benjamin, Walter, 182
Bensaïd, Mohammed, 287
Bensliman, Tahar, 67–68
Berbers, 234
Berque, Jacques, 57, 149
Bilmaun, 156–158
Bouabid, Abderrahim, 286, 288
Bouabid, Maati, 261
Boucetta, M'Hamed, 297
Bourdieu, Pierre, 251–252
Bourqia, Rahma, 8, 243–258
Bouznika, 1993 legislative election in: 267–272; results of, 268; protest about, 269–271
Bowles, Paul, 229
bubonic plague, 207n12
Buck-Morss, S., 182
Bujlud. *See* Bilmaun
Bu Silham ibn 'Ali, 87

Calvin, John, 234
cannon sanctuary, 62–63
Casablanca, Hasan II mosque in, 189–190, 191–193
Casablanca, 1993 legislative election in: 259; in al-Hayy al-Hassani quarter, 261–267, 274, voting procedure in, 262; pollwatchers in, 262–263; results of, 263, 266–267; in Moulay Rachid district, 274; null votes in, 275
CCDH. *See* Conseil Consultatif des Droits de l'Homme
charismatic power. *See* baraka
Charter of Human Rights, 299

Chertaoui, Taieb, 266
Chiappe, Francesco, 83
Chraïbi, Driss, 229
Closed Circle, The (Pryce-Jones), 215
Cohn, Albert, 122n15
colonialism: *dar al-mulk* in, 163–166; organization of power in, 164–167; French, 188. *See also* French protectorate
Combs-Schilling, M. Elaine, 8, 176–214, 216–218
Communist Party, 287
Confédération Démocratique du Travail, 283
Conference of Madrid, 93
Conseil Consultatif des Droits de l'Homme (CCDH), 282, 292, 293–295
Constitution of 1992, 296–297
Cooper, David, 68
Corcos, Abraham, 86
Corcos, Jacob, 86
Cruelty and Silence (Makiya), 216
Culture and Counterculture in Moroccan Politics (Entelis), 216, 218

Dabashi, Ahmed, 216
al-Dar al-Bayda. *See* Casablanca
dar al-mulk, 129–175; as political concept, 133–140, 170; and terror, 139–140; and sainthood, 140–152; and masquerade, 156–159; evolution of, 159; in colonial period, 163–167; after independence, 167–169
al-Darqawi, al-Hajj 'Ali, 143, 144, 145, 146
Delamar, Mordechai, 89, 98n44
democratization, 259–281
Dermenghem, E., 248
development, language of, 250–251
dhimma, 103–120
al-Du'ayyif, 82–83

al-Dukkali, Mustafa, 90
Durkheim, Emile, 184, 185

Eickelman, Dale, 229
El Mansour, Mohamed, 2, 49–73
elections: indirect, 259–261, 279n5; cosmetic role of, 274–275; 1993 legislative, 259–61, 263, 266–267, 297–298; use of null votes in, 275–276; and popular unrest, 276–277
emblem: white robes as, 181, 183; monarchical, 184–189; constancy of, 187
Enaamami, Abdelaziz, 289, 303n21
Entelis, John, 216, 218
Erikson, Erik, 217, 233
Essaouira, 79–80, 81, 85, 91–92
Etienne, Bruno, 252, 254

faith, orienting rituals of, 176–177, 178–179
Family Code, 201, 202, 213n62, 299
al-Fasi, 'Abd al-Qadir, 61
al-Fasi, Allal, 166
al-Fasi, Muhammad ibn 'Abd al-Qadir, 61
Feast of the Mouloud, 140
Feast of the Sacrifice, 103, 152–154
Fez, 55, 56–57; the Fasi *zawiya*, 61–62; shrine of Mawlay Idris in, 68, 246; 1990 riots in, 294
Filali, Abdellatif, 297, 300
Foucault, Michel, 159, 177, 184, 188
French protectorate, 11–12, 63, 68, 165–167. *See also* colonialism
Fromm, Erich, 226, 228, 235

Gannun, Muhammad ibn al-Madani, 76
Geertz, Clifford, 6
Gellner, Ernest, 141, 234

gender inversion, 132, 147–149, 155, 157–158, 208n24
gender relations, ambivalence in, 225
al-Ghazali, 19
gifts, circulation of, 137, 138–139
Goethe, Johann Wolfgang von, 233–234
Goitein, S.D., 106
Goldberg, Ellis, 234
Great Sacrifice, 188
Gregg, Gary S., 2, 215–240
Gulf War, 289, 290

al-Habri, Abu 'Azza, 68
Haddi (Sidi), 150
Hafsids (of Tunis), 20
Halevi, Yehuda ibn Shlomo, 89
Hamilton, V. Lee, 235
Hammoudi, Abdellah, 10, 129–175
Harun al-Rashid, 34–35, 36
Hasan I (Mawlay), 53, 68, 91, 93, 95, 247
Hasan II, 189–191, 195, 198, 199–200, 268, 288; health of, 210n42; reforms of, 282–283, 300; as constitutional monarch, 296–297
Hasan II mosque, 189–195, 252; contributions for, 190–191; construction of, 191–193; size of, 193–194; aesthetics of, 194–195; dedication of, 197–198; role of, 204–206
Hatem, Mervat, 214n63
High Council of the Ulama, 253–254
human rights: constitutional guarantees of, 296, 299; organizations, 261, 292, 299
Humeidan, Raqiya, 269, 271
hurm (sanctuary), 49–70; example of, 52–53; social significance of, 57–58; and temporal power, 58–60; sultan as maker of, 60–63;

hurm (sanctuary) *(continued)*
  erosion of, 64–67; violation of, 67–68
Hussein (interview subject), 221–225, 226, 228, 231, 233

Ibn 'Abd Allah M'an, Ahmad, 55
Ibn Abi Mahalli, 30–34, 43–45nn5,6
Ibn 'Ajiba, 143, 144, 145, 146
Ibn Ariba, Muhammad, 80
Ibn Hawqal, 21
Ibn Khaldun, 13
Ibn Mashish, 'Abd al-Salam (Mawlay), 51, 52–53
Ibn Mubarak, Muhammad, 54
Ibn al-Muqaffa', 30, 38
Ibn Raysun, 52
Ibn Tashufin, 19
Ibn Tumart, 19, 20, 21, 23
Ibn Zaydan, 246, 247
Ibrahim, Abdallah, 167, 285, 288
ideology, role of, 162
Idris (Mawlay), 51, 52, 56; shrine of, 68, 246
Idrisid dynasty, 180, 245
Idrisism, 21–22, 58–60
ikhs, 239n23
ikhwan. *See* Muslim Brothers
Il'al-Amam, 285, 287
independence: *dar al-mulk* after, 167–169; and legitimation, 248–250
Iran, overthrow of Shah in, 289
Islam, typology of, 253
Islamist movement, 254–256, 258n23, 289–290, 301
Isma'il (Mawlay), 10, 34, 38–41, 55, 61–62, 80
Istiqlal Party, 260, 262, 272, 296, 297, 298
Al-Ittihad al-ishtiraki, 265

Jamaï, Khalid, 272–273
Jews: in foreign trade, 79–80; as merchants, 81, 84–85; and *jizya*, 104–109; oligarchic class among, 118–119; emigration of, 125n41
jihad: local aspect of, 22; concept of, 77–78; at sea, 78–79; symbolic role of, 249–250
jizya, 104–109, 110–111, 115–116, 125n37
Juin, Alphonse (Resident General), 166
Junta Selectiva of Tangier, 109–113, 114, 122n14

Kably, Mohamed, 7–8, 17–29, 178
Kaïtouni, Mohamed, 273
Karam, Mohamed, 261
al-Kattani, Muhammad ibn Ja'far, 94
Kelman, Herbert, 235
Khadija (interview subject), 219–220, 228, 233
Khuri, Fuad, 216, 226
Kilito, Abdelfattah, 10, 30–46
Kishk, Shaykh, 221, 232
Kitab al-ansab, 18–19
Knowledge and Power in Morocco (Eickelman), 229
Kovel, Joel, 235
Kutla (Democratic Bloc), 297–298, 299, 300

Lamrani, Karim, 296–297
Lane, E.W., 105
Larache, 63
Laredo, Abraham, 118
Layachi, Larbi, 229
Le Passé enterré (Ghallab), 229
Le Tourneau, Roger, 3
leader, relationship to, 160
left, the political, 285–288; components of, 285; ideology of, 287
legitimacy, 7–8; medieval, 17–29; and independence, 248–250
Levinson, Daniel, 232

Libération, 266
Life Full of Holes, A (Bowles), 229
life histories, synthesis in, 232–236
life narrative approach, 218–219
Ligue Marocaine des Droits de l'Homme (LMDH), 292, 299
Lings, Martin, 149
Look and Move On (Bowles), 229
L'Opinion, 272–273
Lyautey, Marshal (Resident General), 163, 164

Machiavelli, Niccolo, 42
Macnin, Meir, 87, 88–89, 98n44
al-Madari, 145
al-Maghrib al-Aqsa, 19, 25
Mahdism, 23–24
Majid (interview subject), 220–221, 228, 233
makhzan, 53, 57, 59, 65–66, 94, 244–245, 249; in medieval Morocco, 18; centralizing tendencies of, 67, 129, 172n1; commercial monopolies of, 88, 89–90; and *jizya* ceremony, 117
Makiya, Kanan, 216
Malik ibn Anas, 84
Mantle of the Prophet, The (Mottahedeh), 216
March 23 Movement, 287
Marinids, 20, 23, 52, 58, 140, 178, 201
Marrakesh, 79, 91–92; Prophet's Birthday in, 180–181; Koutoubia of, 195
marriage: royal, 211n50; ambivalence about, 225
masquerade, role of, 156–159
master-disciple relationship, 131, 132, 140–152
Mazagan, capture of, 79
meat tax, 112, 114, 118–119
Mecca: sanctuary of, 50–51, 65–66; Great Mosque of, 193–194

Memoirs of al-Baydhaq, 18–19
Mernissi, Fatima, 225
Miller, Susan Gilson, 9, 103–126
mimesis, 182–184
Ministry of Human Rights, 282–283, 292, 295–296
Ministry of the Interior, 271–272
modernism and religion, synthesis of, 235
Mohammed V, 166, 199–200, 247–248, 249, 268, 287–288, 296
monarchy: image of, 209n31; patronage of, 285; in contemporary politics, 290–291; constitutional powers of, 296
Montagne, Robert, 3
Montefiore, Moses, 109
Mottahedeh, Roy, 216, 235
Mouvement National Populaire (MNP), 263
Mrabet, Mohammed, 229
Mudawwana. See Family Code
Muhadarat (al-Yusi), 30–31, 38
Muhammad ibn 'Abdallah (Sultan), 52, 60, 78, 79, 81–82, 83, 88
Muhammad IV, 91
Munson, Henry, Jr., 8, 259–281
Muslim Brothers, 190, 198–201, 218
Muti, Abdelkrim, 289

Ibn Nasir, M'hammad, 143, 144, 145, 148
al-Nasiri, Ahmad ibn Khalid, 63, 88, 93–94, 247
nationalism: movement in colonial period, 165–166; contemporary, 177–178, Shinto, 234
null votes, in elections, 275–276

OADP. *See* Organisation de l'Action Démocrate et Populaire
OMDH. *See* Organisation Marocaine des Droits de l'Homme

Organisation de l'Action Démocrate et Populaire (OADP), 260, 263, 286–287
Organisation Marocaine des Droits de l'Homme (OMDH), 261, 292, 294, 295, 299
Orientalism (Said), 2–3
Ouarzazate, 217

Pariente, Moses, 113–114, 116, 118
parliament: cosmetic role of, 274–275; role of reform in, 298–300; establishing a Senate in, 300
Parti du Progrès et du Socialisme (PPS), 260, 263, 285, 286–287
Patai, Raphael, 215
paternal authority: and sacrifice, 154–156; styles of, 230–231. *See also* authority
patronage: role of, 231–232; royal, 285
Picciotto, Moses H., 122n15
Pinseau, Michel, 211–212n53
piracy. *See* jihad at sea
political culture, psychological dimension of, 216–217
political efficacy, lack of, 274
political prisoners, 282–283, 300, 304n32
political reform, 282–305
poll tax. *See* jizya
poll watchers, 262–263
power, 5–7; representations of, 8–11, 43; in equilibrium, 55–56; *hurm* and, 57–58; *dar al-mulk* and, 129–131, 133, 136–137; sainthood and, 142; in colonial period, 164–165; cultural legacy of, 243–258; of religious symbols, 245–248, 251–256; in era of independence, 169, 248–250; role of language in, 250–251
PPS. *See* Parti du Progrès et du Socialisme

prime minister: role of, 296–297; rotation of, 300
procreation, metaphor of, 149–152
Prophet's Birthday, 179–189; in 1993, 189–203
Pryce-Jones, David, 215

al-Qabbaj, al-Makki, 90
Qadi 'Iyad, 21
al-Qadiri, 'Abd al-Salam, 55
al-Qadiri, Muhammad ibn al-Tayyib, 56, 62

Rachida (interview subject), 225, 228, 233
al-Rahman, Hajj 'Abd, 229
Ramadan, 252
Rassemblement National des Indépendants (RNI), 263, 266, 267–268
al-Razini, Muhammad, 90
Reghaye, Abdelkamel, 267
religion and modernism, synthesis of, 235
religious symbols, power of, 245–248
Riley, James, 107
rites of passage, 152–169
rogui, 14n11
RNI. *See* Rassemblement National des Indépendants

Sacred Performances (Combs-Schilling), 216, 218
sacred time, 54
sacrifice and paternal authority, 154–156
Sa'di dynasty, 20, 24, 28n18, 74, 140, 178, 188, 208n17
Saharan question, 218, 286, 288, 302n13
Saïd (interview subject), 225, 228, 233
Said, Edward, 2–3

sainthood, 3, 10–11, 54–56, 140–152; path to, 142–149
Salmon, Georges, 63
sanctuary. *See hurm*
Schroeter, Daniel J., 9, 74–102
Seksawa, 57, 213n62
Self-Representation (Gregg), 217
al-Shabiba al-Islamiya (Islamic Youth), 289
Sharabi, Hisham, 226, 229
sharia, 64–67
sharifism, 21, 52, 56, 58, 60, 181–189, 245–248, 252
al-Shaykh, Muhammad, 20
Simple Past, The (Chraïbi), 229
sirr, concept of, 248
Smith, W. Robertson, 50
Soufani, Khalid, 271
Spain, expansion of, 74, 76
Sufism, 25, 52, 141, 255
Sufyan al-Thawri, 34–35
Sufyan b. Muhriz, 43n4
Sulayman (Mawlay), 65, 72n28, 83–84
Sullivan, Denis, 269
Sunni Islam, 19, 20, 21, 23, 28n19
Supreme Court, 267, 272

Tabet, Mohammed, 299
Tajfel, Henri, 235
Tangier: tax collection in, 109–116; Jewish population of, 123n17; currency in, 123n19
Taussig, Michael, 182, 184
Tazmamert prison, 282, 283
Tents and Pyramids (Khuri), 216
Thematic Apperception Test (TAT), 223–224
Tozy, Mohammed, 255
Tunisia, al-Nahda party in, 289

UC. *See* Union Constitutionelle
ulama, role of, 253–254
Union Constitutionelle (UC), 261, 262–263
Union Socialiste des Forces Populaires (USFP), 260, 261, 262, 285–286, 285, 286, 297, 298
USFP. *See* Union Socialiste des Forces Populaires

voting procedure, 262

Wad al-Makhazin, battle of, 52, 60
Waltz, Susan E., 8, 282–305
Waterbury, John, 234
al-Wazzani, Abd al-Salam, 68–69
Weber, Max, 5–6, 243
Westermarck, E., 50, 51, 64, 149
white robes: introduction of, 181; significance of, 181, 183–184; maleness of, 183, 186, 202
Willis, J.R., 105–106
women: equality for, 190, 198, 200–201; space of, 199; rights of, 201–203, contemporary status of, 204; in mosques, 212n58; in Algeria, 212–213n59

Yassine, Abdessalam, 255, 289–290, 295
Yata, Ali, 288
al-Yazid (Mawlay), 52, 82–83, 89
Youssoufi, Abderrahmane, 260, 297, 300
al-Yusi, 10, 30–35, 37–43, 45n16, 80, 143, 144, 145, 146, 148–149

Zaïdi, Ahmed, 267, 268, 271
el-Zerhouni, Mohamed, 179
Ziane, Mohammed, 295–296

HARVARD MIDDLE EASTERN MONOGRAPHS

1. *Syria: Development and Monetary Policy,* by Edmund Y. Asfour. 1959.

2. *The History of Modern Iran: An Interpretation,* by Joseph M. Upton. 1960.

3. *Contributions to Arabic Linguistics,* Charles A. Ferguson, Editor. 1960.

4. *Pan-Arabism and Labor,* by Willard A. Beling. 1960.

5. *The Industrialization of Iraq,* by Kathleen M. Langley. 1961.

6. *Buarij: Portrait of a Lebanese Muslim Village,* by Anne H. Fuller. 1961.

7. *Ottoman Egypt in the Eighteenth Century,* Stanford J. Shaw, Editor and Translator. 1962.

8. *Child Rearing in the Lebanon,* by Edwin Terry Prothro. 1961.

9. *North Africa's French Legacy: 1954–1962,* by David C. Gordon. 1962.

10. *Communal Dialects in Baghdad,* by Haim Blanc. 1964.

11. *Ottoman Egypt in the Age of the French Revolution,* Translated with Introduction and Notes by Stanford J. Shaw. 1964.

12. *The Economy of Morocco: 1912–1962,* by Charles F. Stewart. 1964.

13. *The Economy of the Israeli Kibbutz,* by Eliyahu Kanovsky. 1966.

14. *The Syrian Social Nationalist Pary: An Ideological Analysis,* by Labib Zuwiyya Yamak. 1966.

15. *The Practical Visions of Ya'qub Sanu',* by Irene L. Gendizier. 1966.

16. *The Surest Path: The Political Treatise of a Nineteenth-Century Muslim Statesman,* by Leon Carl Brown. 1967.

17. *High-Level Manpower in Economic Development:* The Turkish Case, by Richard D. Robinson. 1967.

18. *Rebirth of a Nation: The Origins and Rise of Moroccan Nationalism, 1912–1944,* by John P. Halsted. 1967.

19. *Women of Algeria: An Essay on Change,* by David C. Gordon. 1968.

20. *The Youth of Haouch El Harimi, A Lebanese Village,* by Judith R. Williams. 1968.

21. *The Problem of Diglossia in Arabic: A Comparative Study of Classical and Iraqi Arabic,* by Salih J. Al-Toma. 1969.

22. *The Seljuk Vezirate: A Study of Civil Administration,* by Carla L. Klausner. 1973.

23. and 24. *City in the Desert,* by Oleg Grabar, Renata Holod, James Knustad, and William Trousdale. 1978.

25. *Women's Autobiographies in Contemporary Iran,* Afsaneh Najmabadi, Editor. 1990.

26. *The Science of Mystic Lights,* by John Walbridge. 1992.

27. *Political Aspects of Islamic Philosophy: Essays in Honor of Muhsin S. Mahdi,* by Charles E. Butterworth. 1992.

28. *The Muslims of Bosnia-Herzegovina: Their Historic Development from the Middle Ages to the Dissolution of Yugoslavia,* Mark Pinson, Editor. 1994.

29. *Book of Gifts and Rarities: Kitāb al-Hadāyā wa al-Tuḥaf.* Ghāda al Hijjāwī al-Qaddūmī, Translator and Annotator. 1997.

30. *The Armenians of Iran: The Paradoxical Role of a Minority in a Dominant Culture: Articles and Documents.* Cosroe Chaqueri, Editor. 1998.

31. *In the Shadow of the Sultan: Culture, Power, and Politics in Morocco,* edited by Rahma Bourqia and Susan Gilson Miller. 1999.